GRAND HOTELIER

Inside the Best Hotels

GRAND HOTELIER

Inside the Best Hotels

As told by Ronald F. Jones OBE
to Eve Jones

To David Patrici

Welcome to our world.

Best wishes

Ronald & Eve Jones

Salute
London

Salute
London

First published 1997
© Eve Jones 1997 & 1998

Set in Times

Printed in Great Britain by
Poole Typesetting (Wessex) Ltd

A catalogue record for this book is
available from the British Library

ISBN 0 9532737 0 9

This book is dedicated to the memory of Sam Wood and John Turpie, without whose guidance, advice and encouragement I might only have got halfway.

And to humble beginnings, the thrill of achievement and the recognition of life's blessings.

The story is mine, the words are Eve's. She waded with me through seven decades of archives, talked me through times and experiences half-forgotten, shared the re-living of the highs and the lows. She tried me out with tape recorders, urged me to make unaccustomed notes, and attempted to break the hotelier's habit of a lifetime – see all, hear all, say nowt! She was my new beginning. She is my happy ending.

Ronald F. Jones
London, 1996

CONTENTS

FOREWORD BY

HILARY RUBINSTEIN*

Ever since, twenty years ago, I began to take a serious interest in hotels and the way in which they were managed, I have held firm to one simple tenet: that good hotels were to be found among those run by a resident owner, and that hotels which were managed on behalf of others – whether a small hotel group or an international mega-corporation – could never aspire to the same order of excellence, however generous the facilities, however efficient the service.

Grand Hotelier has forced me to revise that fixed idea. Good hotels can come in any shape or size or in any kind of managerial structure. My own preference remains for small personal establishments, but it is clear that the many hotels with which Ronald Jones was involved as a General Manager from the Dornoch Hotel, Sutherland, onwards and upwards till he reached the pinnacle of Claridge's, were, for his fortunate guests, as warmly personal and hands-on as anyone would wish.

Some hoteliers are born to the job, inheriting a going concern and a tradition of innkeeping which may go back several generations. Others, some of whom appear in these pages, attain the top job largely through family connections. Ron did not have these advantages, not even the benefit of a degree from a good catering college. He has achieved his success in a harder school, starting at the lowest rung of the ladder and taking his chances as they came. He would, I imagine, describe himself as a lucky man, but he is a fine example of someone who has made his luck, accepting tough assignments as they came his way and making the best of them.

The climb was always steep, the request was invariably that he should 'turn the hotel round'. The Dornoch Hotel hadn't made a profit for 15

---

*Writer and Founder Editor of *The Good Hotel Guide*.

years; the year Ronald came in, it made a record profit. Then came a bigger challenge, the famous resort hotel of Turnberry, which was losing money so fast that unless Ron, now 30, could show a profit in the first 12 months, the place would be sold (a shameful fate!) to Butlin's. He worked his miracle again: within a few years it had become one of British Transport Hotels' most prestigious establishments. And then, as a reward, the sadists at BTH sent him to a real dump, the Royal Station Hotel, Hull. Once again, he surpassed his targets. And so to another flagship hotel, the Queens at Leeds, which looked like a gift-horse till you met the truculent staff and came to understand how a former General Manager had been driven to suicide.

We are all familiar with the sustained boasting which so often characterises the autobiography of someone who has enjoyed a distinguished career. Reading this brief précis of some of the notable struggles that Ronald waged against many varieties of adversity, you might imagine that his memoirs were of this tedious sort. But you have to read these memoirs to know that he is a man of innate and invincible modesty.

The secret of his successes? There's a simple answer. If you turn to pages 96–97 you will find the best summing-up I have come across of the qualities required to be a hotelier. Yes, Ronald Jones knows what it takes, and the good fairy at his christening gave him the dedication, the energy, the sympathetic personality displayed equally towards guests and staff, and of course those dollops of good luck to enable him to fulfil his ambitions, among which must be included the ineffable blessing of his wife Eve.

I would add one more boon from that ever-helpful fairy. Ludwig Bemelmans in his classic *Hotel Splendide* describes the General Manager as 'a type of man, smooth, smiling and bowing, whose face is like a towel on which everyone has wiped both hands.' The smile apart, Ron is nothing like that – thank goodness! He is his own man – at home with himself.

Reading this work, I was constantly reminded of that poem by Wordsworth, 'Character of the Happy Warrior', which depicts so graphically a man of heroic virtues.

> Who is the happy Warrior? Who is he
> That every man in arms should wish to be?
> – It is the generous spirit, who, when brought
> Among the tasks of real life, hath wrought

Upon the plan that pleased his childish thought:
Whose high endeavours are an inward light
That makes the path before him always bright...
– Who, if he rises to station of command,
Rises by open means; and there will stand
On honourable terms, or else retire,
And in himself possess his own desire;
Who comprehends his trust, and to the same,
Keeps faithful with a singleness of aim;
And therefore does not stoop, nor lie in wait
For wealth, or honours, or for worldly state...

That's Ron Jones.

1

From the Sublime

We were put into pens at Buckingham Palace. 'MBEs this way, please', and 'OBEs over here', said the stewards, bossy as collies in a sheepfold. And in we went like lambs to the areas cordoned off from each other with silken cords.

People were whey-faced with nerves or skittish and pretending not to be overawed. Somewhere in the middle distance – the ballroom as I later discovered – a small orchestra played *Nobody Does It Better* and *This is My Lovely Day*, melodies carefully selected to ensure there wouldn't be a dry eye in the house.

This was not my first visit to Buckingham Palace: I had already attended two Royal Garden Parties, at the first of which I got down on one knee and proposed formally to my wife. Yet I don't think I felt any more at home than the other worthies penned in with those silken cords. I relaxed a little when out of a sea of officialdom emerged the beaming boot-button eyes of the duty Guards officer, Major Simon Thornhill, whom my wife had dubbed her 'third adopted stepson' and father of her god-daughter.

Other faces emerged from the crowd waiting to be summoned to Her Majesty's presence. Prue Leith, the restaurateur, whom we knew well, was there to receive her OBE. And playwright Carla Lane, dressed from head to toe in black tat, a fellow-Liverpudlian, kept wandering off in a daze as stewards vainly attempted to usher her to her allotted place.

We were carefully briefed: where to stand, where to walk when we heard our name called, how to approach the Queen and what we should and should not say or do. In an ante-room an official pinned on to the lapel of my morning suit a little hook on which Her Majesty would hang the OBE medal (so that was how she avoided sticking pins into people!). I waited while the CBEs then the OBEs were summoned one by one

1

until I heard: 'Mr Ronald Jones. For services to the hotel industry.' I walked over the red carpet, stopped directly in front of the dais on which the Queen stood, and sensed rather than saw her take the insignia and suspend it from the hook on my tailcoat. I looked up then, as I had a dozen times before when I welcomed Her Majesty to Claridge's, into the bluest eyes anybody has ever seen and she smiled and said: 'And how long have you been in the hotel industry, Mr Jones?'

'Nearly fifty years, Ma'am.' As I turned to my right and exited from the opposite side of the ballroom, my mind raced back over what seemed a very short half-century and I recalled another 'audience' which had filled me with as much trepidation as this one.

'Please sir, can you direct me to the control office? I have an interview with Mr Hawkins.'

It was February 1941. My father had died the week before. I wasn't yet 15 years old, a much-loved only child. My mother had been in her forties when I was born – and I knew how she worried about having to give up our house. An uncle had arranged an interview for me at the Adelphi Hotel in Liverpool. If I could get this job then I would be the breadwinner and we could keep our home.

Red-eyed from grief and lack of sleep, for this was the midst of the Liverpool wartime blitz and most nights were spent in an Anderson air raid shelter, cold and damp and shared with neighbours, I was nevertheless determined to make a good impression. I barely glanced at the grandeur of my surroundings – marbled halls with thick red carpets, ornate bronzed doors, grand balustrades – as I was led upstairs, through the main lounge and along corridors until we reached a long, narrow office on the mezzanine.

I could feel and hear my heart pounding. I *had* to get this job. Those of us who were lucky enough to get good jobs saw them as security for life.

The Adelphi was the finest hotel outside London, one of the great railway hotels that were the equal in every way of the Savoy company's in London. Liverpool had prospered in the nineteenth century to become one of the most important passenger shipping terminals in the world as well as the centre of the immensely rich Lancashire cotton industry. The first Adelphi Hotel had been opened on a corner site in the city centre in 1826 and rebuilt in 1876, and the present Adelphi, one of the first hotels to be built with the controversial steel-framed construction, opened in 1914. Newspapers described it as 'one of the greatest hotels in the world' with 600 bedrooms, a swimming pool, Turkish baths, gymnasium, squash court, billiards room and shooting gallery. Public rooms were air-conditioned, bedrooms had built-in furniture for the first time, and porcelain wash bowls and jugs had been replaced by marble-topped basins with hot and cold running water – much to the distaste of Oscar Wilde, who wrote: 'Who wants an immovable washing basin in one's room? I do not. Hide the thing. I prefer to ring for water when I need it.'

The Adelphi was the hub of social life in the city of Liverpool, a giant wedding cake of a building that comforted and cosseted the passengers arriving on the transatlantic liners of the pre-war era. With its sister hotels all over the country, it promised an exciting and lifelong career for a boy who was ambitious and prepared to work hard. I crossed my fingers and made a silent deal with the Almighty: get me this job and I will put aside any hankering to be a concert pianist or an architect. I wonder how many thousand accountants, clerks and plumbers of that era made similar 'deals'.

My interview was with Mr George Hawkins, the head control clerk (equivalent to the hotel accountant or financial director today). His black jacket, pinstripe trousers and horn-rimmed spectacles made him appear more imposing than his spindly frame and thinning hair suggested. He had a certain fierceness, chain-smoked Woodbine cigarettes and, I would learn later, on his face wore either a smile or a sneer.

That day, he was quite kind. He had known my father, who had been Superintendent for the north-west of England for the dining cars of the LMS railway, under the same ownership as the hotel.

Mr Hawkins gave me a test. I was told to add up – in my head; there were no calculators in those days – the 'daily returns', a document that covered half the desktop, with dozens of columns and headings and a sea of figures neatly inscribed in ink. The total amounts at the base of each column were in thousands of pounds. Maths had been my worst subject at school, yet here I was trying to land a job where most of the day I would be dealing with figures. I tried my best with those endless columns of pounds, shillings and pence, but I knew the answers were wrong.

However, there was one column, headed 'Average Meal and Drink Prices', which required long division – the only arithmetical exercise I could manage with any degree of competence – and I got that answer right. Mr Hawkins peered at me over his glasses and said I would need a lot of practice but . . . he would take me on.

I was to be a junior control clerk, starting in a week's time on 12 February, after my father's funeral and a week before my fifteenth birthday. I would be paid 16 shillings (80 pence) a week.

Remembering that day even now evokes the choking smells of smoke and dust in the city, rubble and charred wood and shattered glass from bomb-damaged buildings. Even a palace of luxury like the Adelphi did not escape. A few days before, Lewis's department store just opposite the hotel had been struck by a landmine, and I recall the incongruous sound of dripping water falling into buckets from the high ceiling of the hotel's main lounge, the largest in all Europe, as I walked through.

Because of the bombing, one wing of the hotel was out of action, the swimming pool would later be turned into a static water tank for fire-fighting, the Turkish baths converted into emergency accommodation with mattresses laid on the marble slabs, and the squash courts and shooting gallery commandeered as storage space for the duration of the war.

I worked hard to improve my maths, and by August I was promoted to Invoice Clerk with a salary of £50 a year. I still have my wages slips, though my pay packet was handed over to my mother, who gave me back a few shillings a week as pocket money. This was normal practice, and many married men continued to hand over unopened wage packets to their wives. At least we were paid! Until the Catering Wages Act of 1948, some hotel staff paid *for* their jobs. When I started work it was not uncommon for doormen, porters and cloakroom staff to pay a weekly amount in return for the right to work and earn tips. Up to the first world war, a carriage attendant in a grand hotel might pay fifteen shillings (75 pence) a week to the management, and a cloakroom attendant as much as £15. A good one, however, could earn between £50 and £100 in tips.

One by one, the men in the office were called up to the Forces, which left the field clear for the girls, all a few years older than me, to be promoted. I was the only male, apart from Mr Hawkins, in an office of 11 females, and it proved an ideal finishing school for a shy and inexperienced youngster. After a while the girls forgot I was there, and their frank discussions about sex and what they referred to as 'women's problems' used to make me blush. I often walked out of the office to cover my confusion.

There was a temperamental Frenchwoman, Jeanette Papon, who every morning used to open the newspaper and read aloud what she called her ''oroscope'. If the oroscope predicted a good day, she was all smiles, but if it forecast a bad one, then I learned to keep out of the way of her Gallic temper.

Maria Martin was the daughter of the famous head chef of Liverpool's

State Restaurant. And another poor girl, who had a shotgun wedding, wasn't quite sure who was the father of the expected baby. We laid odds on it being a married waiter from the fourth floor room service, a quite different man from the one who had the honour of being the bridegroom.

Gorgeous Kathleen Camp became the second head control clerk, the image of Ginger Rogers, with auburn hair, a fine rounded figure, great legs and trim ankles. All the male staff used to race to watch her walk up or downstairs because in defiance of any known physical attribute, her left leg used to positively quiver as she ascended or descended. She had a tremendous following among the troops of all nations, and eventually married an American army officer. Every man in the hotel was a little in love with Kathleen, including my boss Mr Hawkins, a pugilistic head waiter who used to shower her with gifts, and even me, I think, from a safe distance.

In between dates – theirs, not mine – I was allowed to escort the girls to the theatre and the cinema. We always went Dutch; no romance, no necking, just friends.

The hotel's general manager was Monsieur Etienne Cottet, an energetic Swiss who had started at the Adelphi as a waiter and ultimately became a senior manager with the railway company. Cottet was a strict disciplinarian, a dapper man with plump, hairy hands and an eye for the ladies. He insisted they were 'neat and tidy' at all times. Silk stockings were in short supply and used up precious clothing coupons unless the girls had some contact with the American troops who came to Liverpool. But Monsieur Cottet insisted the girls wear stockings to work. To get around this rule, the girls would apply tanning lotion to their legs and paint a line down the backs of their calves with eyebrow pencil. One of my great privileges, when they found I could draw the straightest line in the business (I was a quick learner . . .), was when the girls stood on a chair and got me to pencil in the 'seams'. Always, alas, with strict instructions to begin at the ankle and stop at the knee.

The telephone operators, then as now, were the source of all knowledge and gossip. Even as a young teenager I had to work at night, and I would sit with the night operators for staff supper. They used to listen in unashamedly to guests' conversations and occasionally would allow me to join them. In this way I was able to discover that the tenor Richard Tauber had numerous mistresses while he was married to the exquisite Diana Napier. I could never understand his appeal: here was a man with a gammy leg, a glass eye and a monocle, overweight and in his fifties –

5

married to a gorgeous actress and with hosts of girlfriends. But then, he had this quite amazing voice; enough in itself, I suppose, to attract the female sex in droves.

Noël Coward used to have long, intimate conversations with Princess Marina, Duchess of Kent. Most of it was over my head, but in my naïvety I assumed they were having a passionate affair, instead of being 'just good friends'.

The odd thing is, not only would none of us have dreamed of going to the press with such stories, but we didn't even gossip about them outside the hotel. Not that any of our friends would have been interested. They thought we were mad to work in an industry which demanded such long hours and such utter devotion.

Office hours were 9 a.m. to 6 p.m., with a half-day on Saturday and every other Sunday off. In practice, however, we worked until the job was finished, which meant up to 3 p.m. most Saturdays. It seems slavish by today's standards, yet we still had time for fun. From the wage packet which I handed over to my mother, she gave me back about half a crown (12½ pence) pocket money. It doesn't sound much, but oh, the things that could be done with it! Cinema seats from 6d to 2s 9d, cigarettes 5d a packet, and a good meal for a shilling at the Kardomah Café, complete with music from a string quartet – usually four fierce ladies with moustaches and dressed in black bombazine.

A crowd of us would go the ice-skating rink after work on Saturday afternoons, skate for an hour or two, then tuck into a good tea on the balcony overlooking the ice. This earned us free admission to the evening skating session.

Playing fields and golf courses had been ploughed up and planted with vegetables, so the opportunity for outdoor exercise was limited. Dance halls, on the other hand, were open and packed. There were always queues, as there were outside 'the pictures'. Everyone loved the cinema and it was not unusual to go two and three times a week, since the two films were changed after three days.

Cinemas were not the tiddly, bijou affairs they are today. They were vast, ornate halls seating 2,000 or more. Each had its own Wurlitzer or electric concert organ, which rose up through the stage in a sunburst of sound with a smiling organist to entertain patrons in between films. Some cinemas even had their own orchestras, and a recital would form a part of the programme.

Music and the theatre, then as now, formed an important part of my life. In wartime the great pianist Artur Rubinstein used to perform at the Royal Philharmonic Hall and occasionally at the Paramount Cinema. José Iturbi also played at the Paramount on a couple of Sunday afternoons. I was always at the front of the queue for seats.

The love of music must be in my genes. My great-grandfather on my mother's side was John Ban (Fair John) Mackenzie. He was personal piper to the Marquis of Breadalbane at Taymouth Castle, and won every piping competition he entered, first a bronze medal while he was in his twenties, then silver, then gold. And finally the coveted Prize Pipe in 1849. This earned for him the title 'King of Pipers'. He was not only the finest piper, but described as the handsomest man in Scotland! After Queen Victoria visited Taymouth Castle in 1842, so taken was she by 'Fair John's' piping, appearance and upright character, that she pointedly asked his employer Lord Breadalbane where she might find a piper 'just like him'. Lord Breadalbane naturally had to put the royal request to his piper. According to *The Highland Piper*, published in 1901, the conversation went like this:

> 'John,' he said, 'the Queen wants a piper.'
> 'Yes, ma Lort.'
> 'He must be thoroughly first-rate at marches, and also at strathspeys and reels, just the same as you are yourself, John.'
> 'Yes, my Lort.'
> 'The Queen also wishes her piper to be a fine specimen of a Highlander, tall and handsome, with a fine face and figure; in fact, one something like yourself, John.'
> 'Yes, my Lort.'
> 'There is one other indispensable qualification. He must be sober, reliable, and in every way a respectable man, just like yourself, John.'
> 'Yes, my Lort'
> 'Well, I have now told you all that is required in the man wanted by the Queen. He must be in all respects like yourself, both as man and as piper. Can you recommend any?'
> 'Inteet, ma Lort, there's no sich a man to be found in aal Scotland.'
> 'And will you go yourself, John?'
> 'Na, na, my Lort, na, na.'

However, Queen Victoria clearly did not forget him: 12 years after her visit she presented him with a brooch. John Ban eloped with the daughter of a laird, and fathered a son who followed in his footsteps, winning every piping competition he entered until he died at the age of 30.

Our whole family was musical, and family gatherings in those pre-television days invariably involved a series of performances or 'turns'. My father loved classical music and could play a number of instruments by ear. As a teenager he had played the mouth organ in the trenches during the First World War, and later taught himself to play the piano, organ, violin and a strange contraption called the one-stringed fiddle. This had a horn at one end, and as a child I used to see street musicians play it. The joke was that supposedly vague old ladies used to put pennies in the horn instead of in the musicians' caps, thereby deadening the sound!

Street hawkers, musical and otherwise, were a common sight and sound in Liverpool in the thirties: the muffin man, the jumbo toffee man, the hokey-pokey man selling Italian ice cream in cones. My favourite was the hurdy-gurdy man with his barrel organ and monkey in red waistcoat and fez. Theatre and cinema queues always had a band of buskers to entertain them while they waited.

My mother adored musical comedy and the music halls. She had been what would later be called a career woman, although she would never have recognised such a phrase: she had worked from the age of 14, and when she married my father was manageress of Francis & Mackay, a pastry shop and café in the heart of Liverpool's theatreland.

The tearoom was patronised by most of the stars and actors who appeared in Liverpool productions, and she was a regular theatregoer. As a small child, instead of lullabies I would be soothed by songs from the shows: *Maid of the Mountains*, *The Merry Widow*, her all-time favourite, and *The Belle of New York*. My mother also had a repertoire of Edwardian and Victorian music hall songs.

I was her only child, weighing a mere 5 pounds at birth, or 'two bags of sugar', as my aunts teased her. My older cousin Marjorie said one of them tried to put me into a pint pot, but that's probably apocryphal! My mother was 41 when I was born, and in those days most women started having children in their twenties. She was 13 years older than my father, a fact nobody was aware of throughout her life. She always looked younger than she was, and never had a grey hair up to the day she died at 77. Her complexion was that of a much younger woman, and the only make-up she used was Pond's Vanishing Cream. If it was good enough for the Duchess of Argyll (who advertised it), she would argue, then it was good enough for her. Throughout her life she carefully concealed her age from us all. Then when she reached her seventieth birthday, she decided to be proud of how old she was and how good she looked. From that moment, she divulged her age to everybody she met.

At home we had a pianola, or player piano, with a library of piano rolls. I still have the receipt for the 'Upright Grand Player Pianoforte in Mahogany Case' from Rushworth & Dreaper in Liverpool, to remind me we paid £72 11s 10d for it, including a discount of £1 16s 2d 'as per agreement' in 1935. We sold it finally for £30 in 1984 – still in good condition but too cumbersome to move to a new apartment. Musical evenings played a large part in our lives, because even the wireless was fairly recent. I recall as a very young child my father's delight when he managed to get sound from the 'cat's whiskers' apparatus. Then gramophone records, breakable and easily scratched, became popular. When they became too worn to play, we would put them into a cool oven and shape them into plant pots, with the hole in the centre providing good drainage!

I was sent to piano lessons at the age of seven, but I did not take to it straight away, and neglected my practice. By the time I was 11 and much wiser, I asked if I could go back to lessons. I became a pupil of Madame Ethel Morrey, a well-known Liverpool teacher who ran an academy of music and dance in Broadgreen.

With her encouragement, I entered the Liverpool Musical Festival in 1938 and won the silver medal, just one point away from the gold. The festival took place at the Picton Hall, a beautiful Victorian concert hall in the round. When it was my turn to play, after ten others in the under-14 category, I walked on stage shaking with nerves as I caught sight of the audience of hundreds, including my parents, waiting for me to perform my set piece *The Dance of the Dew Fairy* by James Lyon. But what horrified me most of all was to see that the keys of the concert grand piano were thick with the combined grease of a hundred sweating fingers.

I whisked out the clean white handkerchief my mother insisted I always carry, and quite deliberately wiped the keys clean before I started to play. A ripple of laughter echoed around the hall and I wasn't quite sure why. But I suspect it might have got me an extra mark from the adjudicators.

The following year I was awarded a bronze medal at the Garston Music Festival, having graduated to Chopin's Waltz in C sharp minor, Opus 64 No. 2.

Madame Morrey had told me I did not have an outstanding talent, but that I could make up for this by hard work. She wanted me to try for the scholarship for the Guildhall School of Music in London (our neighbour now at the Barbican) but that was the year World War Two began, and nothing was ever the same again. For millions of young people future plans were shelved, temporarily if you were lucky, permanently if not.

After my father died and I started my first job, with my mother to support, piano lessons were out of the question. Madame Morrey, when she learned I could no longer afford lessons, insisted on teaching me without charge. I went to her studio during my lunch hour, but found it increasingly difficult to practise because of the long, irregular hours I worked and the additional studying I had to do. By then I should have been practising at least two to three hours a day. The lessons came to an end when Madame Morrey and her family moved to Birmingham, and my dream of a career as a concert pianist finally disintegrated.

That first year in the hotel I decided I would be more socially accept-able if I learned to dance, and I enrolled at Vaughan's Dancing Academy. Lessons were sixpence a session, and although I don't know if they enhanced my social acceptability, they certainly taught me to love dancing.

*　*　*

We worked and played hard but could never forget for long the bombs dropping all around us, the freezing, damp nights spent in air raid shelters, and the fact that if the war did not finish within the next year I would be called up to serve my country. I didn't relish the prospect of joining the forces, but neither did I dread it. It was a duty to be done, and I was only one of millions who faced the future with a sense of resignation.

While I waited, I was settling in well to life behind the scenes in one of the world's grand hotels, eager to get on with anything that would speed up my progress. An ambitious lad had to be prepared to do any job he was given – and I was given some lemons.

George Hawkins, at that time acting assistant manager as well as head control clerk, clearly thought my education needed rounding off when he sent for me and told me we were owed money by a prostitute who had ruined the seat of a Louis XV chair in the hotel's elegant foyer. She had 'had an accident' when entertaining a prospective client over cocktails, and although she had inadvertently been allowed to sign the bill for drinks, had walked out without paying.

The woman in question lived in the notorious Lord Nelson Street, just behind Lime Street railway station, the gathering place for local prostitutes. After the war it was said they 'dedicated' the new Jacob Epstein statue – a male figure with an impressive penis – outside Lewis's department store to their endeavours. I found the address and climbed a dingy staircase to the second floor, trying to recall the words to Cole Porter's *Love For Sale* to take my mind off why I was there. I knocked at a peeling, brown-painted door, praying there would be no one at home. But there was. Raised on Hollywood movies, I expected a curvaceous blonde in a tight skirt with heavy make-up, cigarette holder and a come-hither look. Instead, the door was flung open by a blowsy middle-aged woman with tousled hair and a print apron over a shabby pleated skirt.

In a rasping voice the woman asked what I wanted, and with visibly shaking hands I just handed her the bill. She peered at it, then at me.

'Come in, luv,' she said. I hesitated but decided valour was the better part of discretion and followed her into a room with dark red walls, heavy drapes on the windows, antimacassars and fringed lampshades. Much like the suburban sitting room of an elderly aunt, I thought. Told to sit down, I perched on the edge of a worn velvet settee and waited. The woman looked more closely at the bill, brought out a large black handbag, extracted a few notes and said: 'I'll pay for the drinks, luv, but buggered if I'll pay for the chair. Accidents can happen to anyone.'

I got up, grabbed the notes, and ran all the way back to the hotel.

George Hawkins was adept at picking jobs for me that he knew I would hate – but which he also knew I could manage. Petty – and not so petty – thieving was a perennial problem. It was one thing for the occasional item of value to disappear from bedrooms or coat pockets. But quite another when the grand piano was removed from the main lounge by four men in white coats. Only one person had challenged them and they had calmly responded they had been asked to move it!

The hotel's health and leisure facilities included a marbled swimming pool in Romanesque style, with its own entrance and reception desk. There had been a spate of thefts from this area and Mr. Hawkins decided I would pose as a customer and act as his spy.

I took the task very seriously, and was rewarded by being able to swim 'legally' in the hotel pool, which I had previously used only during my lunch breaks if things were quiet and there was a friendly receptionist on duty prepared to turn a blind eye.

In the changing cubicles I realised I was wearing my father's gold watch and would have to hide it. I stood on the seat and stashed it on a high ledge above the small windows which ran along the back of the cubicles. After my swim, during which I kept my eyes open but spotted nothing suspicious, I returned to the changing room and tried to retrieve my watch. I stretched high enough to see along the tops of the other cubicles in the row, just in time to see a pair of legs disappearing through the window a few yards along the row.

I grabbed my towel and dashed to the receptionist's desk, shouting for the house detective. He sprinted outside the changing area and caught the thief. His haul included several wallets and three watches, though happily not mine.

So excited was I at having done the job I'd been sent to do, I didn't realise until later that day when the receptionist and the house detective were chortling over a cup of tea that I'd been running around the pool area with a towel modestly clutched in front of me – but far too small to cover my naked rear.

The house detectives, often ex-CID officers, used to get me to accompany them as a witness when a guest was suspected of entertaining the opposite sex. More often than not it was a naval officer and a Wren. A knock at the door and a polite request always elicited the response: 'There's nobody in here.'

'Hope you won't mind if we take a look, sir?' replied the house detective. In we'd go; the favourite hiding places were under the bed or in the wardrobe. I was the one who would blush to the roots at the sight of a Wren in full naval uniform – or not – clinging for dear life to the coat-hangers, or else with ankles and feet protruding from under the bed.

Another chore I never got used to was the monthly stocktaking in the ladies' cloakrooms. I hated going in there, and the elderly lady attendants did not make it any easier. I'd knock on the door and one of them would shout: 'Come in, boy,' without a thought for the ladies dashing in and out of the cubicles, washing their hands, titivating at the mirrors, more embarrassed even than I was. Checking the supplies of the intimate things women seemed to need – I hadn't a clue what for – was the worst job I could imagine. Yet the two lady attendants were unfailingly happy souls. Every time I went in there, whatever the time of day, they would be drinking tea out of thick china cups. The teapot stood between them on a stool, though I never noticed any milk or sugar. It wasn't until much later that I learned the teapot contained just neat whisky.

Scotch and other spirits gave rise to most of the hotel trade's most

12

successful scams in those days. News filtered through from other railway hotels that the Adelphi was not alone in being gently but regularly ripped off by its employees. In fact it was rather taken for granted. The cellarman at one railway hotel for years got away with watering down the Scotch because nobody was ever able to discover how he removed the metal cap, extracted the whisky and replaced and sealed the cap.

At receptions at the Adelphi when cocktails were popular, some bar staff managed to serve short measures undetected by pouring vermouth or mixers into the glass first and topping it up at the very last moment with whisky or gin, so that the first taste was always good and strong.

Another favourite trick with waitresses during the war was to use their bad handwriting as an excuse for scribbling checks or bills so that they could add their own rounds of drinks to those of the semi-inebriated guests.

When the hotel auditors visited the Adelphi, they would sit at an oriel window overlooking the main lounge and watch to see whether waiters issued bills to patrons having afternoon tea. Often they did not, and if the customer didn't ask for one, the cash would be pocketed.

The kitchen had more fiddles than the hotel orchestra. Legs of lamb, gammon joints, shoulders of mutton would find their way into the garbage pail or the pigswill in the yard behind the hotel, to be retrieved later in the day by a cook or a friend on their way home. I learned that if you saw a member of staff suddenly looking a lot fatter, you often found a fillet of beef strapped to his thigh or a couple of steaks up his jumper.

But don't get the idea that only the staff were on the make. Most of us would confess to carrying out the occasional bar of soap from our favourite hotels, but during wartime it wasn't unknown for guests to leave the hotel with bath towels or sheets wrapped around their waists under their overcoats.

Part of my job was to relieve the night control clerk at the weekend, which meant finishing my own job at 3 or 4 p.m. on a Saturday, and coming back at 9 p.m. to work until 2 a.m. the next morning. During that time I had to collect the service checks from the restaurants, bars, lounges, kitchen and room service; marry the restaurant bills to the cashier's spreadsheets; transfer all these figures to the day book; then balance the day book to the exact halfpenny. Every room in the hotel had its own column, every department its own heading. The huge sheet covered the sloping, Ebenezer Scrooge desk. On busy nights this job could take me until 6 a.m. If it didn't balance, I might still be at it when the day shift arrived at 9 a.m.!

Whatever time I finished, I still had to be back in the office for normal duty on Sunday from 10 a.m. to 4 p.m., back again at 9 p.m., and once again on Monday morning at 10 a.m. Not many teenagers would do it today, but I don't recall feeling particularly put-upon. In fact, the worst part of working those unsocial hours (though whoever decreed nine to five to be social and anything else unsocial I have never known) was simply trying to get some sleep. The hotel was often so busy that no bedrooms were available, and I would have to sleep in one of the curtained cubicles in the Turkish baths, on a mattress laid over a marble slab. There was little sleep to be had, thanks to the snoring and miscellaneous noises that filtered through the curtains all night.

One supposed compensation for being on weekend night duty was being allowed to dine in the Grill Room after the last guest had gone. There was a great shortage of those individuals now euphemistically known as 'rodent control operatives' but then called simply 'rat-catchers'. There were always rats in the hotel, however hard everybody tried to maintain high standards of hygiene – though, to be fair, the Adelphi was not the hotel I once worked in where a live and squirming rat had fallen into the kitchen stockpot. This was not discovered until the stockpot had been emptied. The chef just hoped the soup cook had 'sieved the bugger well . . .' The Grill Room, hushed and empty late at night, had hollow pillars on each side, connected with decorative boxing to hide the supports for the ceiling. The rats used to climb up the pillars on one side, race along the top, slither down the other side, go under the floorboards – and repeat the whole performance over and over again. Not that this put us off our food; rationing was severe and I had the ravenous appetite of a growing teenager.

We were able to keep the Grill Room open during the bombing raids on Liverpool because it was a semi-basement. Other public rooms on that side of the hotel had been put out of action, including the banqueting suites. Always quick to find alternatives, the management decreed that banquets would be held in the Masonic Temple and Masonic Lounge. Several of the larger railway hotels in those days had their own masonic temples, and these were among the most splendid and imposing rooms in the country.

Meals in the staff restaurant were meagre. Food was served in three different areas: the Servants Hall, with trestle-tables covered with oilcloth

14

and seating at long benches; the Stewards Room for office staff and minor heads of departments; and the Couriers Room, which catered for visiting chauffeurs and ladies' maids who took their meals with senior department heads.

I seemed to exist on potatoes and gravy. Sugar was rationed to one teaspoon a day, which I managed to eke out for breakfast, lunch and supper, with a few grains left over to sprinkle on the milk-less rice pudding which was served most days. Occasionally there was 'stew' or 'ragout' but we never dared ask – nor did we really care – what the stew had been before it died.

I did my best to learn as much as I could in the control office but people were often reluctant to teach you in case you took their jobs away from them. I would volunteer to finish off odd jobs when the girls had dates. Gradually, I managed to piece the office routine together like a giant jigsaw. The most difficult job was the collation and separation for payment of the service charge – the ten per cent which was added to all bills for distribution to the service staff according to their jobs and seniority. It was a complicated system, and only the head control clerk and his chief assistant were privy to the intricacies. They certainly were not about to teach them to an uppity teenager, so I used to stay behind at night and go back through the figures until at last I was able to work out the allocation of the service charge. This was as valuable as an additional qualification would be today.

The owners and top management of grand hotels wielded enormous power over their workforce.

The London Midland and Scottish Railway Company hotels, which included the Midland Hotel, Manchester, the Central, Gleneagles and Turnberry hotels in Scotland, and the Queens in Leeds, in addition to the Adelphi, were controlled by Sir Arthur Towle. His father, Sir William Towle, had been manager of the Midland Hotel in Derby in the 1870s, and had introduced luncheon baskets on the trains. This led to the building of smart refreshment rooms in the railway stations, then dining cars on the trains. Sir William's two sons, Arthur and Francis, were also knighted. Sir Francis became the head of Gordon Hotels, which included the May Fair in London, and Sir Arthur took control of the 37 railway hotels. I would eventually work in 15 of them.

The Towle family visited the hotels periodically and we dubbed these visits the Circus. Sir Arthur and Lady Towle, their secretary Miss Oxenford, their personal hairdresser and other members of the household would make a thorough tour of inspection of the hotel. Sir Arthur's barber-factotum, in true Figaro fashion, used to garner gossip and relay it to the Towle family. Miss Oxenford was also a power to be reckoned with; far more than a secretary, she went on to take charge of the interior decoration and housekeeping departments in the railway hotels. She was efficient but without flair, never straying far from red carpets and cream walls. It took years before they were eliminated from the hotels.

In the control office we had to have examples of our work laid out on the sloping desks and be ready to answer any questions that the Towle family – or any member of their entourage – cared to ask.

My job included looking after the accounts of the bookstall, and one day before an expected 'royal visit' I was surprised to find the normal display of books had been replaced by dozens of copies of a new novel called *Madonna of the Seven Moons*, by Marjorie Lawrence. The book-seller explained: Lady Towle was Marjorie Lawrence, and he was obliged during her visits to clear away every other book from the display.

I had to take some papers to the cashier's office and was walking past the lifts in the front hall when out stepped a lady dressed in black knitted silk lounging pyjamas and smoking a large black cigar. The sight shocked me so much I dropped all my papers and had to scramble to pick them up. I forced myself to stop gawping, no doubt open-mouthed, at the big chief's wife looking, to my young mind, so utterly outrageous. Luckily, if she noticed me at all, she didn't report me to her husband. If she had, I might have been fired for impudence – or on any other pretext. In those days it didn't matter much, and somebody could lose their job on the whim of a superior simply for being in the wrong place at the wrong time.

This worked in reverse, too. You soon realised the importance of getting yourself noticed in the *right* way. You had to be smartly dressed and well groomed, the girls in dark dresses or suits which could be relieved with only a small white collar; no earrings, no heavy make-up, no coloured nail varnish, engagement and wedding rings the only jewellery permitted. You had to learn to have 'presence'. A contemporary of mine, Peter Woodcock, happened to be walking through the main lounge of the Adelphi while the Towle family was taking afternoon tea. Peter was always immaculately turned out and carried himself well. The Towles noticed him, sent for him, and he was put on a train that same night to take over as manager of one of the company's smaller hotels the following morning.

With clothes rationing, we were not obliged to wear black tailcoats and pinstripes, just a dark suit, the trousers carefully folded under my mattress each night to preserve their crease. Money was chronically tight throughout the war, and I only accepted that I had to buy a new suit when my kneecaps began to shine through my trousers. My sons in later years, profligate as any post-war generation, found it hysterically funny that we used to press the toothpaste tube with a flat iron to squeeze out the last drop, or meticulously fold used wrapping paper and wind up old string into little spools. There is nothing new about recycling.

Throughout the war the French Restaurant at the Adelphi remained a northern Mecca for the rich and famous. The décor and furnishings and, most important of all, the lighting, followed the examples set by César Ritz: peach-tinted mirrors on either side of the entrance so that ladies could check their appearance before they entered the public gaze. The peach tint also took ten years off their age . . . The restaurant had been one of the most beautiful rooms in Europe, until the Towle family took a trip on the *Queen Mary* in 1936. When they returned, the walls with friezes of cherubs and garlands in different inlaid woods were all stained dark brown; suspended from the ceiling was an oval structure with silk stretched across and lit dimly from above; and wall sconces were glass tubes crossed with chromium bars. It was not until years after the war that the room was restored to its former glory, the faux art deco despatched and the magnificent crystal chandeliers rescued from the Queens Hotel in Birmingham, where they had hung unappreciated for the duration.

I began to learn the rudiments of hotel-keeping by observing in the French Restaurant. I found that people like to sit with their backs to the wall while dining – nobody wants a table in the centre of the room unless they are hosting a large party and want to be the centre of attention. This is why in the Adelphi restaurants there was a sideboard in the middle of the room, never tables and chairs.

Dining chairs, I learned, should have seats that are well upholstered and domed in the centre so that people may sit up straighter and in comfort. César Ritz had been such a perfectionist in this respect that when he opened his hotel in Paris, the restaurant chairs were sent back to the manufacturer on the very morning of the opening to have their legs shortened by two inches. His guests would not sit on chairs which he himself did not find to be perfect in every respect. For the same reason, all chairs without arms had them added.

17

Celebrities were ten a penny in the French Restaurant during and after the war. Michael Redgrave appeared in the uniform of an ordinary sailor, before he was promoted to officer. Laurence Olivier and breathtaking Vivien Leigh, Noël Coward and Jessie Matthews, Jack Buchanan, Ivor Novello and the pianist José Iturbi. The soprano and film actress Grace Moore, tragically killed in a plane crash near the end of the war, was a great favourite with the staff, and the chef used to always prepare her favourite dish – a pâté made from cream cheese and chopped chives – if he was told of her arrival. I often wondered if the poor woman actually wanted it! That's the trouble with guest histories: a visitor only has to mention once that a certain dish or a certain pillow is preferred, and it will always be waiting for him, whether he wants it or not. One American guest who had said he adored raspberry jam years before, only plucked up courage during the last few years of his life to tell the breakfast head waiter that he now preferred marmalade.

Another much-loved celebrity was Jeanette MacDonald, renowned for her duet roles with Nelson Eddy. She sang at the Philharmonic Hall to rave reviews, and I was very disappointed not to be able to afford a ticket.

I once had to deliver a message to Robert Helpmann, and found it hard not to stare at the first man I had ever seen wearing coloured nail varnish. He was in Liverpool to appear with Katharine Hepburn in *The Millionairess* at the Royal Court Theatre. One of my duties as control clerk was to keep the lost property register and make sure the cupboard was locked. However, if any interesting items were left behind by famous people, the girls in the office pleaded to be allowed to try them on, and it would have taken a tougher character than mine to say no. Katharine Hepburn left behind a ruffled silk negligée. All the girls tried it on but, like Cinderella's glass slipper, it just would not fit. Miss Hepburn was willow-slender and quite lovely.

Mae West, on the other hand, could hardly be described as slender. When she arrived to stay at the Adelphi Hotel she sashayed through the front hall on the highest platform shoes I had ever seen, black halo hat and long skirt adding to the illusion of height. She was not young and she was barely 5 feet tall, but her other assets were outstanding – both of them. She was appearing at the Empire Theatre in *Diamond Lil*, way before its time in 1940s England, and because houses were far from full, Miss West left complimentary tickets for the hotel staff.

I got to the theatre early enough to be allocated a seat in the front row. From there I was able to watch Mae West change her costume in the wings between acts. To say she was tightly corseted would have been the understatement of the century. That gal was *loaded*, the show was one of the funniest I have ever seen, and I remained a fan until the day she died.

Roy Rogers, the singing cowboy, endeared himself less to the staff at the Adelphi. He led his horse Trigger through the front hall, accompanied by a fleet of cameramen and reporters, and stood by grinning hugely while Trigger 'signed' his hoofprint on the hotel register.

No VIP visit excited the Adelphi staff half as much as Sir Winston Churchill's brief stay in the hotel halfway through the war. He was everybody's hero; we would have done anything for him and followed his call – as many did – to the ends of the earth for England's greater glory. I contrived to be out of sight of the management behind a pillar in the front hall, just stepping out in time to catch a glimpse of the great man as he walked through, cigar in hand. To my delight, he caught my eye, beamed at me and the girls alongside me, and raised his right hand in his characteristic V-for-Victory salute.

Even with Churchill's inspirational leadership and his great gift for keeping morale up during the darkest days of World War Two, my eighteenth birthday in February 1944 was seldom far from my thoughts. Hopes that the war would be over faded, and I knew I would be called up into the armed services, something just about every young man of my generation saw as part of his coming of age. I expected my call-up papers on my birthday, and every day the buff envelope failed to arrive was a kind of bonus. Although I did not look forward to joining up, it was more because of my mother than for any other reason. In order to make ends meet she had reluctantly taken in a lodger, for whom she provided breakfast and an evening meal. Sometimes she was able to find Anglican sisters through our local church, but the lodger could just as well be, say, a teacher, male or female. There wasn't that great a demand and she was grateful just to have somebody respectable in the house. Even so, it sometimes made her nervous when a newcomer came to stay, and being her only child and breadwinner, I was concerned about how she would cope if I were sent overseas. Like millions of other wives and mothers, she did cope – because she had to – on my naval pay, a gratuity of ten shillings a week from the Freemasons, of which my father had been a member, and the rent from her occasional paying guest.

Six weeks after my birthday my call-up papers arrived, and I had two weeks in which to attend a medical, give notice to my employers and say my farewells to friends and relatives, before joining the Royal Navy. I had chosen the Navy for several reasons. My father had volunteered for the army when he was 16 years old and lied, like many other young men anxious to serve their country, about his age. Only occasionally had he spoken to me about trench warfare, but it was enough to instil such horror that I wanted nothing to do with the army. As a result of being wounded and temporarily blinded by mustard gas, he remained an invalid and died at the age of 44 without having received a penny in pension or compensation from a grateful government, despite winning the Military Medal for bravery. He was one of the lucky ones. His lungs were damaged beyond repair, but at least he was able to go on working as a superintendent of the railway dining cars, including the Royal Train, until a few months before he died.

The Royal Air Force held no immediate appeal. The other option was to become a Bevin Boy, the alternative to joining the armed services, but going down the coal mines was even less attractive. I had always longed to travel and see the world, despite the words of the old song: 'I joined the Navy to see the world, and what did I see? I saw the sea!' And surely I'd be guaranteed a clean bed to sleep in aboard ship. Well, that much was true – even if the clean bed was no more than a makeshift hammock strung like washing on a clothes line cheek by jowl with hundreds of other able-bodied but often seasick seamen.

2

Butlin's, Bombs and Battleships

Looking back, it's hard to decide which was worse: being shelled on board a battleship or spending six months on the Isle of Man. At least the shelling was soon over. Our exile on the island felt like six years. It was a bleak, grim and unfriendly place to teenage boys away from home for the first time, and it seemed always to be raining. I can remember no warm or sunny days, although there must have been some.

The inhabitants were as pleased to see us as we were to be there, and who could blame them? Boarding houses, hotels and even private homes were requisitioned as billets for thousands of servicemen. The war turned us into unwilling and unlikely guests and the islanders, accustomed to a bustling tourist trade, into unwelcoming hosts. Perhaps the powers that be, in their infinite wisdom, realised that after six months on the Isle of Man, we raw recruits would be ready to experience whatever the real war demanded of us.

I had opted for a communications course in the Navy and was on the island for training as a wireless telegraphist. To make our course, held in the Palace Hotel and Ballroom, more interesting, our chief petty officer instructor dictated passages from a magazine called *Health and Efficiency*. This was aimed at naturists, and was illustrated with pages of black and white photographs of nudists of all shapes and sizes, pretty unprovocative despite the nakedness. The chief reckoned this would hold the attention of our motley crew of randy and lonely young sailors more effectively than reading from *Motorcycle Maintenance* or *Engineering Monthly*, and that our skills in Morse code would improve more rapidly. Good thinking on his part, since I passed the course with 94 per cent and went immediately out to splurge 9s 5d on a gold-wire badge – much smarter than regulation issue.

On miserable route marches around the island we used to pass the camps where the aliens, mainly Italians, were interned. We sang as we marched, and everybody would sing up as loudly as breathlessness and exhaustion would allow when we drew level with the camps. I used to wonder, until his autobiography revealed his period as an internee was limited to the very early years of the war, if Lord Forte might have been one of the internees who were cheered – or otherwise – by the sound of our singing, and what he thought of our patriotic rendition of *Colonel Bogey* and other wartime songs whose words we changed, as sailors will, out of all recognition.

The highlight of each week in Douglas was going to the Salvation Army canteen for a fry-up, followed by a visit to the local cinema to cheer ourselves up with such epics as *Lifeboat* with Tallulah Bankhead or *Sailors Three* with Tommy Trinder.

Visiting the island 50 years later, it was easier to see its attractions for holidaymakers: the horse-drawn trams still plied the prom, sea vistas from every vantage point, the hinterland is verdant and there are some fine buildings on the seafront. I took my wife to see the hotel set at right angles to the promenade where I had been billeted in 1944 and recalled sleeping eight to a room meant for two, so exhausted from a day's drill, studying and kit cleaning that sleep was instantaneous and dreamless despite the sights, sounds and smells emanating from 100 teenage boys around, above and below.

The odour from Ken Keithley's boots was so pungent we took it in turns to put them outside on the window sill after he fell asleep. I recalled the innocent words of my anxious mother: 'I hope you don't have to share a room with someone you don't like, dear . . .' Her concern would have been quite different had she known about the desperately uncomfortable dhobi rash which affected her only child because, never having washed his own underwear, he did not realise that one rinse is not enough.

Accustomed to the more benign disciplines of civilian working life, I learned the hard way that in the Royal Navy an order is an order, to be obeyed instantly and without question. Three minutes late on parade and my punishment was to scrub, with a small hand brush, zinc pail of water and bar of household soap, the six flights of bare wooden stairs and landings of our billet hotel. Sooner that, however, than the fate of a fellow resident who fell out with his room-mates. They blackleaded his private parts, upended him and dunked his head in the wc pan for good measure. Another public-school tradition that lived on amongst the lower orders in the Royal Navy!

The discipline did not always work – or did it? For our passing-out parade the Admiral of the Fleet for the Western Approaches came to take the salute. Our squad was selected to parade in front of the Admiral's platform. We had been gruellingly drilled day after day for weeks to stand rigidly to attention whilst the Admiral made his speech, then to turn left on command and march smartly away. Whether our sadistic master-at-arms was merely human enough to be nervous or not we never found out, but at the crucial moment the speech ended he bellowed: 'Squad right turn!' instead of left. Half of us remembered our drill and with Pavlovian alacrity turned to the left. The others, more afraid of the wrath of the master-at-arms, turned right, and the parade ended in shambles. I don't think anybody was sorry to see our lot depart the following day on our way to the Pacific.

Before the Isle of Man we had already done our basic training for a month in Skegness on the Lincolnshire coast, where they had turned me from a pasty, unfit sprog into an able-bodied rating.

The railway stations in those days had posters proclaiming *Skegness – it's so bracing*! The extremes of temperature were unbelievable; at night it was bitterly cold, but in the afternoon the sun would beat down on us poor square-bashing squaddies. It's the only time in my life I've had to treat myself simultaneously for chilblains and sunburn.

We were stationed at Butlin's Holiday Camp, which I vowed never to visit again as long as I lived, and drilled until we were stiff and blistered. When we thought we would die from exhaustion we were put to cleaning our kit – boots were blackened and belts blancoed to within an inch of their, and our, lives. I learned that 'spit and polish' was not an empty phrase, and it's still the best way to shine shoes. I was proud of my uniform, but the regulation-issue underwear of thick flannel drawers and vest, off-white and hairy, was only produced, neatly folded, for kit inspection.

As new boys we learned to avoid being singled out for ridicule by bleaching our smart square collars and the sailor's vests, which had a blue stripe at the neck, to make them look less new. And to perch our hats at a slight angle in defiance of regulations or, a much more serious offence, at the back of our heads. One could also, at a price, buy a fair reproduction of a navy vest cut lower at the neck to reveal a little more of a manly chest and impress any gullible girls. Rumour had it that abroad one could even buy these vests with false chest hair peeping over the top.

23

Early in 1945 we were ordered to HMS *Collingwood* at Fareham in Hampshire to await our draft to the Pacific. The short winter voyage from the Isle of Man across the Irish Sea showed that I had been born with one natural advantage that beat the hell out of any silver spoon: I was almost the only sailor on board who wasn't seasick. By the time we were loaded on to a troopship three weeks later, some of my mates began to go a little yellow about the gills as soon as they walked up the gangplank.

Our ship was the *Empress of Canada*. She had been the *Empress of Japan*, but for obvious reasons had been renamed, although all the notices about the ship were in both English and Japanese. On 10 March we sailed for Australia. Virtually everybody on board was suffering from either seasickness or flu. I was one of the lucky ones – I had flu. I never realised until then that people do literally turn pea-green when badly seasick, and still remember how it felt to be suspended in a hammock at close quarters, with the end of your canvas touching those of your neighbours on both sides, while they lean out and throw up.

After the roughest two weeks imaginable, we reached the Panama Canal. Everybody felt better, and revelled in the joy of freshwater lakes. The small luxury of a good wash in clear water was the stuff of life after washing and showering in salt water.

On 9 April we sailed into Sydney Harbour, and the beauty and warmth of Australia and its people took us all by surprise. In fact it was to change my life.

I was billeted at HMS *Golden Hind*, which was, in civilian gear, the racetrack at Warwick Farm. We lived under canvas and when it rained our tents collapsed because the pegs could not support the ropes and canvas in the deep mud. I had signed up for a telegraphist's touch-typing course, because the Americans were using an automatic Morse transmitting system which was too fast for us to take down messages in longhand. There was the usual examination at the end of the course, but this time with a prize: the top student got to take the pretty young teacher out to dinner – all expenses on her. I missed the coveted prize by one mark, but still have the certificate to prove that at one time at least I was a fast and efficient touch-typist.

Time off in Sydney was a very different affair from the Isle of Man. Off duty we would make a beeline for the British Centre in Hyde Park, where there was a good restaurant staffed by volunteers, occasional live entertainment, and often dancing in the evening. Better still, local families would leave invitations for British sailors to enjoy some wonderful Aussie hospitality. There would always be a party to go to, a family to visit, a weekend on offer, or an evening out with Sydneysiders anxious to look after visiting Royal Navy personnel. This was so typical of the warmth and kindness shown wherever we went in Australia.

My pal John Seville and I were also entertained by relatives of a neighbour back in Liverpool, a large family with two grown-up daughters. One decided to teach John and me to dance properly. The correct technique, she assured us, was for the man to hold the girl closely at the hips, and to demonstrate this she would place a gramophone record between her hips and those of her dancing partner. I'm afraid I broke the record – more than once. John did much better and was invited to dance regularly.

The Knights family were particularly kind to me. There was a huge confectionery company of that name in Australia but it never crossed my mind that Mr. Knights owned it, for in England it would have been unusual to be entertained by somebody of his business and financial standing. In Australia the class system did not exist.

Alan Knights asked me, when he and I had become friends, what I would do after the war. 'Well,' I said, with fingers crossed behind my back and thinking I mustn't disappoint him, 'I'm going back into hotels and I'm going to become a manager.' Afterwards, I berated myself for telling a whopper. I had been told in no uncertain terms that somebody of my education and background should forget any ideas of becoming a manager. However, the Australian way of life had begun to change me, and by the time I got back to England, the determination I felt during that conversation with Alan Knights stiffened my resolve to make the promise come true.

Although Britain celebrated VE Day in May of that year, the war in the Pacific was not yet over. On 16 June I joined the battleship *King George V*, flagship of the British Pacific Fleet, and a week later sailed north to join the American Third Fleet. We were out of sight of land for three months, the longest period a major ship had been at sea, revictualled and refuelled by a line from supply ships.

The second time I was late on parade was on board the *KGV*. I can't recall why, but I do know it was only by a few minutes. However, it was important to relieve your opposite number at the right time and the offence was a grave one. This time my punishment was to climb up the main mast along with another offender, to clean the ceramic aerial holders right at the top. The sea was rough as I started to climb, hand over hand, each foothold more precarious than the last. The higher I got, the more the mast swung and swayed and the more my stomach churned. Think of climbing up a seven-storey building that won't keep still! I didn't dare look down, and the ceramic holders got a very quick wipe-over before I scrambled down again, relying on the fact that no officer or master-at-arms was going to voluntarily climb that benighted mast to check on me . . .

The Royal Navy was working closely with the American fleet. Our orders were to bombard the aircraft factories and coast of Japan – the allies' task was to wipe out the surviving units of the Imperial Japanese Navy and avenge Pearl Harbour with air and sea bombardment. We sailed as close as we could, well within the sight of land, and on 17 or 18 July began our attack on Hitachi. I can recall the brilliant light of the moon as the Japanese retaliated by shelling us from the shore while their kamikaze pilots dive-bombed us from the sky.

During the first big battle I learned what war was all about and, had I been able to think at all, might have yearned for the Isle of Man. The noise on board was indescribable, so bad there was no room inside your skull for anything except that and sheer terror. My action station happened to be the ship's chapel above the magazines. There was just one light at the far end of the chapel, illuminating the crucifix on the wall. The bombardment intensified and we all threw ourselves face down on the chapel floor. I remember praying: 'Please God, don't let me die now. I haven't started to live yet . . .'

The message must have got through, but I have never in my life been quite as frightened as I was at that moment.

President Truman had taken the decision to drop the atom bomb on Japan. The entire ship's crew silently awaited the news that the Japanese had surrendered, and the *King George V* became the first ship to sail into Tokyo Bay on 29 August 1945. My diary records.

I never dreamed I would be doing this . . . even a few months ago. It was an awesome sight . . . all the battleships and other ships sailing in formation. The predominant feature of the land . . . was Fujiyama, it is the Japs' sacred mountain. It is a volcano, and when the clouds cleared we could see the shape of it, a cone shape with a flat top covered with snow. As we got nearer the shore we could make out the trees and the buildings. The sea is full of flying fish.

They jump out of the water and glide along in the air for a few yards, and dive in again.

The prison camps had opened their gates and the allied prisoners of war had been released or escaped. They got to the edge of the water, and those who could, swam out to the battleship. Most of them couldn't. They were too weak and too ill, starved and beaten, skeletal figures unable even to walk. When they could only crawl, they crawled. All they knew was that their personal hell was over and they would be rescued and taken home.

Aboard ship we all helped pull those who had been able to swim, out of the water. Even they were emaciated beyond belief, and I do not know where they found the strength or the will to swim the distance between the shore and the ship. It was several decades before I could bring myself to speak to a Japanese person.

On 2 September the formal surrender of Japan to the allies was signed on the SS *Missouri* in Tokyo Bay, with the *King George V* in attendance. Our twin battleship *Duke of York* carried Admiral Fraser to sign on behalf of Great Britain and the Commonwealth. We all felt this was a terrible injustice; the *King George V* had been the first ship into Tokyo Bay, and this should have been our piece of history. In a letter to my mother I wrote:

A lot of the chaps on board are a bit sore at the Duke going in first, as we should have had the honour, because we have been at sea nearly three months, doing strikes etc. while the Duke has been in Sydney and only raced up here when the surrender was announced.

. . . One of the destroyers which has been with us most of the time went alongside the Duke . . . and the destroyer's company showed their disapproval by throwing spuds at her and shouting at the chaps on board. You can imagine the situation, a destroyer throwing spuds at the great battleship. Of course the C. in C. did not like this, so a signal was sent to the effect that all the ship's company of the destroyer should get three days punishment.

To celebrate Japan's surrender and the end of the war, we spliced the mainbrace: all those over 20 were given an extra tot of rum, while we teenagers had to make do with plain water – not even an additional ration of lime juice. The big treat was tinned peaches for supper. Also

27

anchored in Tokyo Bay was the destroyer *Whelp*, on board the young Prince Philip of Greece. He was already conducting a fond correspondence with Princess Elizabeth, though he would enjoy a period of immense popularity as one of the world's most eligible bachelors in Australia before being posted back to the UK.

The war now over, some of us were given shore leave to visit the naval base of Yokasuka before we sailed for Australia, and a letter I wrote to my mother recorded my 18-year-old's impressions, going ashore with my mate John Seville, thinking ourselves rather splendid in snow-white tropical gear. Yokasuka was almost overrun with American sailors by the time we stepped off the tender.

The poverty and filth of the place and the people was terrible. The Japs are small compared with us and were dressed in rags, and those 'shoes' which are a piece of wood held on the foot by a piece of cord in between the big toe and the next one.

I don't think I saw one clean person ashore, the men seemed to let the women do all the work. The children were quite different from the grown-ups, some of them seemed quite sweet, but the adults were ugly. They lived in shacks and there was not a decent-looking house in the town. I never thought that human beings would live in such filth.

There were some shops (or what they called shops) in the town, they had open fronts and the Japs squatted on the floor with their wares around them. I only saw one food shop, and there were a lot of women queuing up for what looked like dog biscuits, to me. That is the only food we saw in the town. All the other shops and shacks were selling souvenirs for the benefit of the Yanks and ourselves. There were even little kids sitting in the road selling all sorts of trash. They were asking a tremendous price for the things, but a packet of cigarettes or a bar of soap would be worth to them about ten yen which we exchanged on board for four shillings and twopence.

. . . Bartering is not allowed but I think everyone managed to take some cigs to exchange ashore. The Japs have plenty of yen money, but they cannot buy anything with it, so cigs, soap etc. are worth a lot to them.

As one of the lucky few who got shore leave, I had to promise to bring back as many souvenirs as I could find for my shipmates. I went back on board with my shorts bulging on each side and my shirt stuffed with the things I had bought in Yokasuka. I recall vividly the sights and smells and sounds of that day, the narrow mud streets with open drains set into the middle, single-storey buildings made of wood, tiny rooms inside separated only by paper screens, crowds of people not aggressive or resentful as we had expected, but friendly and eager to communicate. Market stalls had been set up in a hurry to sell souvenirs to the naval personnel: hundreds of paintings of Fujiyama, ceramic pots, ornate paper fans, Samurai warrior dolls. I bought gifts for my mates, and for myself a splendid Samurai warrior figure, which, alas, disappeared on the journey home, a small folding Japanese screen and an opium pipe, all bartered for cigarettes.

Our battleship, camouflage removed, sailed for Sydney, and for us, too, the war was at last over. I began to contemplate demob and a speedy return to civilian life, but the Royal Navy had other plans.

During the few months before we sailed for Tokyo and that final year I spent in Australia, I was never left to spend leave or even nights off alone. The Aussies overwhelmed us with hospitality – they must be the kindest people on earth.

However long my demob took to come through, I knew I must prepare myself for a return to hotel life. My job would have been kept open for me and I felt a slight change of course would help me gain good experience. I became an admiral's clerk, which made full use of my touch-typing skills and gave me practice in dealing with correspondence. I was assigned to the release office, which dealt with naval personnel who had decided to stay on in Australia. Some had married Australian girls, others did not want to return to the UK, so changed had they become by the Australian way of life. My job wasn't particularly interesting, but I felt I was doing something positive to help people settle down after the war. It wasn't very onerous, either, and I resolved to have the time of my life that year in Sydney.

Eager to see more of the country, I spent a few days' leave visiting the capital, Canberra. Even there, in the hotel after dinner I got into conversation with two families who insisted I join them sightseeing in their car next day and for a picnic the day after.

Friday 13 September was a black day indeed. My friend John Childs and I, with long weekend leave, had to start seeking out all those people who had looked after us like sons so that I could thank them and bid them farewell. Each family had planned something special – a picnic, a day in the country, a dance, a farewell lunch party. Mrs Knights had even baked a cake for me to take home to my mother. When we sailed on HMS *Chitral* on 24 September, with friends waving goodbye from the dockside, it felt like leaving home all over again.

* * *

Life on board the *Chitral* was far from arduous, with only a few duties on watch and in the wireless room. For me it was a voyage out of the pages of *National Geographic*. We had shore leave in Colombo, walked along the Galle Face Esplanade, past the hotel to the Slave Island district, where we found '. . . *the natives look very dirty and live in hovels but there are not too many beggars, only chaps who want to be a guide.*' This was the red-light district but my diary records solemnly, '*We did not see any visible signs of it, maybe it was too early in the day but I think we missed the worst area.*' If I was disappointed there would be compensation later when, returning from the Salvation Army Hostel to the ship in time for dinner, we were accosted by Sinhalese who '*tried to tempt us to the lust of the flesh. Black women, white women, hula-hula, jig-jig etc . . .*'

We sailed into Aden on 16 October in the early hours of the morning and anchored offshore. Hordes of small boys swam out to the ship and shouted for money, and when we threw it, they dived for the coins and stuffed them into their mouths and shouted for more. In the Red Sea it got so hot we were allowed to sleep on deck, and I remember sunbathing when we arrived at the entrance to the Suez Canal on 20 October, astonished to see on the western side strips of verdant green land, and on the eastern side, pure desert. Bumboats would pull up alongside for the entire 99 miles and 12 hours it took us to sail from Suez to our berth in Port Said, and I shouted myself hoarse bargaining with them, ending up with not much more than a zippered leather shopping bag for 30s and a wallet for 2s 6d. The boatmen were great fun, yelling 'Ach awa' Mrs. Macgreggor' and 'OK, send down the bloody money'. Ladies – for there were Wrens or 'officers' perks' as we called them on board – were addressed as 'Mrs. Simpson' as they were plied with leather pouffes, suitcases, Turkish delight, sandals and cigarette cases. I retired early that night with 'a thin wallet and a dry throat'.

Our next port of call was Naples, and there was great excitement on board when we spotted the dark outline of Mount Etna looming on our port side on a grey, wet afternoon. Mount Stromboli put on a show for us that night by sending showers of sparks and spitting flames high into the air, receding into the distance as we sailed past, a red glow like the tip of a cigarette in the dark. Next morning as we approached the Porto Militaria we heard the band strike up to welcome the Italian prisoners of war who were disembarking.

There was a small crowd of people to greet them. The women were rather hysterical and were anxious to know if their particular friend or relation was aboard. The waterfront had been badly hit during the war, and there were quite a few wrecked ships in the harbour. The Stazione Maritime was a complete ruin. The Castel Nuovo was slightly damaged and it was in the balance whether we would be allowed ashore or not.

Our Lieutenant Commander Guthrie approached the authorities, and returned with the good news that we could go on shore from 11 a.m. until 3 p.m. The sun was shining and the view of the bay of Naples was spectacular, with Vesuvius gently smoking in the distance.

We went ashore and up the Piazza Municipio. It was a colourful scene but the streets were dirty and the smell was not sweet. There were stalls on the narrow sidewalk offering jewellery, cigarette boxes, and trinkets for sale. I bought a necklace and a bracelet for 60 fags and a scarf for 50 . . . We were accosted (everywhere we went) by men, women and children who wanted us to sell them cigarettes, sterling money, or to . . . entice us to pretty girls.

. . . We found the Royal Palace (which now housed the NAAFI canteen) at the end of Via Roma and made straight for the bar by the front entrance. It had been dubbed the George & Dragon, because of the old English-style beamed roof, stone walls and floor and dark wood tables and settles. Beer cost about three lire a small glass (about fourpence) and we had a few rounds before going into the Palace proper for lunch.

The entrance hall was really grand with a wide marble staircase on each side running up to the first floor. There, a terrace ran round a square well and was richly furnished with easy chairs for 'the boys', and there were stalls selling films, cakes, toilet accessories. The lounge was furnished in palatial style and we passed through this into the [NAAFI] restaurant, which must have been a small ante-chamber in the days of royalty. The paintings on the ceiling were beautiful and depicted Minerva and some other wenches that are unknown to me. There were long mirrors on the wall and paintings, one of Bacchus God of Wine. Our lunch was very good, soup, roast mutton, French beans, pumpkin, roast potatoes, currant slice and custard.

After lunch we . . . strolled to the Gardens of Litoranea where we were stopped by a photographer who wanted to sell us a collection of the filthyest [sic.] postcards I have ever seen. We had a look at them but did not buy.

My mate Geoff and I had crammed a lot of sightseeing into that short day in Naples, and when I returned there with my second wife on our honeymoon in 1978, I was able to show her many of the places I visited 33 years before. We sailed that post-war night past the beautiful Gulf of Naples, leaving behind the smoking Vesuvius, the dark outline of Capri and one of the most memorable sunsets I have ever seen. We caught glimpses of Gibraltar, Spain and Portugal before a calm passage through the Bay of Biscay – and home.

I emerged from the Royal Navy as I had entered – a virgin. It's not that I was unaware of the real or imagined joys of sex, nor that I wasn't interested. A colleague of mine in the control office at the Adelphi Hotel confessed that his first time had been over a bag of spuds in the veg store while he was working in the kitchen. There were always known females in the hotels willing to initiate the young men into the mysteries of sex: a still-room maid at the Adelphi, a breakfast cook at Gleneagles, a head receptionist – no less – at Turnberry and a restaurant cashier at the Midland.

I resisted the temptations of the hotels, the Orient and the Antipodes due less to any personal sense of honour and more to the horror stories I heard and the misery I saw result from casual port-side encounters. We young sailors used to be shown awful films on the dangers of venereal disease, and issued with thick rubber condoms that had to be powdered with French chalk to keep them from perishing in the Tropics. The MOs took sadistic pleasure in sending chaps back to the mess deck with their affected member bandaged to look like a huge sore thumb, the loose ends of the bandage tied in a natty bow.

3

The Making of a Hotelier

Back in Civvie Street in my ill-fitting grey, chalk-striped utility demob suit I recalled what I had confidently told Alan Knights in Australia – I was determined to become a manager. Now I had to do something about it. I resolved to work hard and to do – with a smile – anything and everything I was asked to do for the next six months, and see where it led me.

I reported to George Hawkins at the Adelphi Hotel and explained that I had three months' leave due, since I had not had any holiday since I was called up. Mr Hawkins replied that if I wanted to work in my old office again, I would have to forgo my leave and return to work within a week. Taken aback, I reminded him as politely as I could that everybody returning from active service was entitled to leave, and that their jobs were guaranteed. Yes, he said, the job is guaranteed – but not necessarily the same job. I would have to move to another hotel, probably in London. Still giddy with delight at being back in my home town, I forgot about my eagerly anticipated holiday and returned to the control office that week, joining the ranks of returned servicemen disillusioned with the lousy rates of pay they were now receiving. I was on 35 shillings a week, whereas my naval pay had been just under £5.

The people in the control office were all new to me; many of those who might have returned from the forces found hotel pay so low they left in search of better prospects. The attitude of the new team was that they were in charge now, and I could see a danger that I would end up at the back of the queue for promotion. Planning my career became paramount. George Hawkins had by that time been made assistant manager of the hotel, and I approached him with some diffidence to ask if I could be considered for the company's official management training scheme. No chance, he told me. 'You haven't the education or

33

the background, no public school, no university. Forget it. You'll just have to soldier on as I did and make the most of things.' And be lucky to be an assistant manager at the age of 42? That was the moment I decided I *was* going to become a manager – and of the very best hotels.

Within the year I had been promoted to number two in an office of 13. Those official management trainees who had their careers interrupted by the war all had to spend a few months in the control office, and I helped them all I could. Some had been accepted because of influential parents who were clients of the railway hotels or friends of the directors. There were a few failed university students and playboys or chaps who were 'good with people' (even today the only qualification fond parents think necessary for hotel life) whose parents had put them into hotels in much the same way as aristocratic families used to put the idiot son into the church. They didn't all fall into that category, and I enjoyed teaching the techniques of the control office to the bright ones. Harry Berry, for example, who became one of the youngest managers at Gleneagles and later returned to the Adelphi and to the Midland Hotel, Manchester, as general manager. Dennis Aldridge followed Harry at Gleneagles shortly after marrying the daughter of the Chief Hotels Manager. And Eddie Williams, from Southport, close to my own home town, became manager of the Queens Hotel in Birmingham, the Great Western Royal and the Great Eastern in London and the Central Hotel in Glasgow when these hotels were grand and important. Able though they were, I knew I was just as good. If they could become managers, I reasoned, then surely there was a chance for me.

My education or lack of it was a shortcoming I could do something about. Although my formal schooling had been brief, it had also thrown up some valuable experiences. I was bad at sport, hopeless at gymnastics, due mainly to a sadistic sports master. His sarcastic manner and constant ridicule ensured that I couldn't do anything right in PE. And yet when another master took over, I had no difficulty in performing the feats demanded, including vaulting over the dreaded horse. This became an early lesson that stood me in good stead throughout my own career: always encourage, never bully, if you want to get the very best out of a person.

Art was my best subject, and another encouraging master, Mr Moorhouse, considered me good enough to take the scholarship for the Liverpool School of Art. Before I could take him up on this, war began and my school was evacuated to Wales. As I lived outside the Liverpool city boundary, I did not have to go with all the other pupils into, as it seemed to me, exile.

Lessons for the four boys left behind were conducted in our own homes twice a week in two-hour sessions by teachers either too old or not suitable for the services. My father considered four hours a week pitifully inadequate, and at enormous personal sacrifice sent me to a private school, Skerry's College in Rodney Street, Liverpool.

Now it was time to build on that frail base. I knew I'd have to brush up my French, so the first step was to enrol in the beginners' then the advanced course at the Liverpool College of Commerce. I sought out the only evening catering courses on Merseyside, at Wallasey Technical College. They offered two-year City and Guilds Certificate courses 150 and 151, and I persuaded two colleagues from the control office to join me, twice a week after work. We felt rather at a disadvantage since all the other students were working full-time in catering, but we were more at home with the theoretical side, and had great fun taking our cooked dishes home, although my efforts often arrived even more exhausted than I was. I used a leather bag I had bought in Port Said, and the flavours of the cooked food I was carrying used to permeate the bus, ferry and tram. Once, a delicious hotpot tipped over out of the bag and trickled down the stairs of the bus, much to the passengers' amusement. My punishment was to clean up the mess with my dishcloths – and go without a tasty supper.

The two days a week I used to go to Wallasey College began at 9 a.m. in the office. I left at 6 p.m. then had to travel by tram, then ferry, then bus to reach Wallasey in time for class at 7 p.m. At the end of two and a half hours of cooking and lectures I was dead beat, and then had to look forward to that endless journey home – bus, ferry and tram this time. Often I would just catch the last tram, fall asleep, and end up with the conductor shaking me awake at the terminus, leaving me to walk the three miles home lugging my Gateau St Honoré or Blackcap Pudding. Never did food lie more heavily than those dishes in my tired arms.

Was it worth it? Definitely. Even though my two companions retired hurt after a few months. I obtained my precious City and Guilds certificates after two years and two exams, and I was reminded of them when I read recently that Dr Mary Archer, wife of Jeffrey, had told pupils at her old school, 'If you think studying is a grind, it's nothing compared to the grind of growing up ignorant.'

I told my general manager, Frank Collins, what I had achieved. His

35

comment was that the certificates 'were not worth the paper they were written on, without practical experience'. Well, I asked, not unreasonably I thought, might I now have the chance to gain some practical experience? He fobbed me off with the excuse that there was 'a long waiting list'.

I had by this time been promoted to head control clerk, the equivalent of the hotel's accountant today, but because I was only 20 and far younger than any other in the 32-hotel company, I was told I would be called 'acting head control clerk' until I was 21.

When Mr Collins moved on, the new general manager, Chudleigh Pritchard, allowed me occasionally to relieve as assistant manager. However, my big chance came when the Chief Hotels Manager Etienne Cottet paid a visit to the Adelphi. He had been general manager of the hotel when I started work there in 1941, and I was surprised when he sent for me, wondering what I might have done wrong. I would have been less surprised had I recalled my only experience of anything approaching hotel management. As head control clerk I had to be around on busy banqueting evenings, because of all the cash bars, dressed in black tie and dinner jacket like the assistant managers. At one major function with 900 guests expected, I witnessed Etienne Cottet becoming so upset with the assistant managers because things were not going well that he ordered every one of them off duty in a fit of pique. I made to leave with them when Cottet snarled, 'Not you.' That was how I came to supervise my first big banquet.

Mr Cottet was basically a kind man, although very strict, and the offending assistants were forgiven the following morning. He was a typical Swiss, a fine and demanding hotelier, prone to taking ten-minute catnaps throughout the day. Sitting in a chair, he would just nod off and precisely ten minutes later would be wide awake and bright as a button.

Now, as the most senior 'establishment' figure I knew, Mr Cottet interviewed me in suite 201. He had been watching me for some time, he said, and thought I had done extremely well. Had I never considered becoming a manager?

'Consider?' I managed to blurt out. 'But it's all I've ever wanted to do!'

'Leave it to me,' said my guardian angel. 'I will arrange your training programme.' This was to be the last thing Mr Cottet did before leaving the company to run the May Fair Hotel in London for Gordon Hotels. Coincidentally, his secretary there was a lovely blonde girl called Davida who subsequently married one of our good friends, Herbert Striessnig, who became general manager of the Savoy Hotel.

I had told Mr Cottet I would like to spend some time in France, if possible in a kitchen, and he arranged an exchange with the Hotel George V in Paris, where I would be a commis or trainee cook. Just my luck that on a brief trip to Paris before taking up the appointment I caught jaundice, or hepatitis – through drinking out of a cracked cup – and was confined to bed for several weeks. By the time I had recovered sufficiently to return to work, I had missed my chance – another management trainee had gone instead, to allow the French trainee from the George V to take his place here. Instead, I would start my official management training in the kitchens of the Adelphi Hotel.

The structure and the hierarchy of a traditional hotel kitchen has changed hardly at all since Escoffier's time, though today, with simplified menus and a tendency away from full à la carte service, the unit is less labour intensive. The chef and his brigade of cooks have French titles, orders are given and acknowledged in French, and kitchen French is the common language. The Adelphi kitchen was ruled, often despotically, by the chef, usually French or Swiss, assisted by one or more sous (under) chefs. At the Adelphi in 1952 it was Emile Neuhaus, an immaculate Swiss in towering white toque, pinstriped trousers and highly polished black shoes, even in the kitchen. He had an outwardly fierce and bad-tempered disposition, but was always kind to me, his ill temper no doubt explained by severe gout brought on by his fondness for port. Traditionally the *aboyeur*, or barker, calls out the orders for food as they are received from the dining rooms and checks each finished dish before it leaves the kitchen. In our case the *aboyeur* also had the job of keeping a half-pint tumbler of port full to the brim on his desk, so that every time the head chef passed, he could take a swig. This didn't improve his gout or his temper, and although he found it increasingly difficult to walk, he worked long after normal retirement age in order to support his daughter and her children.

Chef Labarbe was also elderly and immaculate, and had a glass eye. He had worked with Escoffier and came over from France for a few months each year to divide his time between the Adelphi and Gleneagles. His sauces and fish dishes were probably the finest I have ever known. He was unstinting and used only the very best ingredients; during rationing it wasn't unusual for him to lavish his entire month's supply of cream or eggs on one special party.

Labarbe loved his English ale, and the job of his commis was to keep chef's glass topped up and frothing. If he had to leave the kitchen Labarbe would remove his glass eye and leave it beside the beer – Chef's way of 'keeping an eye on things' when he wasn't there. I added to my vocabulary of French curses when one afternoon Labarbe returned to find somebody had dropped the glass eye into the beer.

One of the sous-chefs was inordinately proud of his male member. He seldom wore anything but a short shirt when walking around the male staff changing room, and he took sadistic and good-humoured delight, when a new waitress came into the kitchen to serve breakfast, in fishing out this famous member, plonking it on to a silver salver and covering it with a domed lid, asking the unfortunate female: 'How would you like a nice sausage for your breakfast, girlie?' And they say sexual harassment is an invention of the 1990s! This (married) man had had a long-standing affair with a still-room maid who was as thin as a stick insect, and we all used to speculate about how she ever managed to accommodate his admittedly enormous 'sausage'.

Each 'corner' of the kitchen is presided over by its own *chef de partie* (department) – the *chef saucier*, arguably the most skilled, in charge of sauces. The chef poissonnier was often an artist too, his speciality fish and seafood. The *entremetier's* domain was the veg, egg dishes and pasta; the *garde manger* or larder chef was responsible for the 'cold kitchen', cold meats, collations, pâtés and pies, hors d'oeuvres and canapés, and the elaborate buffets. The *chef rotisseur* roasted or grilled the meat, and the *chef tournant*, an experienced cook, acted as relief chef in any department. The chef patissier had a small department of his own where he and his brigade would work on the intricate *pastillage* and spun-sugar work as well as desserts, ice cream, tea pastries and puddings. The butcher and the baker had their own domains, too, in the days when any hotel or restaurant worth its salt butchered its own carcasses and baked its own bread.

This team of professionals was assisted by a battery of lesser mortals. As a commis, I was almost the lowest of the low. Only the kitchen porters and dishwashers came further down the social scale.

The Adelphi Hotel kitchens were cavernous, with hard-tiled floors and walls. Coal-fired boilers and huge ranges made them constantly roasting hot, steamy and uncomfortable, and a network of metal pipes and batteries of bright lights criss-crossed the ceiling. There was no natural daylight and we were permanently soaked in sweat. Even after a bath or shower and a change of clothes I felt I reeked of meat and fish.

Meat was rationed and scarce, and my admiration for the results some of these men achieved was boundless. Veal, for instance, was not available, but rabbit was. You can imagine, then, the technique of taking a saddle of rabbit, flattening out the two pieces, egging and crumbing them – and selling the finished dish to hungry and gullible guests as *Escalope de Veau*. I can't remember anybody among our distinguished clients ever questioning the authenticity of the 'veal', even though they must have known it barely existed.

I used to spend hours with a razor-sharp knife cutting, carving and scraping every shred of meat from a cow's head to make into a stew that would 'see us through the week', as the wags in the kitchen put it. Without benefit of trade descriptions acts and health and safety acts and hygiene regulations as we know them today, we got away with murder – almost literally. Chickens were delivered completely frozen and we would plunge them into hot water to make them more manageable – a technique which in the days of salmonella would have the health inspector apoplectic but which then was the least of our worries.

We always knew when a goat had arrived in the kitchen (not a live one, I hasten to add) because the stench of this strongest of meat permeated most of the lower floors of the hotel. However, the carcass would be transformed by those adaptable cooks into delicious stews, ragouts, fricassées and pâtés. The skin was greatly prized because it could be cleaned and dried and made into rugs, and the cooks used to throw dice to decide who would take it home.

In those days the French influence was paramount – in fashion as well as food, in décor and design. Cuisine was expected to conform to the dictates of Escoffier and Saulnier's *Repertoire de la Cuisine*. Complicated sauces, elaborate garnishes and formal presentation were the most desired attributes. '*Le sauce faire passer le poisson*' was how the French put it. 'If it ain't classical it ain't s—' was an American equivalent. During and after World War Two with the rigours of rationing, this was no bad thing, and if your banquet started with a first course of half a grapefruit, or the fish course comprised half a fillet of sole for every guest, the presentation – sometimes the disguise if, say, rabbit was masquerading as veal – *was* important. The closest those chefs of the 1950s were allowed to self-expression was to give a slight tweak to the recipe of a classic dish and name it after the hostess.

The French influence extended to service, and French waiters were the most sought-after by the grand hotels and their patrons. Although they could be superior and arrogant, French waiters *were* usually the best, for the simple reason that theirs was a respected profession in France, while it was regarded as a job for people who could do no better in this country. Service was equated with servility, an attitude that prevailed until recently. After the French, Italian service staff were considered the best, and one grand hotel only agreed to promote a very capable British head waiter on condition that he became known as "Luigi".

Most hotel chefs of repute were either French or Swiss. No head chef that I met was under 40 years old – it would not have done. They would not have merited the respect nor have gained the experience they needed, was how the thinking ran.

In the early 1950s the Adelphi sauce chef was Joe Cerutti, a homespun philosopher, musician and raconteur. Joe was a lapsed Catholic because he did not approve of the church's 'unreasonable' birth-control laws. What if, he said, a man just rolled over in his sleep and committed the act before he knew it? Joe could conjure up magical sauces from practically nothing to complement the fish which was about the only thing not strictly rationed. There were practically no eggs, hardly any cream or butter, but Joe would make a reduction of fish bones and with top of the milk and his secret ingredient – nobody ever found out what it was – produce a sauce fit for a king.

At large banquets the fish course was almost invariably *Filet de Sole Belle Otéro*, and while I was Joe Cerutti's commis I must have scooped out thousands of baked potatoes, placed a folded sole in the cavity with a few shrimps and covered, or napped, this with one of Joe's special sauces, piped potato around the dish and flashed it under the salamander.

All this was a good 20 years before what I like to think of as the Chefs' Liberation Movement of the 1970s when Michel Guerard, Paul Bocuse, the Troisgros Brothers and others in France, then Anton Mosimann, Michel Bourdin, Richard Shepherd and Nico Ladenis in England, brought chefs out of the closet and into the public domain. Along with the cult of the cook came instant accessibility to a stupefying range of fresh produce from the world's markets, riches undreamed of by their predecessors in the 1940s and 1950s. At the same time came their departure from the classic repertoire with its emphasis on rich, complex sauces and ornate garnishes. Although he may be still classically trained, today's chef – or more often, cook – as media personality is just as likely to be self-taught or to have served a token apprenticeship in the kitchen of a culinary superstar.

The head chef of a large hotel, however, now as then, has to be far more than just a cook. Customers are often unaware of his name; he might not have his own television programme nor have written a best-seller. But he will be a man manager, an accountant, an ace trainer of young people in a very demanding craft skill. Like the good hotelier, the good chef is judged by his acolytes worldwide. He is his own finishing school. If a young person can add to his CV a stage in the kitchen of Michel Bourdin at the Connaught, Anton Edelman at the Savoy, Peter Kromberg or Bernard Gaume; or time spent with the Roux brothers or Anton Mosimann, he or she will find it much easier to step into the job of his or her dreams.

That's another difference. When I was growing up in hotels, the only females allowed near the kitchen were waitresses collecting food for the restaurant or still-room maids whose job it was, in a separate pantry or still room, to make tea, coffee, toast and prepare fruit juices.

Today's chef must be an expert in food technology, health and safety and food hygiene regulations, employment law and local authority regulations. He might have a brigade of a hundred and to them he is employer, mentor and father confessor. He must hold his own around a boardroom table at management and planning meetings, account for an important part of the establishment's revenue, and plan meals for hundreds daily, banquets for perhaps a thousand quite often. Every day of his life he risks being professionally torn to shreds by critics and the media, often without the opportunity to respond. And he is still expected to be a good and creative cook.

Unlike their counterparts of half a century ago, in today's grand hotels there is no room for temperament or the kind of eccentricity to which managers used to turn a blind eye. The chef with his own restaurant may do as he pleases – insult his customers, kick his staff, run amok with the meat cleaver now and then. The *mâitre chef des cuisines*, or executive head chef, of an important hotel needs instead the skills of a craftsman, the dedication of an Olympic athlete and the temperament of a Buddhist.

With only occasional lapses Marjan Lesnik, who four decades later was *mâitre chef des cuisines* during my term at Claridge's, had all of those attributes. He is the thinnest, wiriest and one of the strongest men I know. While I have known many wonderful cooks, Marjan has the additional talents that make him a good manager. He had another great asset at Claridge's in his sous-chef John Williams, an affable but tough

Geordie who took over when Lesnik moved on, to become the first British head chef in a Savoy company hotel.

One of the major contrasts between these men and the kitchen brigade of the Adelphi Hotel is that while the latter had great talents and skills, these did not include teaching the tricks of their trade to snotty young management trainees. Look, listen and learn was the order of the day, because most of the chefs – Joe Cerutti was an exception – were afraid to show anybody how to do things lest the newcomers did them better or, even worse, took their jobs. As a trainee I was often told: 'Why should I bother with you when I know that in a few months you'll come back as a know-it-all assistant manager and start bossing me about?'

I tried always to remember this later in my career, and made sure trainees on their way up the management ladder showed respect and appreciation for people behind the scenes whose jobs might be tedious, repetitive or disagreeable. While the trainees spend only a few months there, for the others that is as good as it gets.

Food preparation skills were hard to learn when the cooks used to create sauces or whisk up beautiful desserts with their backs deliberately turned to you. The art of management was even harder to come by, with no proper manuals, no courses, none of the help that today is so readily available. Then it seemed to be a case of trying to *stop* young people getting on or getting ideas above their station. Every question I asked, every request for information, was countered with an order to go and do yet another menial job around the kitchen.

I searched for a book that might help me get through to the old-timers. All I could find was the American Dale Carnegie's *How to Win Friends and Influence People*. It seems an innocent, outdated affair now, but it was way ahead of its time in England in the 1950s. I spent every spare hour studying the Carnegie method, and I targeted the sauce chef.

During the war, when most of the men in the hotel had been called up, women became wine waiters and lift attendants. As a control clerk before I went into the Royal Navy, I had to present bills to be paid for any mistakes or shortages on the part of waiters – especially wine waiters. One of these was Jenny Hodgson, very popular with the guests but not very efficient when it came to charging properly. There were many occasions when I had to ask her to make up the shortages in her bills.

Later on, when I went into the kitchen as a management trainee, I found her brother was the sauce chef. My reputation for the relentless

42

pursuit of his sister's shortages had gone before me. Bobby Hodgson would have nothing to do with me, and I knew I couldn't learn the indispensable skills of sauce preparation from him. His second in command was a little more approachable, and I decided he would be the man to teach me all he knew. Armed with the Dale Carnegie method, I began to draw him out, asking about his family, his interests, his opinions. So engrossed were we that it was some time before we wheeled around, noses a-quiver, and yelled, 'What's that awful smell?' He opened an oven door and found several heaps of shrivelled, blackened meat – all that remained of six baked hams. Dinner was a little late that evening, but the sauce cook became an ally and taught me everything he could in the short time I spent in his corner.

When I felt I had learned the basics in each department, I would ask Chef Neuhaus if I could be moved on to the next. The pastry and bakery departments were run by two brothers, Bill Spofforth the baker and Sid Spofforth the *chef patissier*. Bill was relatively easy to work for – perhaps because he needed all the extra help he could get to bake the thousands of vienna rolls, meat pies, loaves of bread, afternoon tea scones and teacakes not only for other hotels in the city but for the railway dining cars, station refreshments rooms, even the ships that steamed out of Liverpool.

Sid, on the other hand, did not lightly give away any of his professional secrets of chocolate work and *pastillage*, spun sugar and delectable desserts. He wanted me to do useful jobs like cleaning out the fridges, scrubbing the floor or, worst of all, polishing the yards and yards of copper pipes until they shone. I forced myself to smile and get on with it, and if I finished these chores quickly Sid might relent and allow me the privilege of scooping ice cream, occasionally making fruit salad or baking apples and, greatest compliment of all, teaching me how to use the Bunsen burner to crisp the top of a meringue or finish a crème brûlée.

A popular sweet was the Beehive, a scoop of ice cream around which meringue was piped then quickly flashed on top with a Bunsen burner before it was sent out to the restaurant. One of the pastry-cooks was an affable one-eyed Swede with a snuff habit, and I swear two out of three of those desserts went out with a sneeze garnish.

Working in the kitchen meant split duties, and I had a couple of hours off each afternoon when I would retreat into the cushioned silence of Liverpool's great Picton Library to read all I could about food and wines. On Wednesdays, however, I often allowed myself an afternoon off to go to the tea dance at Reece's Café, which had a full orchestra and lovely girls. There a young man could forget about work for an hour or two.

I usually persuaded a friend or two from the kitchen to come along, and there we'd be, waltzing around with the girl of our dreams, when one or other of us would glance at his watch, see it was 5.20 p.m. and realise we would have to be back in the kitchen and changed into our whites in precisely ten minutes. There was nothing for it except, Cinderella-like, to blow a farewell kiss, call a reluctant goodbye – and leave the poor girl stranded in the middle of the dance floor, thinking me anybody but Prince Charming.

*   *   *

The first Grand National Ball to be held at the Adelphi after the war was a star-studded affair. A thousand guests, including all the major racehorse owners and countless celebrities, were served in the main court of the hotel, with balconies on two sides, and the French Restaurant. I was working in the pastry department, and we had our ears glued to the radio in the afternoon to hear which horses won the main races. Not to see whether our wagers had been worthwhile, but so we could then look at the newspaper to check the winning owners' colours. Sid Spofforth, the pastry-cook who confected the most brilliant chocolate horses, could then decorate them with the appropriate colours.

The florists meanwhile got to work on the long tables to be occupied by the winners, where they created 'jumps' made out of foliage, over which the chocolate horses went through their paces.

The Grand National was a spectacular occasion for Liverpool, and the Grand National Ball one of the highlights of the year for the Adelphi Hotel. The arrangements for this, as for all other banquets, were supervised by the banqueting head waiter, Sam Wood, later to become my father-in-law. Sam was much more than the title implies, and today would be called banqueting manager, probably the best I have ever known. He was like a general on the battlefield. Every waiter and waitress including the 'extra ducks' brought in to serve at evening parties, would be drilled and thoroughly rehearsed in every detail prior to the banquet. He spoke to each of them, inspected their appearance and checked the condition of their white gloves. They were expected to move with military precision, and woe betide any who were out of step with the others – especially should they begin serving their table before the top table had been served. There were two service entrances at the far end of the main court at the Adelphi, and at a given signal from Sam, two absolutely straight lines would enter together, one from each entrance, walk briskly to their tables and stand behind the first guest's chair until, at another signal, the top table was served. A third sign from Sam indicated the also-rans could be served, in strict formation. All this took only seconds, and to watch it was to watch a well-choreographed ballet or a Busby Berkeley musical.

One of the regular guests at the ball was a colonel whose party piece was to balance a magnum of champagne on his head and, from a standing position, bend over backwards, limbo-style, until he lay prone on the floor. He would then slowly rise again, magnum still unwavering on his forehead, to cheers and handclaps – and a battery of bread rolls, none of which ever hit the bottle!

At the end of the evening, when the dancing had finished and the guests had been sufficiently lubricated with champagne, the favourite game was to toboggan on tabletops down the twin staircases leading to the main court. Massive wagers would be laid on which tobogganer would reach the bottom first, and I was always amazed that no more damage was done than the occasional broken arm or dislocated shoulder. Any damage to the premises, of course, went on the bill.

The hotel was stretched to capacity during Grand National week, serving up to 2,000 meals a day for 600 resident guests plus banqueting and restaurant meals.

For the New Year's Eve Gala a pageant was rehearsed by the hotel staff. In 1952–53 the theme was Coronation, the part of Elizabeth I being played by Mrs Pritchard, wife of the general manager. The year before the theme had been Mr Pickwick. A bridge was built between the twin staircases and at midnight all the Pickwickian characters, beautifully spotlit, would cross the bridge in front of a giant clock face. All went well until the night telephone operator who played Mr Pickwick contrived to get himself spectacularly drunk, and was only prevented from falling off the bridge down into the court below by fellow-Pickwickians holding on for dear life to the back of his trousers. Guests' attention was diverted from the fracas when thousands of balloons descended from the ceiling.

Those of us who had worked through the evening still found the energy to enjoy our own celebrations after the last revellers had departed. We feasted on lobsters, oysters and caviar left over from the banquet and saved for us by the waiters, drank champagne, and danced until we had to be back on duty.

For the Gardenia Ball the ballroom was decorated with thousands of gardenias, their heady and exotic scent pervading every corner of the room. Gentleman guests wore a gardenia buttonhole, and every lady a corsage.

Some affairs were smaller but equally memorable. Room 155 on the first floor was a popular venue for exclusive private parties. Sam Wood was in charge and the service was always impeccable, but his second in command had a bit of a drinking habit and was not always up to the mark.

One busy evening, Sam satisfied himself that everything was in order, the clients happy, and left the carving of the roast duck to his deputy. Sam returned to check progress just in time to hear the No. 2 shout to his commis waiter as he carved the duck: 'Take this duck back to the kitchen! Look at it – it's raw. Look at the blood on it!'

Sam sized up the situation, glared and growled: 'Shut up, you silly bugger. You haven't been carving the bloody duck. You've carved your own bloody finger – that's what the blood is.'

I would have cause to be grateful to Sam Wood for the rest of my life and I loved him like a father. He proved a mentor and a friend whose wise advice and guidance remained with me throughout my career. More than that, he introduced me to his daughter.

Before the Christmas party given for the Adelphi staff in 1949, the manager Mr Pritchard invited heads of department to bring their spouses and grown-up family for drinks in a private room. Sam Wood brought his son and daughter, who were 15 and 17 years old, or so I was told. I remember thinking how sophisticated and grown-up Jeanette – or Jean, as everyone called her – was for somebody so young. She was slender, with a beguiling smile. I had been told she was engaged to be married, so although we got on famously and danced together during the party, I said goodbye that night with no thoughts of seeing her again.

Then in September the following year Sam himself told me his daughter was, in fact, 21. Her engagement had been broken off and he invited me to the twenty-first birthday party he was giving for her at the Seacombe Hotel. Nervous as I always was before meeting new people, I called in at a pub to have a beer for Dutch courage before catching the ferry over to Seacombe. At the hotel the dinner party for family and close friends was coming to an end and the guests who, like me, had been invited to the dance waited for the speeches to be over.

Sam had recruited the banqueting waitresses from the Adelphi for the evening. They had all known me since I was 14, and they plied me with whisky and ginger ale. Before long I began to feel dizzy and decided to go home. Then, as fate would have it, the champagne was poured, I drank a glass without thinking – and it cleared my head like magic.

Jean and I danced every dance, and within a week I had asked her to marry me and she had accepted. We were married 11 months later, and with a husband's responsibilities I now had more reason than ever to want to get on.

4

The High Road

The Adelphi was undoubtedly the finest hotel outside London, and I still felt proud to work there, but when I had the opportunity to spend a season, Easter to October, at Gleneagles as part of my training programme I couldn't have been more excited. I would only be flying, if not out of the frying pan into the fire, then out of the kitchen and into the dining room – as a waiter – but the craft skills needed 'front of house' are just as important as those 'back of house'. I wanted to be sure there was no job in the hotel which I had not experienced when I became a manager.

Gleneagles was like a temple dedicated to the goddesses of elegance and leisure (for the guests, that is). Britain's finest golfing hotel, renowned worldwide, a Versailles-style château set in 700 acres of Perthshire countryside. The hotel had been built by the Caledonian Railway Company, which saw no reason why Scotland should not boast a resort hotel as prestigious and luxurious as those in Switzerland. The Swiss might have skiing – Scotland had golf.

Not only was Gleneagles – the valley of the eagles, appropriately enough – a perfect natural site for three right royal golf courses, but it was on the main railway line between London and Inverness and London and Aberdeen. Work began in 1913, and ceased the following year with the outbreak of World War 1. It was 1922 before the directors of the railway company formed their own team of builders, craftsmen and decorators, eschewing the use of outside contractors, and in just ten months completed the building, decoration, fireproofing and furnishing 'with not one inch of jerry work.'

The hotel opened on 5 June 1924, and thanks to its proximity to the railway, discerning travellers could dine lavishly in London, sleep off the effects in a comfortable first-class compartment, and wake up to breakfast in Perthshire.

From the very beginning the restaurants provided the best of Scottish and French cuisine based on fresh produce straight from the local hills, glens and farms to feed 'the hungry and the fastidious'. It must have also fed the very poetic, judging by the preface to a booklet published about the hotel in 1924:

> Is it the magic hour ere dinner is served? Walk through cool gardens and avenues, pace the green lawns, watch the mountains fade to violet – whilst a strutting piper in all his glory pours forth a stream of pibroch, lament, fling or reel, and stirs you with skirling.

I couldn't help thinking my great-grandfather John Ban Mackenzie, King of Pipers, would have felt at home there.

Alas, although the panelled interior of the hotel had been described as 'the last spoken word of an exquisite and civilised art' with 'every hall, every room, every fitting, every piece of furniture a harmonious note in a carefully wrought symphony', the author of the fulsome booklet might have changed his tune had he glimpsed behind the scenes 30 years later. While he had found 'every bedroom is a separate creation – individual to you. It folds to your personality; not a hotel room at all – but *your* room', I was introduced to rather different accommodation.

I was allocated a bed in an attic room shared with 15 other male staff. Even by Royal Navy billet standards it was stifling and utterly fetid, with only two tiny skylights providing light or such air as there was. A dog shouldn't have been expected to live in such conditions and I was damned if I was going to. I asked to see Harry Appleton. He was now assistant manager at Gleneagles and I had taught him the rudiments of hotel accounting while I was head control clerk at the Adelphi. I can't recall what I said, but it must have had some impact – either that or he took pity on my still being a mere trainee – because he arranged for me to share another attic room, this time with only one skylight and only one other occupant, the veg cook, whom I had known at the Adelphi.

Staff 'dined' in a room they called the Snake Pit, a windowless basement underneath the main lounge service pantry. When I first clapped eyes on the pit I could hardly believe the squalor. Filthy dishes caked with leftover food were piled in festering heaps on every available surface. Before you could eat at a table you first had to clear a space, and people just shoved a heap of dirty plates to one side before tucking into their own food, surrounded by the debris.

Again I asked to see the assistant manager, and again he got me

49

transferred, this time to the Couriers Room, where I would eat with the maids and the chauffeurs of the hotel guests. Not much consolation for the other poor devils who still had to eat and sleep in such appalling conditions, but their turn was to come.

I worked under the supervision of the restaurant head waiter, Louis Tapiro, who in the winter was the number two at the Adelphi. He made me commis waiter to a very experienced waitress called Laura, who had the busiest station, or group of tables, in the room. It was essential to have close at hand, long before the guests arrived, all the equipment you were likely to need during the meal service. Laura and I always got to our station at least 15 minutes before anybody else. Our sideboard was soon heaving with silverware, china, condiments, cold sauces and everything else we might need for the four- or five-course meals which were the norm in those days. There would be no time to fetch anything we had overlooked once service was under way. We worked non-stop.

There were 8 tables in our station, one of which sat 10 people, and a total of 30 diners. The usual number for gueridon (a small wheeled table) and silver service, using a spoon and fork to serve from a silver 'flat' or tray is 20 guests per station. Laura taught me how to be quick, and I was an eager student. We prided ourselves in being swift, efficient and polite, even to those guests who didn't deserve it and who certainly were not polite to us in return. The old saying *pas devant les domestiques* was quite true – some of these people had conversations that would make your hair curl (I still had some in those days); others would discuss business or politics; and we would overhear nuggets that today would probably be sold to the tabloids for thousands of pounds.

After each meal we would lay the table for the next, three times a day covering tables with pristine cloths, folding napkins Carlton style, standing proud like triangular pointed hats, polishing glasses and silver cutlery until they shone. We could never leave the dining room until after the last guest had gone from our station. After starting work at 7 a.m. to prepare for breakfast and working through to lunch, we were lucky to manage three hours off in the afternoon from 3.30 to 6.30 (the guests were on holiday and could enjoy leisurely meals). We seldom finished before midnight and it could be much later. Laura, well into her fifties, was a trouper, and if she ever felt tired she did not let it show. I hope I didn't, either, but I lost a stone in weight in my first month.

Rationing was still in effect, yet the chefs at Gleneagles, with the help of all the fresh produce from the countryside around always managed to make the menus outstanding. The head chef was a Swiss, efficient and a stickler for discipline. But it was the larder chef, a bad-tempered highland Scot, for whom I had the greatest regard. He worked 20 hours a day, fuelled on neat whisky, preparing fabulous pâtés, raised pies, decorated hams, galantines and chickens, and his magnificent Sunday luncheon buffet took my breath away.

My initiation into the special skills of the banqueting waiter came soon after I arrived, and it was obviously thought that as a management trainee I should have the nous to tend the top table without too much danger of doing the wrong thing. The first course went without a hitch, and I thought the game was a dawdle. The second course was soup. When I got hold of the plates I learned what my initiation rite was to be: the plates were red-hot, blistering the fingers of both my hands. Fixing a smile on my face to mask the grimace of pain, I carried them to the top table – dropping them would have been an offence beside which first-degree burns on the hands of a commis waiter were as nothing. In any case, there was a whole line of other waiters behind me in strict formation. The first couple I was to serve were deep in conversation, heads together, and I was supposed to discreetly wait for a break. There was none and I couldn't hold on any longer or the plates would have been welded to my hands. In desperation I slightly touched the lady's bare arm with my plate. Galvanised, she soon made room for me to serve and I counted myself fortunate that she didn't have me fired.

That was 1953, Coronation year, and on the day itself I was determined to see something of the ceremony even though Laura and I had 28 luncheon guests to look after. We set up in record time, and I escaped from the dining room and hared down the corridor to the guests' television lounge – just in time to witness the crowning ceremony from the doorway and hear the resounding closing bars of *Zadok the Priest* and the choristers of the Abbey singing *Vivat Vivat Regina*. When I attempted to sneak back out, I was spotted by Jimmy Petrie, the head hall porter, who chased me back to the restaurant and threatened to report me. Luckily for me, he didn't, because in a hotel like Gleneagles, intruding on guest facilities was a gross misdemeanour.

The general manager of the hotel was Harry Berry, whom I had helped to train in the control office when he was a management trainee. Gleneagles was a top job and Harry handled it with typical aplomb. His was another of the many railway hotel marriages; his wife Margaret had been the ladies' hairdresser at the Midland Hotel, Manchester, while Harry had been assistant manager there. Years later Harry returned to the Midland as general manager until his retirement.

Those few months at Gleneagles taught me the enormous differences between a city centre hotel like the Adelphi and a resort hotel. The most important is that whereas in a city hotel guests stay for only a night or two, seldom as long as a week, and are out and away from the hotel for most of that time, in a resort hotel where people come to have a holiday or play golf, they are yours 24 hours a day. They stay for two or three weeks, sometimes more, and they take three meals a day in the hotel – four if you include afternoon tea, and most of them did. Menu fatigue, however good and varied the chef's food, is a hazard. Falling out with fellow guests and the minor squabbles and petty jealousies that develop when people are living at close quarters, however luxurious, is another. And the weather is the worst. Scotland's weather, undependable at the best of times, is the scourge of golfing hotels. One year we had to transfer the entire Gleneagles/Saxone pro-am golf tournament to Carnoustie, the only course in Scotland that wasn't waterlogged. When it is bad enough, and it often is, rain may stop play. And walking. And sightseeing. And other outdoor pursuits apart from a limousine trip to Edinburgh for shopping. Husbands, wives and children are forced to fall back on each others' company, and an indoor swimming pool and billiards room were not enough when the windows and the beautiful views were obscured by rain. Fresh diversions had to be constantly offered: games, quizzes, treasure hunts, competitions or concerts. The hotelier's lot is made worse when reservations are cancelled or guests are summoned urgently back to London or Manchester by a convenient telegram or family crisis.

*   *   *

Gleneagles really marked the end of my official management apprenticeship, and from there I was set on the first rung on the ladder of promotion: relief assistant manager at the Royal Station Hotel in York then the Exchange Hotel, Liverpool. I spent only weeks at each of these, and as a wet-behind-the-ears manager I found it difficult to work with some of the long-serving staff. We call them 'old soldiers'. It would be a rare young manager indeed who could ever get one over on these stalwarts who had clocked up years of experience of dealing with a passing population of young shavers like me.

I went to the Midland Hotel, Manchester, in the winter of 1954, excited at the prospect of working in the busiest hotel in the company. The acting general manager was George Hawkins, who had been my original employer. 'I didn't know you were coming,' was his greeting. 'We don't want another assistant manager.' Not quite the welcome I was hoping for, but head office at St Pancras Chambers in London confirmed that I should be there, acting as relief to one of the six assistant managers. They were a lively lot, those assistants, hard workers but fond of a good time and even fonder of the opposite sex. I was a newly married man so not in their league, but I used to observe their exploits with amazement and not a little admiration. The number of affairs going on between these eligible bachelors and the female staff – and guests, come to that – was impressive. One man managed to involve himself with three different women in one evening, one a waitress in the Wyvern Room, another a hairdresser from the Steiner salon in the hotel, and the third a receptionist. Somehow, he managed to avoid being found out, although he did look extremely tired the following day and appeared for breakfast in dark glasses.

Her Grace the Duchess of Bedford, who was a loyal guest at Claridge's years later, revealed in her autobiography how she was awakened as a woman by a three-day encounter with a smiling silent stranger at the Midland Hotel. I wondered if it was one of my colleagues, but never had the heart to ask the charming Nicole Bedford.

The assistant managers at the Midland knew they had an ally and protector in Ben Martin, the head night porter. He had spent all his working life at the Midland and nothing escaped him. If the general manager happened to be around when one of the assistants came back late at night the worse for wear, dear old Ben would sneak them into the cubby-hole storeroom behind the porter's desk. He would even arrange for black coffee before releasing the young man to stagger through the front hall and up to his room.

The Midland was staffed by the nationals of 17 countries. Mr Hawkins was promoted soon after I arrived to general manager of the Midland Hotel in Derby, his home town, and the new general manager was John Turpie, the man who was to have great influence on me and my career. He was full of the most wonderful ideas, unfailingly efficient and courteous to staff as well as guests, a true gentleman, and the most accomplished hotelier I have ever met. He transformed the Midland Hotel with his fresh thinking and ambitious schemes. Under his direction the French Restaurant, Trafford Restaurant and the Grill Room were refurbished and equipped with innovative new menus so that in a relatively short time they once again became the finest restaurants of their kind in the North. Front of house and what would nowadays be called 'guest relations' were J.T.'s particular forte; he had an unerring sense of what the guest really wanted. For the first time, arriving guests were greeted personally by a manager and shown to their room, instead of being handed a key and left to wander the corridors. I worked with him for only a few weeks on that occasion before he sent for me and told me I had been promoted.

* * *

Three weeks before Easter 1954 I returned to Gleneagles in the bitter cold of a Perthshire spring, this time as assistant manager with formal status and the great bonus of being able to take my wife with me. Jean and I found a small flat above the post office in the village of Blackford. The postmistress had been doing a number with a retired colonel who ran the local pub. He might have sweet-talked her into licking his stamps, but when he got one of his barmaids into 'trouble', the romance came to an abrupt conclusion. The postmistress was a kindly soul and made us welcome in that small community. Just as well, because Jean was left pretty much on her own while I worked the hotelier's extended hours. I usually managed some time off in the afternoon – time enough, it seems, because our first son, Graham, was born in a Merseyside nursing home the following January.

I had made a rod for my own back at Gleneagles; the first job I was given was to put right all the things I had complained about as a trainee the year before. The entire exercise stood me in good stead for the future, and I always made it a priority to see that the staff have decent conditions for eating, sleeping, changing clothes, and relaxing while they're off duty.

Life was quite different as a manager, even the most junior. Dressed in black jacket and pinstripe trousers by day, dinner suit and black tie in the evening, I was dealing with guests face to face instead of with spoon and fork in hand. Best of all was being able to use my initiative, to make things happen and to feel I could contribute to the fortunes of the hotel.

There were invaluable lessons in what came to be known as 'crisis management'. The reception manager disappeared into the wide blue yonder one day: just didn't appear for breakfast and was never seen again. We imagined all sorts of problems with his love life until the general manager discovered he had overbooked not one but three major conferences, one from the US. Somehow, with all of us pitching in, we managed to persuade the Americans to stay in America, the second conference to switch to another of the company's hotels, and the third we kept – but only by evacuating the living-in housekeeping and management staff and hastily converting their rooms into additional guest accommodation.

Although I had seen scores of celebrities at the Adelphi Hotel, now I was able to meet them and observe them at close quarters. Not just film and stage stars but the aristocracy, fashionable people, society stalwarts like Barbara Cartland. At that time she was still Mrs Hugh McCorquodale, and even in middle age she made quite a stir when she entered a room. For Gleneagles she dressed appropriately in tweeds, but these tweeds were in every colour of the rainbow and topped off with a Robin Hood hat sprouting long multicoloured feathers at the back. She looked like a technicolour galleon in full sail – as she continued to do when I greeted her, in her nineties, every week at Claridge's.

Another redoubtable annual visitor was Jennifer of 'Jennifer's Diary'. In real life Betty Kenward was as charming and charismatic as her *Tatler* and later *Harper's & Queen* diaries were precious and gushing. She, too, was a regular visitor to Claridge's nearly half a century later and I never ceased to admire her. She had the gift, envied by everybody who knew her or read her columns, of almost total recall of the names, correctly spelled, titles, background and family history of every person she met. She never carried a notebook or pencil, never seemed to ask for a name to be repeated, yet there the Diary would be, month after month until she was in her eighties, with every detail correct. Her energy was boundless well into old age. She usually managed to take in at least three parties a day, and there was hardly a débutante mother in London who didn't consult Mrs Kenward on her daughter's coming-out programme or solicit her advice on any important guest list.

Lord Inverclyde played a major role in life at Gleneagles. He had been married to the actress June and divorced because, according to the press, he was impotent. In spite of – or perhaps because of – this, women threw themselves at him, queuing up to see whether they might not become the next Lady Inverclyde.

Cowan Dobson, the portrait painter, used his wife, a famous beauty of the 1920s and 1930s, as his canvas, painting her face every morning and every evening with white make-up and scarlet lipstick and slicking back her black hair. The poor woman, undoubtedly beautiful at one time, looked as though she would be more at home in a circus. I don't believe it brought the artist many commissions.

The Duke and Duchess of Argyll always created a frisson when they entered a room, especially in full Highland dress. The Duke had a florid face, described by one of the staff as looking 'like a fairmer's erse on a frosty morning', while the Duchess had a skin white and smooth as alabaster. No wonder Ponds had her advertising their cold cream!

One of the most tiresome guests was the Hon. Lady Gamage. She arrived in August for the shooting season, and at the end of her stay always hosted a lavish dinner party in the French Restaurant. Her table, the largest we could find, had to be in the centre of the room so that all the other guests had the honour of gazing in towards hers. She was dressed by Norman Hartnell, the Royal couturier, and one year he created for her a crinoline gown in pink shot through with grey – a difficult colour to wear. We were given a week's notice and the general manager, Dennis Aldridge, all his assistants, housekeepers and head waiters set to hunting down tablecloths, candles and flowers to match her ladyship's gown. Difficult enough in London or Manchester, but in the wilds of Perthshire in the midst of a busy season . . . We did manage to track everything down except the promised carnations. On the very morning of the party, our florist in Glasgow finally managed to find them – lovely big flowers, pink with a tiny and very subtle grey stripe.

Lady Gamage insisted on the best table in the restaurant *and* the best table on the gallery of the ballroom. Before she arrived in the summer of 1955, we'd had guests from America who had booked for a month and were enjoying Gleneagles so much they extended their stay through August. This Mr Brown was known as 'the pineapple king' because he lived in Hawaii and owned most of the pineapple plantations there. Mr Brown's favourite table on the ballroom balcony was the same one that Lady Gamage demanded.

He was a charming man, good-natured, expected the best and appreciated good service. He was a keen football fan, and when he learned that the hotel had a football team, decided to do something for it. At his behest we fixed a match with the Central Hotel in Glasgow, about 40 miles away. He insisted on paying for the team's transport and for all the prizes, and was invited along as guest of honour. Glasgow's cinder pitch was a killer, and most of our players returned with severe grazing to legs and arms and thighs, and were treated to drinks at Mr Brown's expense.

A return match was played on the Gleneagles pitch, a much better one, and our benefactor presented a silver cup and silver tankards to all the players. That evening he also sponsored a dance in the clubhouse which all the staff could attend.

He was a larger-than-life character and a generous tipper. If somebody was sent into Auchterarder to buy him a newspaper, for instance, it wasn't unusual for him to proffer a five-pound note – and that, 40 years ago, was a week's wages. He brought many distinguished Americans to stay as his personal guests, including Errol Flynn and Patrice Wymore and Alice Faye with her husband Phil Harris. Always a pin-up of mine, Alice Faye delighted me more than 30 years later by signing the sheet music of my favourite of her songs, *You'll Never Know* with the words 'To Ronnie. Thanks for everything!'

All this will give you an idea of why Mr Brown was our most popular guest. It will also introduce you to one of the hotelier's dilemmas: who has priority?

Reluctantly Lady Gamage, whose reservations were jealously guarded from year to year, must have her druthers: Mr Brown and his lady, Miss Winona Love, were relegated to a table on the floor of the ballroom below to make room for Lady G and her party. Mr Brown left the ballroom early. I had a call at 5.30 the next morning to say he wanted to say goodbye to me. He, his valet and his maid had packed his trunks during the night, and they would be leaving at 6 a.m. It was a good few years before Mr Brown could be persuaded to return to Gleneagles.

Lady Gamage, *au contraire*, remained a regular visitor. She often wore low-cut Hartnell gowns and carried a lace scarf or stole made to match, with which she covered her cleavage whenever a waiter approached the table. She needn't have bothered; there was much to conceal but none of it even remotely provocative.

The restaurant manager sent for me one evening and I approached Her Ladyship, who was standing, gowned in black lace, décolletage revealed, surrounded by her 11 guests and shrieking, 'It's been pinched. I tell you it's been pinched.' I wondered if she meant her hallowed cleavage, but it was her modesty panel which had disappeared and which she was accusing the restaurant staff of 'pinching'. She was furious as she swept along the grand corridor, shouting as she went. As she waddled up the three steps leading into the ballroom the black lace scarf tumbled from the folds of her gown and fell to the floor.

I picked it up, handed it to her and said: 'Your Ladyship, the scarf just fell from the folds of your gown.'

She snatched it out of my hand and snapped: 'I don't believe it.'

There were glittering events aplenty during the spring and summer months, guests vying to outdo each other with the lavishness of their parties, and important charity dinners and balls. The Friends of France Council under the chairmanship of Lord Inverclyde staged an Entente Cordiale Ball for which Christian Dior brought over an entire fashion show. This was followed by supper and a dance, the menu was as lavish as the Master's post-war fashions, and the event was sold out months in advance.

Christian Dior was addressed as Master and treated like a god; he stayed only one night and left the following morning laden with gifts from the Chief Hotels Manager. I cherish the memory of one of his most elegant models screeching like a fishwife at one of her better-endowed cohorts, who was about to step on to the catwalk showing a little too much décolletage.

'*Mon Dieu!*' she cried. 'Zose teeties! Don't let ze Master see ze teeties . . .'

The event that caused most excitement, however, was the first television show to be transmitted direct from Gleneagles. It was to feature golf in the morning, pony trekking in the afternoon, and in the evening music performed by Henry Hall and his dance band, famous for his radio programme *Henry Hall's Guest Night*. He used to open all his broadcasts with the announcement: 'This *is* Henry Hall and tonight *is* my guest night', because he had arrived late for one important broadcast after his plane was delayed, and somebody had to stand in for him at the microphone.

Henry Hall had first played at Gleneagles in 1924, and his name was still a great draw on its own, never mind a live television broadcast. The world and his wife descended on Gleneagles that day. We served 450 afternoon teas. The lounge was full and I arranged for extra tables and chairs to be placed along the grand corridor. The staff were stretched to the limit but they coped admirably; the doughty waitresses with years of experience and a black leather moneybag under their white pinnies would not even entertain the idea of extra staff being brought in lest their tips be diluted. Not all, but many a waitress at those grand hotels retired to a life of luxury to live out their declining years on the cash accumulated and invested or hidden beneath the mattress.

Like all hotels, Gleneagles had its share of scams. We managed to stamp out some of them; others we lived with, and the rest died the death with the advent of each generation's new technology. Room-service waiters had the task of stocking every suite with a full bar – spirits, mixers and beer. We almost never had a complaint, yet we knew full well that the waiters would take frequent nips from the spirit bottles and either top them up with water or just hope nobody noticed. With the aid of the hydrometer which measured the specific gravity of each bottle's contents, and random checks, we were able to reduce this practice to a minimum.

No self-respecting Scottish hotel would be without its complement of pipers. Gleneagles had – and still has – some of the finest. When I worked there, all the pipers were great characters whose love of the pipes was exceeded only by their love of a wee dram. After every party, I used to send up a prayer of thanks that they had all managed to stay upright, given the amount of whisky they needed to lubricate their pipes. Of course, the night came when they didn't. One piper managed to support himself against a pillar and play on, while a second collapsed in an ungainly heap, his chanter inextricably entangled in his sporran.

Because Gleneagles was so isolated, recruiting and keeping staff was a nightmare. The hotel was an hour's drive from Edinburgh or Glasgow, slightly less from Perth, and in any case, the most staff could hope for in the way of transport was a bicycle or the loan of one. Villages like Auchterarder and Blackford, only just within walking distance, were devoid of entertainment. Inevitably, staff created their own.

Little did the famous golfing guests at Gleneagles dream that their hallowed turf doubled as the favourite spots for staff to do their courting. The bunkers well hidden from view were the choice locations for hanky-panky, as were the rhododendron bushes that surrounded the hotel. It was one of my jobs to patrol the grounds and pull out of the bushes ignominiously by the ankles any offending male member (you should pardon the expression) of staff, then to obligingly turn my back while his female companion picked herself up, dusted herself off – hopefully not to start all over again. All of this under the windows and in view of the hotel guests.

A later general manager, Jimmy Bannatyne, a wonderful Scot and a great friend, had the kind of wry humour that was always getting him into trouble. He described the favourite leisure activity of the Gleneagles staff as 'a knee-trembler up the Braco road'.

I also heard him admonish a rather stern spinster housekeeper, on her knees tending a spot on the stair carpet the day before the hotel opened for the season: 'Och, it's all sex and scrubbing in this place, m'dear – and you get all the scrubbing!'

You could hardly blame the staff for occasional lapses of protocol, and although discipline had to be meted out, I could barely suppress a smile when I came upon a coven of housekeepers trying on every item in the wardrobe of Mrs Billy Graham, wife of the celebrated evangelist. It was quite a wardrobe, too, packed from stem to stern with designer labels and expensive clothes.

Staffing the massive kitchen and back-of-house area was the major headache. Every Thursday afternoon Mr Curran, the Area Personnel Officer, would ring from the St Enoch Hotel in Glasgow to let us know a number of new staff were arriving on the next train. It was always Thursday; that was the day the notorious Barlinnie Prison in Glasgow used to let out its minor (and sometimes, we found, not so minor) felons. We did have strict rules about who we employed: they had to breathe. We welcomed them with open arms and stitched-up pockets, especially if a big banquet or conference was scheduled for the weekend.

Sometimes this form of recruitment had dreadful consequences. If you had to dismiss some of these hardened characters, and yes, that was one of my jobs, too, they tended to resent it somewhat. One of the kitchen porters, a graduate of Barlinnie, decided to wreak revenge by running amok with the meat cleaver, not, as in Arnold Wesker's play, around the kitchen, but all over the hotel, front and back of house, along guest corridors. It was me he was looking for, and once again I got lucky: it was my evening off. He managed to break every window on the staff staircase before he was caught, imagining no doubt it was my head he was smashing in.

*　*　*

When Gleneagles closed for the winter in 1955 I returned to the Midland Hotel, Manchester, under the stewardship of the great John Turpie, as assistant manager. I learned more about management and the art of hotel-keeping from observing and trying to emulate the way John ran his hotel than I had in all my training. He encouraged me at every step, and just as I had at school, under his kind and wise tutelage, I blossomed and matured. He even unwittingly improved my knowledge of fine food and wine, when he and his wife Doreen, a former railways hotel housekeeper whom John had married after they met at the Tregenna Castle Hotel in Cornwall, entertained in the hotel. Their private party menus were always the most exciting and creative selections, and by testing these dishes and their wines before they were served (and by filching the leftovers, if I'm honest) I improved my palate immeasurably. That is one lesson you learn early in hotels: if you want to eat well, eat fast! The crumbs from a rich man's table take on a whole new meaning when you are a growing lad on low wages and surrounded by epicures.

From a sound middle-class background and with all the right educational attributes, John Turpie nevertheless abhorred the thinking I had encountered before Etienne Cottet stepped in. John saw no reason why I should not become a manager – not only a good manager, but a top one. His words were music to my ears and I am convinced John Turpie's faith in me and his discreet supervision played a major part in any success I later achieved.

When confronted by an especially challenging dilemma I often stop for a moment and think: what would JT have done? When he achieved his ambition and retired at the age of 60 the hotel industry lost a star. When he died in Cornwall in 1995 I lost a friend.

Not that everything always ran smoothly even with a great hotelier in command. The Blue and White Ball was the event of the year in Manchester, raising vast amounts of money for Jewish charities. A thousand people attended; all the banqueting rooms on the main floor and the public rooms were commandeered, leaving only the French Restaurant to cater for hotel guests.

As often happens, it was just one seemingly small mistake that nearly ruined the entire event. Guests were given a choice of main course. Waiters were to make a note of those who wanted Dover sole and those who wanted chicken. Now the waiters might well have made mistakes, but I am convinced what actually happened was that when the chicken was served and they saw how good it looked, many of the guests decided to switch from their original choice. Before long guests were standing on the chairs shouting for food. The message was clear: never, regardless of pressure from the host or the organiser, give a choice of menus at a large party.

Nearly 40 years later I made a not too dissimilar error of judgement at Claridge's. One of our regular patrons brought the wedding reception of a grand-daughter to the hotel. The bride's mother could have haggled her way out of a Marrakesh souk. After a succession of meetings at which costs were shaved well below our normal levels and we agreed to let the lady bring in her own flowers, waive the room hire and charge only minimal corkage for her own champagne, we were asked to replace some of our usual elegant and not inexpensive canapés and savouries with such popular items as samosas and miniature pizzas, baked potato skins and dolmades. As the price came down, the numbers went up. And up. Greatly against my better judgement I gave in to unrelenting pressure from the bride's mother to have the reception from 6.30 p.m. to 9.30 p.m. I tried to explain that you could not invite 320 people from all over the UK to a reception at Claridge's in the middle of the evening and expect them to go away and find their own dinner!

The chef prepared double the estimated number of canapés, and not 320 but 450 people showed up. Worse, photographs and subsequently the receiving line were delayed for nearly an hour. Hordes of guests like avenging angels surged into the reception room without waiting for a glimpse of the bride and groom. I expected the waiters as they emerged through the service swing doors to be devoured along with their silver trays of food. As fast as the kitchen produced more and still more savouries, they disappeared without trace, the waiters barely able to set foot in the room before their trays were emptied with the speed of a vacuum cleaner sucking up dust.

The hotel of course got the blame, if not for the behaviour of the guests, then for not producing enough food. My comeuppance, for making a wrong decision and giving in to pressure from a sweet old lady, was that after a succession of thoroughly unpleasant meetings the bride's mother ended up with the cheapest wedding reception in history.

Some problems that are experienced in any business, can pose a particular dilemma in hotels. We took on a liftman at the Midland who had excellent references, was a thoroughly nice man and very good at his job. We learned, however, that he was far from clean in his personal habits, and one of the guests emerging from the lift sent for me to complain. 'You must do something about this,' he said. 'I mean, it's not exactly Balenciaga!' I took the liftman aside and gently pointed out that he must change his socks and bathe his feet during the day because standing as much as he did, it was understandable that his feet became sweaty and unpleasant. To be honest, I also had him transferred to the staff lift.

I could hardly do the same with the banqueting head waiter, immaculate in white tie and tails and one of the best in the business. He had the incurable habit, while waiting for guests to arrive, of picking his nose with one hand and scratching his backside with the other. He would instantly fling open his arms with the arrival of the first guest, bow and beam: 'Madame! Welcome! How wonderful to see you again . . .'

One of the happiest parties I remember from that time was thrown by the very young Tommy Steele. Topping the bill for the first time at the Palace Theatre, he invited a large party of relatives and friends from London and gave them the party of a lifetime in the Marie Antoinette Suite. He was little more than a teenager, and I thought this gesture fairly typical of the very kind-hearted and down-to-earth man he became.

*   *   *

I am glad that John Turpie was the one to break the good news to me, early in 1956, that my first major opportunity to show what I could do had finally arrived: I was to be relief manager at Dornoch Hotel in Sutherland for a few weeks. The general manager had been ill but was expected back at work before the season got properly under way. Happily for me, he found another job and did not return.

Up to the Scottish Highlands with me came my wife and son, then six months old. On the way there I had to break the journey to relieve for a long weekend at the Royal Station Hotel in Inverness. The keys were left with the hall porter, but no instructions or messages as to how the place was run. This was typical, as I learned when I took over at other hotels later in my career. Handovers, if they had been invented, were unheard of. The King is dead, long live the King, seemed to be the order of the day with the railway hotels.

My brief experience at Inverness was enough to teach me not to allow dogs into public areas. One of the permanent residents had a collection of miniature Pomeranians. They took the best seats in the main lounge, and when I went over to speak to her she said: 'Oh, I must get the dogs to perform for you!' At a signal from her several of the dogs scrambled off the settees and performed a series of undignified pirouettes around the lounge carpet. The performance over, they jumped back on to their soft berths on the brocade sofas, much to the disgust of the other guests, who nonetheless, did little more than glare.

At first glance, Dornoch Hotel was beautiful. To me, any hotel that gave me my first crack at management would have been beautiful! However, it was not particularly well built, and although in those days most general managers were expected to live in, little thought was given to their accommodation. Our quarters comprised a small sitting room with bathroom at one end of a guest corridor, and a bedroom at the other, cheek by jowl with the visitors' rooms. The walls were so thin we could hear people in the next room turning over in bed, let alone snoring. Our baby son slept in a cot in our room and when he woke up in the night – as he invariably did – I had to jump out of bed and dash helter-skelter down the corridor to try to pacify him in the sitting room out of earshot of the sleeping guests. We soon found the only remedy, to which I believe many parents succumbed in those innocent days, was a mixture of hot water, sugar and brandy.

We opened the hotel a week early to accommodate an important local wedding. I briefed the waiters and waitresses so that the service should be impeccable and, with Sam Wood's military precision in mind, impressed upon them that they must not start serving until I gave the signal. The minister was barely halfway through a lengthy Scots grace when the service door burst open to reveal the waitresses bearing the first course. In my haste to stop them I caught my shoe in a hole in the carpet, slid all the way across the small dance floor and landed stumbling convulsively right under the nose of the minister, who was just getting to the 'amen'. 'Mr Jones, the new manager,' he added for the benefit of the assembled guests, 'has now been well and truly launched into our midst.'

The hotel had not made a profit since before the war and I was convinced, sleepless nights notwithstanding, I could change that. Believing firmly in the personal touch and that every guest, irrespective of his standing in life, wants above all else to be made to feel welcome and important, I personally 'met in' and said farewell at the end of their stay to all of them. I also spoke to every guest in the restaurant at luncheon and dinner; I don't believe the golf or fishing story exists that I haven't listened to a hundred times and smiled. I worked hard at persuading visitors to extend their stay. This was a good ploy if they had teenage children, because I offered a little-used part of the male staff wing, separate from their sleeping quarters, as an annexe for young people and charged them reduced rates. The company was always curious about how we attained 130 per cent occupancy some weeks!

I took only one evening off, on our wedding anniversary in September. And the hotel that year made record profits.

Sometimes I found it hard to believe the staff had the same objectives. The head waiter, a hard-working character with a limited vocabulary, used to mutter every time I saw him: 'Bloody window tables. Bloody picnic hampers. Bloody dogs' dinners. They'll be the bloody death of me.'

The area was a great fishing centre, not far from the Shin Falls salmon leap. It was a tradition that when fishermen returned in the early evening their catch was displayed on silver salvers in the front hall. There were a lot of fishermen and a lot of fish, but they always urged us to make quite sure their particular fish was served to them. Hard on the chef, since the fish didn't exactly have name tags, but we got through it without too many diners recognising 'their' fish at another table.

One of the *specialitiés de la maison* was 'twice-poached salmon', the fish being left outside the kitchen door at night by prior arrangement with the chef, then poached in the more conventional way for guest meals. The shifty suppliers of these prime comestibles would arrive at the back door every weekend to collect anonymous little brown envelopes.

I managed to upset a lot of the suppliers and tradesmen at Dornoch because, with my background in control offices, I checked all the invoices as they came in and queried any amounts I wasn't happy with. It taught me to be very careful with people. The chef was the proverbial crocodile with a permanent smile which, after my regime of checking began, became a permanent snarl.

One of our regular visitors was Mr Whitlow, the Savoy Hotels meat buyer. There was great excitement when he was due; he had the best suite in the hotel, the best table in the dining room, and was treated like royalty. He came up to select his beef on the hoof as the cattle grazed serenely on salty Highland pasture. This was why the Savoy company was always renowned for the quality of its meat. The local squire, Captain Bob Grant, was also owner of the famous butcher's shop in the town, and when he entertained Mr Whitlow most lavishly, I was fortunate to be occasionally invited to join them.

Other guests, perhaps sensing how hard I worked to ensure they had a good time and knowing about the ungenerous rates of pay meted out by the railway hotels, were equally kind. I used to compensate Jean for working such long hours by taking time off in the afternoon, while the guests were fishing or playing golf or out for drives. William Moss, of Moss's Empire Theatres, was a particular ally. He had a wonderful old-fashioned Rolls Royce and he used to offer me the use of it, with his chauffeur, to take Jean to some of the local beauty spots.

In those days there was severe class distinction between white-collar and blue-collar workers, never mind between staff and guests, and there was a scandal of ridiculous proportions when the head housekeeper, a woman of considerable refinement, had an affair with the handyman who stoked the fire in the boiler house. This was a great source of double entendres, but neither of them deserved the gossip and sniggers their affair caused.

You will find me a pretty tolerant fellow, but there is one above all of God's creatures that I heartily detest – the bat. One evening at Dornoch I had a frantic phone call to say there were bats in the female staff quarters. The girls were terrified. Please would I go up there *right away*. I found one absolutely enormous bat flapping around the room, undoubtedly more terrified than the girls who stood cringing and shrieking, some of them standing on chairs, which only brought them closer to bat height.

'Be brave, Jones. Have courage,' I muttered to myself. (I remembered that scene from *Ben Hur*.) I grabbed the nearest 'weapon', which happened to be a tennis racket, and a towel, chased the bat for dear life, hit it hard, tossed the towel over it and flung it out of the window. I was shaking, but that may be the one and only time in my life I was hailed as a hero by a crowd of adoring women.

At the end of the season we threw a party for the staff to which we invited some of the local suppliers to send representatives. The trouble with not being a local myself was that I didn't realise some of those businesses were not small-time employers of two or three people. They took our invitations at face value and extended them to all their employees, sometimes as many as 30 or 40. Highland Scots are never ones to miss a ceilidh, and our staff party was overrun to such an extent within the first half-hour that we had to close the doors. Undeterred, those inside opened every reachable window to admit their less fortunate friends. The kitchen did an amazing job of catering for 250 people in a room designed to accommodate half that number.

* * *

I returned to the Midland Hotel in Manchester for the winter not displeased with events at Dornoch, and I was able to act as relief manager for John Turpie while he went abroad to recruit staff. I felt it was a privilege to stand in John's shoes even for a short while, and I must have acquitted myself well because in February of 1958 I was given my most important assignment to date.

I couldn't believe my good fortune when I learned I was to be appointed general manager – at just turning 32, one of the youngest in the company – of one of its most prestigious establishments: Turnberry Hotel on the Ayrshire coast, an important resort hotel with golf courses every bit as hallowed as those at Gleneagles.

There the similarity ended.

Turnberry was glorious, no doubt about it. As you approached the hotel from the coast road from Prestwick, or over the hills and side roads from behind, it seemed to welcome you with open arms. Today, 40 years later, it still has that feeling for me. It sits on the brow of a hill overlooking the Irish Sea; the building is white, the roofs red, the surroundings vibrant green. Between the hotel and the sea is one of the world's most challenging championship golf links – far more exciting, many say, than Gleneagles. Looking out to sea, your eyes rest on the Ailsa Craig, a giant granite rock that looks like a battered bowler hat, half-submerged. They say if you can see Ailsa Craig, it's going to rain. If you can't see it, it *is* raining.

When my appointment was announced somebody sent me a cutting from the *Daily Express* with a headline: 'FLOODLIGHT LUXURY LOSES RAILWAY HOTEL 300 POUNDS A WEEK'. The article claimed this beautiful hotel was virtually empty all winter, a drain on railway resources and a burden to the taxpayer. My brief from Frank Hole was to turn its fortunes around. I must show a profit in the first 12 months, or else it would be sold – to Butlin's, as an extension to their 'luxury' holiday camp 16 miles away in Ayr.

What hotelier could resist such a challenge?

That first February weekend at Turnberry showed the newspaper article had not exaggerated. In the restaurant built to accommodate 250 people, there was one solitary diner. Fortunately for me, it was Niall Hodge, who appointed himself my protector and became my friend until he died in Edinburgh the night before he was to be honoured by Queen Elizabeth the Queen Mother at Holyrood House.

Niall was the chairman of Blackwood Hodge, the earth-moving and industrial conglomerate, and lived in a modern house converted from the old air traffic control tower at Lands o'Turnberry, the former airfield near the hotel. He was a great character, a bachelor philanthropist who liked to use his vast wealth to help the old and the young who needed it most. He took the seemingly outrageous step of building a combined luxury old-people's home and public restaurant close to his home. Malin Court was designed so that the elderly with or without means could live in some comfort in single or double rooms for as long as their health and mobility allowed. If they became ill or needed long-term care, there were round-the-clock nursing facilities in a separate unit. Whatever happened, they need never move from their home.

The dining room, decorated and furnished by interior designers, with Turkey carpets, soft lighting, polished wood tables and fine chairs, was open to the public for lunch and dinner most days. This ambitious project enjoyed some success, though few had faith in the venture to begin with.

Niall Hodge often threw open his house and grounds for the benefit of the children's home at Bridge of Weir. He would sponsor gifted children through public school and further education, and at one time adopted a lad from Bridge of Weir and sent him to Gordonstoun at the same time as Prince Charles. This boy grew into a fine young man, worked with Niall in his Malin Court project for some time, and eventually entered the priesthood.

'The most valuable thing you can give to your guests,' Niall Hodge told me at our first meeting, 'is your time.' I put into practice 'the Dornoch regime', meeting every guest on arrival and speaking to each one in the restaurant or in the ballroom after dinner. I discovered my greatest asset as a hotelier was not efficiency or talent or even hard work but being a natural listener. People respond to this, and when you add to it the acceptance that one man's luxury is another man's necessity, you have the key to good hotel-keeping. Luxury is an experience which exceeds the individual's expectations of personal and physical comfort levels. People will pay for the level of convenience they are accustomed to, and good hotel-keeping reflects the times we live in. In the 1990s, for example, hotel guests are likely to have marbled bathrooms, jacuzzis or saunas, air-conditioning, and telephones in every room in their own homes. Those things, considered luxuries even 10 or 15 years ago, are basic requirements for many travellers today.

At Turnberry, my immediate goal was to fill the hotel in those quiet winter months when the wild south-west coast of Scotland holds limited appeal. I made a huge effort to publicise weekend terms which were the bargain of the age: for five guineas (£5.25) we offered two nights inclusive of all meals, free golf and the return rail journey from Glasgow. Soon we were full most weekends. I extended the offer to midweek, which attracted some lucrative conference business, and as news of the hotel spread, we were able to fill the rooms with little trouble and increase our rates to a more sensible level.

There was a wonderful atmosphere at Turnberry, and the village of Maidens along with the nearby town of Girvan made it part of a small, close-knit community. The local golf society members were our neighbours and often our suppliers as well as important year-round customers. This brought its own problems, since the feeling was that their business brought with it proprietorial rights over the hotel (and its manager), along with the right to more for less – food, drinks, accommodation for their friends, special terms for private parties and club events. If they couldn't get what they wanted from me, they simply went over my head and contacted Reggie Turnbull, the Scottish Hotels Superintendent. He had been general manager at Turnberry some years before, and still visited the hotel most weekends with his family. Almost invariably, he sided with the Turnberry residents in any argument over prices, and I listened to each new request knowing full well that whatever I said, it could be overturned by the superintendent.

Turnberry rapidly gained a reputation for small but prestigious conferences where the delegates could combine golf with business. Ford Motor Company executives did themselves proud with one of the most magnificent buffets I have ever seen. And SMT, one of Scotland's leading transport companies, reminded me of a lesson I first learned by listening to the Fats Waller song: 'Find out what they want, and how they want it – and give it to 'em just that way . . .' The SMT executives were a nit-picking bunch much given to issuing detailed instructions suited to a five-year-old. These had to be taken down verbatim by me in a notebook; a previous manager had failed to do so and nothing, they claimed, was exactly as they wanted. I was happy to do it their way, and their annual meetings became a valuable source of revenue to the hotel.

Billy Cotton, the radio bandleader, used to come up to entertain conference delegates and important parties. He had a special connection with Turnberry, having been in the air force in the First World War and flown in and out of Turnberry airfield. He recalled the golf courses being used as an airfield during both world wars, and remembered the hotel – as I did, when I spent a holiday in Girvan as a boy – as a military hospital.

Turnberry, like Gleneagles and Dornoch, was a resort hotel, and we were always looking for new diversions for guests who stayed for long periods, or when the weather precluded evening golf. There was dancing every night except Sunday during the season, and I considered it one of my less arduous duties to dance with every lady guest whose husband or escort had two left feet. With *My Fair Lady* playing to packed houses in London, I arranged a *My Fair Lady* evening, and many of the guests managed to fashion costumes at short notice from the contents of their wardrobes. A florist from Glasgow came through with a vanload of violets, dressed as Eliza Doolittle and handed out posies to every lady in the restaurant.

One annual occasion that allowed the ladies to dress up yet still be outclassed, was the *Concours d'Elégance*. Frank Hole, the Chief Hotels Superintendent, hosted a grand luncheon before the event – always what I consider the ideal summer menu of local asparagus, poached salmon and fresh strawberries. The parade would then assemble, the Rollses and the Bentleys, the Lagondas and the Hispano-Suizas graced by a lady dressed in the same colours.

I shook hands with my first American President when Dwight D. Eisenhower came to play golf. He was being honoured at nearby Culzean Castle, presented with a ten-room apartment for use during his lifetime, as a gesture of thanks from the nation for his work in World War II.

Ike arrived with his friend, the President of the Pepsi-Cola corporation and sometime husband of Joan Crawford, and Reggie Turnbull and I greeted them and escorted the pair to the clubhouse for some refreshment before their game. Asked what they would like to drink, both chose Pepsi-Cola (I should have known . . .). 'Och sir,' the waitress clapped one hand over her mouth and whispered to me, 'I hav'nae got any o' *that* stuff in *this* bar.' I told her to send one of the caddies over to the hotel to fetch some and run back all the way. The poor lad hared across the road, up the 85 steps leading to the hotel and back down again in record time. Even though his panting could be heard all over the clubhouse, Presidents Eisenhower and Pepsi were too polite to notice. Pepsi-Cola has been served in the clubhouse ever since.

There was another momentous event during my three years at Turnberry. Within months of our arrival Jean found she was pregnant again, and our second son, Russell, was born in June of 1959, in the same Merseyside nursing home as his brother. We and everybody else were so sure this child was going to be a girl that when they rang me to announce Russell's birth my perfectly serious response was: 'A boy? But I've *got* one!' The planned Louise Margaret became Russell Brent, and Jean arrived back in Ayrshire carrying the plumpest, blondest creature we could have imagined. *We* might have been thrilled, but his older brother had other ideas. Graham was now four years old and deeply resented the interloper into our little family. He expressed his disapproval in various ways, despite our best efforts to appease him. We arranged for a new bicycle to be delivered to him the day the new baby was brought home but he chose instead to sail his little clockwork boat in the fountain in front of the hotel entrance. It was such a hot day that when the boat slipped out of his reach he climbed over the low wall and waded in to retrieve it. Excited that the cool water came up to his thighs, he resisted all the efforts of the stern hall porter, Charlie Graddidge, to fish him out. Every time poor Charlie compromised his dignity by making a lunge for him, the boy would scoop another load of water over his uniform.

Always good with his hands even as a small boy, Graham liked nothing better than to follow the joiners and handymen around the hotel, and they made him his own miniature tool kit and tool bag so he could 'help out'. They also used to let him sit with them during their tea breaks, and no doubt soon forgot he was there. We, however, were reminded when one evening Jean and I were entertaining important guests in the hotel and our four-year-old burst in, pyjama-clad, and announced: 'I've lost my f—ing fire engine. I can't find the bugger *anywhere.*'

Another member of our family who caused ructions with the guests was Buster, our West Highland terrier. We had bought Buster just weeks before Jean became pregnant and they do say 'buy a new dog, get a new baby'. By the time he was a year old Buster had developed an alarming fixation for ladies' silk stockings. So long as they wore trousers, long skirts, or any other type of hosiery, the dog took no notice. The moment he sensed silk, that was it! I might meet guests while out walking the dog and be deep in conversation when I'd hear a shriek and the lady would jump halfway into my arms: Buster had struck again, sniffing discreetly then cocking his leg up against the silken calf.

Turnberry threw up its share of characters, both behind and in front of the scenes. I inherited a restaurant manager who knew by name and by sight all the lavish tippers. When these people arrived he would lead them straight to the very best window tables overlooking the bay. Anybody else, however celebrated or loyal to the hotel, was banished to the secondary tables behind pillars at the rear of the restaurant. I was having none of this, and managed to contrive a sideways promotion which returned him to Glasgow. I recommended a young station head waiter for the job; too young, many thought, but I had known him as

71

a commis waiter at the Adelphi Hotel. I firmly believed even then that a good manager should learn to trust his own instincts and judgement, and should never be afraid to be innovative, to take chances and to give chances. Otherwise he is liable to miss the potential stars in the firmament around him.

Ronnie Hamblett proved an excellent choice and remained at Turnberry until he retired. His son Raymond followed him into the hotel industry, through the British Transport Hotels apprenticeship scheme. He became one of the finest young classically trained hotel chefs of his generation and the catering world was devastated when he died of a massive heart attack at the age of 32 in 1989, leaving a wife and baby son. He was at that time head chef at the Gosforth Park Hotel in Newcastle, and had worked in several of the most notable British Transport Hotels.

The Turnberry years were memorable ones. I had the satisfaction of turning a business with flagging profits into one of the company's most prestigious hotels. We had been successful enough to plough money into the refurbishment of those beautiful bedrooms and suites overlooking the sea and the Scottish countryside, the fine restaurant, ballroom and lounge, and the indoor sports facilities. Local people with money to spend were once again in evidence, along with fashionable visitors from all around the country and overseas. We enjoyed living in beautiful surroundings just minutes away from the beach, and the afternoons we were able to spend there with the two boys, our tranquillity disturbed only by the occasional guest who firmly believed hotel managers should be on listening duty 24 hours a day.

So far as I was aware I had only one serious black mark against my name. During President Eisenhower's visit my parents-in-law were up in Turnberry to visit their grandchildren. Sam was still Banqueting Head Waiter at the Adelphi Hotel in Liverpool, and as such considered to be a member of the service staff. He happened to be in the crowd that assembled to see the President, and was unfortunately visible in a press photograph, though only those who knew him well would have spotted him in the crowd. The Scottish Hotels Superintendent reported Sam's inadvertent appearance in the press to Etienne Vacher, Chief Hotels Manager, and I was summoned to Edinburgh and severely reprimanded for a breach of what was considered proper.

Nothing gives me greater satisfaction today than to return to Turnberry, which we try to do at least twice a year, and see it once again restored to its former glory, after a period of decline during the sad years of the railway hotels in the 1970s. It is now under the stewardship of Chris Rouse, a young trainee manager during my time at the hotel. He loves the place as much as I did, has Scotland's best chef, Stewart Cameron, and a talented management team around him, and has seen Turnberry blossom under Japanese ownership as nobody believed it would again.

5

The Pennine Way

I knew that managers' careers with British Transport Hotels tended to move in three-year cycles. Nevertheless I secretly cherished the hope that since I had done so well at Turnberry I might be allowed to stay a little longer. However, a telephone call – not even a visit – from Reggie Turnbull, the Scottish Hotels Superintendent, informed me in 1960 that I was to be transferred to the Royal Station Hotel in Hull.

My heart sank as I contemplated exchanging the beauty of the west coast of Scotland and my beloved Turnberry for a city and a hotel which nobody seemed to know much about. Before the amalgamation of the railway hotels in 1947, the Royal Station Hotel had belonged to the London and North East Railway region. I had been trained in the London Midland and Scottish tradition, which was considered far superior!

When Frank Hole, the Hotels Controller, next visited Turnberry, I asked him 'Have I done something wrong here at Turnberry? Because this doesn't strike me as a promotion.'

Mr Hole told me no, I hadn't done anything wrong, quite the contrary. But I had not had any experience of general management in a city centre hotel. The Royal Station Hotel, which had been built in 1851, needed improvement in virtually every area; and the company was anxious to re-establish it as a centre of social life in the city, a position it had long since lost. I would have their full support for any improvements I recommended, and what seemed to me at the time an almost limitless budget. It was, he said with more than a hint of hesitation, 'a challenge'.

I might have taken all that as an omen of what was to follow. If my three years at Turnberry had been full of optimism and good things, the next three were to prove a test of endurance, physical, mental and emotional.

As I danced around the ballroom for the last time, careful as always to partner every lady guest who expected it, I wondered how the four of us would adapt to such different circumstances. On the dull and rainy morning we left, the staff and the guests lined up in the courtyard to wave me off. The family piled into the car, but the tears in my eyes, along with the rain on the windscreen, must have made me lose concentration. The car skidded violently on the rainsoaked drive, almost pitching us over the grassy bank and down the steep hill below.

I took a few days off with my family in Liverpool, visiting my mother and my in-laws to show off their latest grandson and his five-year-old brother, and asked the AA for the best route from Liverpool to Hull. The distance was not great as the crow flies – 130 or so miles from west to east – but this was in pre-motorway days, and the route the AA prepared for us was tortuous, using side lanes and country roads up and over the Pennines. Bad enough had our journey been during the summer, during the day, and in good weather. But the weather was foul, wet, grey and cold. Fog soon blanketed the whole area and I could barely see a hand's length, let alone a car's length, in front of me. My wife pacified our two small sons as best she could but they cried for most of the six-hour journey.

After what felt more like six years, we arrived in the centre of Hull and found the hotel. We were directed to the back entrance. I got out of the car, walked into what I took to be the station waiting room, and found I was in fact in the indescribably dreary main lounge of the Royal Station Hotel. Everything was dark wood. Melon-shaped plastic lights in hideous colours dangled flaccidly from the ceiling. We were late and the outgoing manager did not appear pleased to see us. He told us he was glad to be leaving the hotel and the city.

We were shown up to what passed as the Royal Suite and assured that Queen Victoria had slept there in 1854. Clearly it had not been decorated since.

The boys hated it on sight. There was no separate bedroom for them, only a camp bed for Graham and a cot for Russell in the dismal sitting room. They cried all night. Jean and I cried all night, too.

After such a beginning, things could only get better. Or could they?

Taking over the management of any major hotel propels you into the centre of the community that surrounds it. Hull's main industries were fishing and timber, both thriving at that time, and the city was full of wealthy business and professional people. It was my job to encourage them to direct some of that wealth towards 'my' hotel. The Royal Station had once been fashionable, at the centre of all the city's major social events. I tried to convince myself that it could be again.

I embarked on a major programme of redecoration. First to go was the dreadful main lounge. I designed a scheme, drew an artist's impression of what I wanted, and submitted it to Frank Hole. He asked Nicholas Hill, the London interior designer whose distinguished father John Hill had been responsible for the transformation of many of the railway hotels, to come and see me, and I felt we were on our way. Out went the two pillar boxes and stamp machines which had pride of place in the lounge. Dark panelled corridors, brown screens, threadbare fitted carpets gradually gave way under Nicholas Hill's supervision to areas of light and shade, bright upholstery, patterned carpets, happier colours and, almost the most important, discreet and stylish lighting. I have always been a disciple of César Ritz in believing that the right lighting can do more to enhance a room – and its occupants – than any amount of smart furniture. It conceals a multitude of sins, highlights best features, softens the environment, and takes years off a woman's age.

There was even more urgent work to be done behind the scenes. Venturing into the hotel kitchen was a feat of endurance for anybody not used to working there – especially managers wearing wool three-piece suit, stiff collar and tie. Everything was antiquated – hard brown floors, lavatorial white-tiled walls spider-webbed with cracks, the network of hissing, rumbling steam pipes, stone washing-up sinks and out-of-date machines. Only the stove was a thing of beauty – an old-fashioned range which had to be regularly blackleaded, solid-topped with miniature manhole covers over each burner and a naked flame beneath that shot up when the plate was removed. Scant relief was given to the 30 or so men who worked in the kitchen by a huge skylight, so that at least they worked in natural daylight, but conditions were close to unbearable, the temperature well over 100 degrees. The whites of the cooks and the clothes of the kitchen porters who had to stoke the coal-fired boilers were permanently wringing wet.

My plan was to replace the coal-fired boilers with gas ones, which would immediately moderate the intolerable heat. The job was done – and the kitchen grew hotter. Nobody could fathom out why, not the chef, the gas board, the boiler engineers. Until I happened to be in the kitchen before six o'clock one morning a few weeks after the conversion. I watched the old kitchen porter painstakingly lighting every single gas jet and burner in the kitchen, leaving it turned full on. He had always, he explained, lit the fires under the coal boiler at the same time every morning so that the stoves and hotplate burners were full on by the time the breakfast cooks came in. Nobody had told him this wasn't necessary with gas. The kitchen soon cooled down and I learned a valuable lesson in communications: never assume somebody will know what to do. Instructions for every job must be spelled out.

Experience at the Royal Station Hotel taught me how important it is for hotel managers – or any other employers for that matter – to acknowledge that everybody has a different level of competence and ability, and you cannot drive them beyond that. Their 100 per cent might not be your 100 per cent, but if they are giving all they can, you must be content.

The hotel's Royal Suite was high on the priority list for refurbishment. I had read with some amusement an account, from the *History of Hull* published in 1864, of Queen Victoria's visit to the hotel ten years earlier.

The Directors of the Railway Company placed their magnificent hotel at the disposal of the Corporation for the accommodation of the Queen and her suite. Upholsterers were set to work to fit up in a becoming manner a throne-room, bedroom, drawing-room and boudoir for the Queen; and the Royal children's sitting and sleeping-room . . . Next morning, the Corporation etc. ranged themselves in front of the hotel. When the Royal party appeared on the balcony, 10,552 Sunday School children and 1,210 teachers sang the National Anthem.

I wondered what Her Majesty would have thought of the Royal Suite named in her honour had she caught sight of it a hundred years on.

Another pressing matter was the provision of more bathrooms. A mere dozen of the hotel's 150 bedrooms had private bathrooms, which even in 1960 was well below the standard expected in a good hotel. Most rooms still sported carpets and curtains from the 1920s. And many of the guest bedrooms were heated by little gas fires with coin-in-the-slot meters.

Local people who had long since stopped using the hotel for important events or dining out responded to the Royal Station's rebirth and began to bring back their business.

The first person to extend the hand of friendship was the Medical Officer of Health for Humberside, Dr Alexander Hutchison. He came to see me on my first day and said: 'I know you are new here and things could be tough for the first few months. But remember you have a friend in the city, and let me know at any time if I can be of help.'

'Hutch', as everybody knew him, was a Glaswegian who had studied medicine at Aberdeen University. A year or two after our arrival in Hull there was an outbreak of polio. Our boys were seven and three years old and, like all the other parents in the city, we anxiously watched them for any signs of illness. Things became so serious the city was isolated, no one allowed either in or out. Hutch, as MoH, was at the centre of the crisis. He decided to use the controversial Salk vaccine. Clinics were set up in schools, church halls and public buildings, and the entire population of Hull was vaccinated, adults as well as children. Long queues formed at every temporary clinic. We swallowed our vaccine on a lump of sugar. And we waited.

Hutch's hunch paid off. There were no further outbreaks of polio. We called him a hero. Modest man that he was, he would have no part of such acclaim. He went on to become an important member of the World Health Organisation, honoured by the Queen with the OBE for his work in public health, and in his retirement Hutch and his beloved wife Pat, always enthusiastic and intrepid travellers, went to live in the Solomon Islands, where he became Medical Officer of Health. Then retired in earnest to Monaco where Hutch died in 1987 and news of Pat's death reaches us as this book goes to Press.

Through Hutch we made other medical contacts who remain close friends. John Norman, now a leading maxilla-facial surgeon, author of several standard textbooks, and a professor of surgery in his home town of Sydney, was then one of those young Australian dentists who seemed to proliferate in the UK during the 1960s and 1970s. Clearly destined for greater things, John and his beautiful blonde wife Verity were Hull's golden couple. Verity had exotic taste in clothes, and stunned party-goers in this conservative city with saris and silks from all over the world.

Hutch had formed a circle of doctors who held a monthly meeting and dinner at the hotel. He explained to me: 'Ronnie, doctors don't like to pay an enormous amount for their meal. But their bar bills . . . well, their bar bills more than compensate.' He was right. The average spend per head on drinks, particularly at their annual dinners, seemed to me an all-time record, outdoing even the Licensed Victuallers, who had the reputation for record liquor consumption at their annual events.

There was nothing wrong with the banqueting facilities at the Royal

Station Hotel, and there were two restaurants, the main restaurant and a grill room. I introduced a pianist to play in the evenings, and dinner dances on Saturday nights. During weekends when, as in most city centre hotels, business was slack, we were able to use the main restaurant as an additional banqueting suite, and gradually I set about winning back the business that I knew was in the gift of the timber merchants and trawler-owners. People in the timber trade were particularly tight-fisted. They had used the hotel for years and resented any increase in rates. I had the temerity to put the beer up by a penny a pint and it caused uproar, so used had they become to low tariffs along with the low standards.

There was also an important Jewish community in Hull. I had been accustomed to kosher catering in Manchester and Liverpool, and I encouraged the community leaders to use the hotel more, until it became a fashionable venue for weddings, some of them the most lavish the city could remember. I persuaded hostesses to have not only the wedding, but an engagement party, too. This practice caught on, and mothers and mothers-in-law-to-be vied with each other to make their invitations the most sought after and their parties the most lavish. We decorated the banqueting suite with fountains and lily ponds and increasingly extravagant themes. One bride's mother wanted us to provide something nobody else had ever done. With the help of our florist and maintenance man, I designed an ornate gazebo of white wire, lavishly decorated with intertwined white flowers and greenery. In the midst of this would sit the four-tier wedding cake, lit from above. The hostess was so pleased she made us promise not to use this for any other party because she had two more daughters and wanted the gazebo to remain exclusive.

Our bar mitzvah business increased, too, and I was often invited to the synagogue for these special occasions.

At one important all-male dinner in the hotel restaurant, the host complained that the whisky – which they had been consuming in generous quantities – was watered. I explained that we had been serving the railway company's own brand, Royal Scot, and that it was a very pale whisky, but they clearly weren't happy. I suggested an on-the-spot blind tasting and presented four different brands for them to try. Royal Scot was chosen unanimously as the best.

Hull lies at the end of the line, on the east coast. Having reached it, you can go no further, and this helped make it unique as a city. In many ways it retained the atmosphere of a village. Divisions between the very rich, the rich and the not-so-rich were clearly defined, but they all came together for weddings and charity affairs, dinners and balls. Every year the wife of the Sheriff used to perform a really slick cabaret act, with two other ladies from the upper echelons of Hull society. They would rehearse for weeks with a professional producer and a full band. Tickets were a sell-out and they raised thousands of pounds for local and national charities.

Partly due to the geographical location of the city, the Hull Theatre had a struggle to survive. The actor Ian Carmichael, a son of the city, helped a great deal, with personal appearances and encouragement for their productions. Ian's family owned a de luxe gift store in Hull, nicknamed 'the Asprey's of the North' and a must for the wedding list of every self-respecting bride.

Another 'local lad made good' who returned to support the theatre was John Alderton, at that time married to an actress from the television series *Emergency Ward Ten*. He later married Pauline Collins and they enjoyed great success in *Upstairs Downstairs* and a host of theatre and film productions.

Jessie Matthews, the musical comedy star of 1930s and 1940s, came to appear in a play at the Hull Theatre, having seamlessly made the transition from flapper roles through the daily radio serial *Mrs Dale's Diary*. And the lovely Anna Neagle, later made a Dame, also came to stay at the hotel. We noticed when she was interviewed she always sat with one hand lightly propped under her chin, and speculated that this was perhaps to hide the odd neck wrinkle. Much later I learned the mannerism was to help conceal the early onslaught of Parkinson's disease.

* * *

Our three years in Hull threw up more than their share of unhappiness. During our first year my beloved mother died. She was 77 years old, had hardly a day's illness in her life, and still boasted the dark brown hair of her youth. After a coronary thrombosis she died within a few weeks of going into hospital in Liverpool.

At the time, while based in Hull I was also acting relief manager to John Turpie at the Midland Hotel, Manchester. This meant I was able to drive over to visit my mother in hospital every afternoon. It was a 70-mile round trip and I got a speeding ticket on one occasion, but I will always be grateful that I was able to spend those last weeks with my mother and to be by her side almost up to the end of her life.

My own health began for the first time to be a problem. Every winter

80

I suffered severe coughs and colds, and our second winter in Hull, I began to spit blood. A bronchoscopy revealed an oedema, or polyp, on the upper bronchus of my right lung. The doctor said I would be admitted to hospital, they would nip it out and I would be home within a few days. I was pretty relaxed about it.

When I woke up after the 'simple surgical procedure' I felt cast adrift on a sea of pain. I couldn't move, couldn't think, didn't know where I was or why. I realised this had been no nip-and-sew job. When I eventually got to speak to a doctor, I was told I had undergone major surgery involving the removal of half of one lung. The good news was there was no malignancy. Later I came to understand the reason the pain was so intense was that even after major surgery, the lung has to go on working; there is no let-up to the breathing process in order to let the lung rest and heal. All I knew then was utter disbelief that a human being could stand so much pain without passing out. As it swept over me in sickening, engulfing waves, I kept thinking I would faint – I *must* faint. But I didn't, and inevitably it passed.

Ben Chapman, a Yorkshire antiques dealer in the next bed, had just had the same operation on the opposite lung. We became known as the bookends. We shared the same sense of humour, threatened to burst more than a few sets of stitches among our fellow-patients, and became friends for life.

Our ward was run by a sister descended from a long line of drill sergeants. Each day the physio would give us exercises for our chest and arms which were excruciatingly painful to perform. Apart from the bending and stretching exercises, they included one particularly suited to the torture chamber, where we would lean over a gymnasium horse while the physio thumped us hard on the back to make us cough and get rid of the phlegm that accumulated on our lungs. Each day the stentorian tones of sister would ring through the ward: 'If I see a bent old man hobbling down the street next year, I'll know it's you, Mr Jones!'

She was quite right, of course. Those ghastly exercises which we persevered with only under her stern direction, ensured that we got back the complete use of our lungs and our limbs very quickly.

Our younger son was little more than a toddler but Graham, at seven, was enrolled in the local school. In Hull, schools were zoned and we had to send him to a little school by the railway sidings, where he fell into the proverbial bad company and ended up making a pretty serious attempt to burn down the school by setting fire to the perimeter fence.

We felt we had no choice but to send him to a private prep school as a boarder, where, to our delight, he blossomed. He loved the school, excelled at sports, became top cricketer, and was seriously embarrassed when, playing for the father's XI on sports day, I managed to be out for a duck.

Jean had never been strong; she had always had what we used to call a delicate constitution. When we met she was a shorthand typist for a shipping company in Liverpool, and was advised by her doctor to give up typing at the age of 19 because her wrists were weak. However, she carried on, with her job and with the normal life of a young woman and a young wife. Although it meant little to us at the time, after we were married she found it increasingly difficult to cope with the housework that a wife in those days accepted as her lot. This hardly mattered, since we lived first with my mother, who was the epitome of the house-proud Scottish widow, and later, when I was training away, she went to live with her own parents. After I became a manager we lived in, with maids and often room service to provide most of what we needed. Her increasing tiredness and lack of physical strength and energy were perhaps concealed for longer than they might have been. At the same time, she was apparently healthy; we both assumed that she was simply not a strong person.

After our second son was born, Jean's strength declined still further. During the year after I came out of hospital in Hull, she lost a great deal of weight; but both of us put that down to worry over me. She could walk only a short distance before her limbs would, almost literally, lock and she had to be helped back home. Later, I sometimes had to leave her leaning against a shop window while I went back for the car. Looking back, all the early signs of multiple sclerosis – which was not to be diagnosed for another two years – might have been recognisable to anybody who knew about medical matters, but in our naïvety we ignored the signs. Had we been able to recognise them, there is still nothing that could have been done to alleviate them or to prevent the inevitable progress of the condition.

We adapted to a not disagreeable life in Hull, and by 1963 the hotel had regained its position in the community. With the profits made from the earlier improvements, I had been able to plan an additional restaurant and bar with their own kitchen and separate street entrance. The new Brigantine restaurant was more informal, could seat 75 people, and featured two waterfalls cascading over an underlit display of plants and rocks. We acquired a series of David Hockney drawings of *The*

Rake's Progress for the restaurant, which caused a sensation in ultra-conservative Hull. Letters were published in the local press about 'this scandalous pretence' that might have been anything but certainly wasn't art! Complaints were made to the hotel and to the railway company, protests of unsuitability from all quarters, threats never to set foot in the hotel again. Years afterwards, of course, the collection was sold off at an enormous profit to help the railway pension funds.

I had surpassed the targets set for me, and I might have expected the usual three-year promotion, but for my health record the year before. A summons to see the Hotels Superintendent at St Pancras Chambers set my hopes jangling once more.

Slipping through the revolving doors of the pink Victorian Gothic folly in the Euston Road, I took the undersized lift up to the second floor. Frank Hole sat behind a huge oak desk at the far end of the longest room I had ever seen, about the size of the garden of your average suburban semi. The room was dark – the only window was at the far end – and it seemed like several minutes before I reached Mr Hole's desk, his noble head silhouetted, Caesar-like, behind it.

Although the usual grapevine flourished within BTH, it often got things wrong. It had predicted I would be sent to Tregenna Castle in Cornwall in 1958 when in fact I was posted to Turnberry. This time, I had heard a whisper or two that Ian Jack, general manager of the Queens Hotel in Leeds, had said I was the only man he would allow to take over 'his' wonderful property after nine years under his stewardship. That was a plum job within the company.

When Frank Hole confirmed that he would like me to go to the Queens Hotel, I enthusiastically accepted. He rose from behind his great desk and walked me back to the door of his room, where there were deep leather settees and chairs. He invited me to sit down and shared his thoughts on the direction in which I might take the hotel.

Throughout that interview and all the others I had with Mr Hole, Etienne or 'Papa' Vacher had been present. I could always sense that Mr Hole had over-ridden his opinions, because I had never been a favourite of Papa's. However, the appointments were always confirmed by Vacher as Chief Hotels Manager, and he always ended his letters with the words: 'I will call and see you soon to discuss the immediate problems', which I considered pretty negative and discouraging. He and Frank Hole had never been fond of each other, and Vacher always gave me the impression of being jealous and resentful of the senior man.

Leaving St Pancras Chambers that winter afternoon I was in high spirits. The Queens Hotel was one of the most modern and prestigious city centre hotels in the provinces, rebuilt in 1937 and designed by the same architect as The Dorchester in London. All 206 bedrooms had not only private bathrooms but telephones, central heating and air-conditioning. The hotel had been built on a triangular site adjacent to the main railway station, and every modern device was incorporated to reduce noise levels to a minimum: rubber cushioning in the door rebates, sound-resistant flooring, double windows and suspended ceilings within the hotel, even rubberised paving bricks on the station approach. The exterior was of white Portland stone, and the décor and furnishings were state of the art, with a magnificent French restaurant and, in the banqueting suites, walls lined in soft kidskin. This was a city centre hotel with a difference, and I couldn't wait to get my hands on it.

Jean and I had made a pact when I first became a manager that 'home is where I hang my hat', and, with her father firmly on my side, I had told her I would never refuse a promotion. Leeds was not an unpopular move, the city itself no better and no worse than Hull, and with the advantage of being closer to her parents' home. The Yorkshire Moors and Dales were also easily accessible.

There would be the inevitable problems of new schools for the boys; this had to be faced after each move. The children of hoteliers, like the offspring of diplomats or soldiers, must remain portable throughout their young lives, making friends where they can, longing to live a normal life. It is to their credit that ours survived this educational caravanserai more or less unscathed.

6

In Scotland Again

It was easy to see why the Queens Hotel was regarded as a great prize. It had been extensively redecorated by John Hill, father of Nicholas Hill who had worked with me at the Royal Station Hotel in Hull, and the front of house was looking great. The people and places behind the scenes, however, told a different story. Insufficient capital investment had been made available in the recent past for anything but top show. Kitchen equipment was in a bad state, and the staff facilities not much better. I was dismayed with the areas that the paying guests did not see.

Although for once the outgoing manager, Ian Jack, had insisted on a two-week handover, he was moving on himself to Gleneagles Hotel, and after a few days found there was an immense amount of work to be done in moving his family, arranging a new home and new schools and getting to grips with a new job after his years in Leeds. Instead, John McCleverty, the Area Engineer, was my guide to the most up-to-date hotel I had ever worked in. Mac's pride and joy was the boiler house. He was never happier than when down there, and we often wondered if he had a share in the boilermakers' company. Mac's mission in life was to explain the intricacies of a system that had clearly been designed by somebody more experienced in ocean-going liners: six massive boilers, only two of which were ever used, in an area so vast it could have housed an underground cathedral. The air-conditioning plant was on a gigantic scale, too, with great chambers which washed the air, and a series of cotton blankets through which the clean air was blown before being circulated throughout the hotel. During our three years at the Queens not one of the family suffered from a cold – as good a case as I know for clean air.

I was less enthralled when Mac took gruesome satisfaction in showing me the underground river which flowed beneath the hotel, and the exact spot where Paul Vacher, brother of the Chief Hotels Manager Etienne Vacher and the general manager before Ian Jack, had blown his brains out with a shotgun.

Mac was equally at home with the hotel's complex plumbing system and I called him to ask why it was that there were bidets in every bathroom – but none of them worked. Simple, he explained. The water pressure was so fierce that if guests used the bidet 'it would boil their kidneys and blow their hats off'. Notwithstanding, I asked him to adjust the pressure and reinstate what was becoming an increasingly popular facility.

The staff at the Queens seemed set in their ways and did not appear to be stretched or challenged.

I inherited an elderly secretary who believed in minimum hours and minimum work; my new ways did not suit her, and I was constantly reminded that 'we never did things that way before'. She and others canonised my predecessor to such an extent that I began to loathe the sound of his name – even though I liked the man. As the secretary was approaching retiring age I felt I had to put up with her, and in any case I always advocated a period of look, listen and learn when I took over a hotel. New brooms often sweep a little too assiduously in their haste to make an impression. However, when I was on a week's leave I had a call from my assistant manager: the secretary had been refusing to do his work and threatened to give in her notice. I urged him to get it in writing, and her replacement created a far more helpful and pleasant atmosphere in the management corridor.

I likened the staff situation to a set of pigeon-holes; each head of department operated within his or her pigeon-hole without any interest in what went on in the others. I was astonished to learn while sitting in the barber's chair that he, with 20 years' service, did not know the name of, and had not spoken to, the Grill Room manager with 25 years' service.

My first priority was to change the outlook of the staff so that they worked as a team, and to give them decent equipment and good conditions to work in. It took longer than I thought. I remember late one night sitting on a bench in City Square with my old friend Ben Chapman, looking up at the façade of the Queens Hotel and asking, 'How can I make a difference to that hotel?' Ben as always cheered me up and predicted an early improvement. In one way at least he was right. The Queens Hotel had the dubious record of the highest number of suicides in all the railway hotels; mostly guests, but also that one manager. This was put down to the fact that soundproofing of the bedrooms was so effective that people felt isolated and depressed. In three years we didn't have a single suicide – though there was one three weeks after I left.

A new kitchen was planned. Up till now any replacement equipment had come from the Area Engineer's stock of surplus gear thrown out by the railway refreshment rooms. Now everything from the flooring to the dishwash would be the most modern available. The staff restaurant was next, then their outmoded dormitory accommodation was replaced by single or double rooms with fitted furniture and carpets, bright curtains, and utility and sitting rooms for their off-duty hours.

The chef when I first took over was an elderly person who had been promoted during wartime and whose cuisine still had the taste of austerity. When he retired, his replacement was an eager and talented French chef, Henri Serieys, who not only loved and understood food, but was a great teacher. Young commis cooks blossomed under his tutelage, and two of them won the Apprentice of the Year Competition – first Eddie Murcha, then a young Yorkshireman called Michael Quinn, who went on to become head chef of the Ritz Hotel in London. As the Queens cuisine reached new heights, so did the business. The oval Harewood Restaurant was full of affluent diners and the art deco Grill Room was a favourite venue for businessmen.

Downstairs the Brasserie and Quick Lunch Bar thrived under the watchful eye of Miss Gates. In her 40 years with the company, she had come to know three generations of hotel clients. Parents entrusted their sons and later their grandsons into Miss Gates's care when they travelled home from their boarding schools to or through Leeds. 'Gatesy' would personally meet them and see they got on the right train and, as often as not, made sure they had a little extra pocket money as well. Grateful parents showed their appreciation in various ways, and the boys themselves grew up into faithful and adoring clients of Miss Gates and the Queens Hotel. More than one young man temporarily short of funds found her a soft touch, but a severe glare or a slightly frosty greeting at the right time ensured the debts were always repaid.

The ballroom could seat 650 and had been built with no pillars to obscure the view of and from the top table. The Variety Club of Great Britain held an annual ball with a different theme each year, the ballroom transformed into a circus big top, the Wild West, or a Parisian nightclub. Two of the young business dynamos behind these gala events were Michael Land and Ian Brill, both of whom remained supportive clients at each hotel I managed, becoming as fond as I was of the Athenaeum and Claridge's and perhaps never quite appreciating that it was guests like them who made the hotels the special places they were.

The *Yorkshire Post* Literary Luncheons held in spring and summer attracted the best speakers – and lots of ladies. From the balcony it was like looking down on an exotic flower garden since in those days it would have been unthinkable for a lady to lunch without a hat.

Eddie Waring, the Rugby commentator known for his 'up and under' catchphrase, used to treat the cocktail bar as his office, setting up camp by the telephone every day he was in town and nursing a small glass of cider.

The arts were well represented in Leeds, the theatre attracting such stars as Lawrence Olivier and Vivien Leigh, Anna Neagle and Evelyn Laye, who all stayed at the Queens Hotel. There was also a young star in the ascendant called Cliff Richard who was besieged by hordes of teenage girls. Sometimes they managed to force their way in the front door, almost hysterical, and we would have to hide Cliff, only a teenager himself, behind a pillar, then whisk him out through a side entrance. Not long after his visit I was asked to accommodate the four members of a wildly successful new group, the Beatles. However, I had heard from other hoteliers of their reputation for attracting mobs of teenage fans, so I turned down the booking. I don't believe my two sons ever forgave me.

By the 1960s railway hotel staff were under increasing pressure to become unionised. Most of our workforce would have preferred not to join and took little interest in union affairs. But a small group enjoyed the unaccustomed power conferred by membership of a union committee, and the prize was to be elected chief shop steward with the authority to go straight to the general manager.

There was a Grill Room waiter who was a bit of a loner, an oddball with few friends, just efficient enough to keep his job but without enough aptitude for promotion. To everyone's surprise he was elected chief shop steward, though I found out later that nobody else wanted the job. He would come to me with petty complaints, which were dealt with swiftly and amicably, but one day he saw his chance to become a champion of the workers. The two main hotel restaurants had separate brigades of waiters. The Grill Room was packed midweek, but quiet from Friday night for the weekend. Both rooms were overstaffed, and it made sense to amalgamate the brigades. No one would lose their job, and there would be an opportunity to make a little more money in exchange for greater flexibility.

After a presentation to the staff and as much individual counselling as they wished, the plan was to proceed. However, the chief shop steward stepped in and just after lunch service he announced that all the Grill Room staff, including him, were going on strike as a protest against the new work plan. I told him I would like to speak to the brigade right away and asked him to assemble them in an area just outside my office. While he was doing this I summoned my two assistant managers and issued instructions.

I surprised the chief shop steward by announcing I would speak to each man personally and in private. My office had two doors and my assistant ushered the waiters one by one through the main door. As I suspected, every man admitted he was reluctant to go on strike and had only agreed because nobody wanted to be in the minority. After each brief talk the waiter would exit by the side door and was escorted back to the Grill Room without having the opportunity to confer with his colleagues. Dinner that night was served on time and with good grace; the staff knew as they had always done that I would do everything in my power to help them, and the chief shop steward left soon afterwards, no doubt to find a flock of more biddable sheep.

In 1966 another visit to the Gothic halls of St Pancras and an affable interview with the managing director culminated in his telling me he wanted me to leave the Queens Hotel and take over the management of the Central Hotel in Glasgow. Right away. That day.

I asked if I might not have a week to clear up my affairs in Leeds, but in his charming way Frank Hole made it clear that I was needed in Glasgow. I could have 'a week later on', he said, to tidy up in Leeds. Through my mind flashed frenzied pictures of what that would mean: one week in which to pack up our home in the hotel. Luckily I knew I could rely on my mother-in-law to help, because Jean was increasingly weak and unable to do much. I would have to take the boys out of their schools and arrange for new ones in Glasgow. The office would have to fend for itself. In typical railway hotels fashion, my successor would have to step in without notice and do his best to take up the reins where I had left off. And I was about to do the same.

The Central Hotel was the busiest hotel in Scotland. Its Malmaison Restaurant had been known as one of the finest outside France, and the two banqueting suites were in constant use. As a promotion, it represented a first-rate opportunity.

The building was a Glasgow landmark, soot-blackened and wrapped around two sides of the railway station. It had been intended as an L-shaped block of luxury offices when the station opened in 1879, but its potential as a hotel was spotted and after a further four years work the Central Hotel opened with accommodation for 420 guests. The planners did not stop there, and by 1921 had added enough additional rooms for 550 guests and 300 staff. The hotel boasted a grand total of 50 lavatories and 40 bathrooms and corridors 343 feet long. I inherited a staff of 470 and 5 assistant managers.

Frank Hole had whetted my appetite for the job by telling me it would include helping to plan a new hotel to be built on 'stilts' overlooking the River Clyde. An American architect had prepared the plans and it promised to be an exciting project. Alas, soon after taking over, I was advised that the plan for the new hotel was proving too expensive and it was abandoned.

There were very few other surprises at the Central: the relics of a static management style, an uninspired chef, and lack of investment behind the scenes.

The chef turned out to be the son of the personal barber/factotum to Sir Arthur Towle, Controller of the LMS hotels, the Figaro in an opera without music that I described in an earlier chapter. Although chef was an agreeable man, he lacked the special flair demanded of a restaurant like the Malmaison. He decided to move to a very good but much smaller hotel. His replacement was Jean-Maurice Cottet, a dapper young Frenchman who wore the tallest white toques I've ever seen to give the illusion of height. He was energetic, brimful of ideas and inspired tremendous loyalty in his brigade of cooks. His sous-chef in particular hero-worshipped him and they made a formidable team.

We got on well from the start. New menus were designed for all three of the hotel restaurants and imagination and flair applied to devising the finest banqueting food in Glasgow. Jean-Maurice made headlines in the city when he introduced Fondue, both Swiss and Bourguignonne, and Raclette to La Fourchette, the more informal restaurant. He eventually became head chef at Gleneagles, the job he always wanted, and now has achieved his other ambition – he and his wife run their own restaurant with rooms in the Haute Savoie.

My own immediate ambition was to have the curiously attractive Victorian building – black with accumulated decades of city centre grime and railway soot – cleaned and restored so that its large windows, carved pedestals and ornamental balconies would be a landmark once again. The time was right, I reasoned, because the railways had been electrified and there were few steam trains. Sadly, this was also a time when the railway company was beginning to draw in its horns, and I only managed to have the front entrance cleaned and polished. Later, when Glasgow was undergoing its renaissance in the 1970s, the Central was fully restored, along with some of the other beautiful Georgian and Victorian buildings in the city centre, but today it is a barely recognisable relic of the great hotel it once was.

Being a business hotel, the Central had a much lower room occupancy at weekends, but the lounges were packed, with scarcely enough seats. I found it odd that the food and beverage receipts did not reflect this high usage. It appeared that only soft drinks, tea and coffee were served, yet customers seemed to linger over these from about 7 p.m. until the lounge closed at 11 p.m. I questioned the waiters and waitresses, but they all seemed perfectly happy, and I learned why from one young waitress: the customers were exceptionally good tippers.

I asked the house detective, a taciturn man when he was the one being questioned, if he could offer any explanation. Reluctantly he explained that the hotel lounge on Friday and Saturday evenings was the social venue for the homosexual community. 'They all behave themselves,' he argued. 'There are no fights and the waiters and waitresses are happy with their tips.'

In the 1960s homosexuality had scarcely been legalised, and other guests who might have increased the drinks and snacks revenue in the lounges were reluctant to come in. I realised this was not what the managing director had had in mind when he briefed me to make the Central Hotel the social centre of Glasgow. The following weekend I had the house detective stationed in the front hall and the assistant manager at the station entrance to the hotel, explaining that the lounges in the evening were for the exclusive use of hotel guests. Business did increase, as other guests felt comfortable in the lounge and their orders were more likely to be for early cocktails or champagne and after-dinner brandies. This seems harsh now and I doubt if the situation would arise, but 30 years ago we all lived in an even less enlightened society. Two men travelling together were allowed – often reluctantly – to share a room, but never with a double bed. Odd, when you consider that up to Victorian times any number of men slept together stark naked when they stayed at an inn! Even in the 1960s, if a male and female asked for a double room but gave different names, they would be shown politely to two single rooms – on different floors.

Another example of what would soon be outmoded thinking occurred when I had a call in our apartment late one Saturday night. The Malmaison head waiter, a very proper person indeed, was having trouble with a very irate customer and please would I come and help. This in itself was unusual, since senior staff prided themselves on being able to deal with any situation and rarely called for the off-duty general manager. I learned that a couple had come in asking for a table in the busy restaurant and the lady was – horror of horrors – wearing a trouser suit! *They* still had not been legalised and no lady was permitted to enter a formal dining room so improperly dressed.

I changed back into my dinner jacket and dashed downstairs. There, I was confronted by one of the most beautiful women I have ever seen, dressed in a gorgeous black velvet pants suit, standing coolly by while her apoplectic escort ranted at the head waiter, much to the amusement of the diners. Had I been on duty, I'm afraid I would have bent the rules and led them to a quiet table. As it was, I had to support my head of department, and expressed regret that we were unable to seat the couple in the restaurant. I offered to open the hotel dining room on the floor above and serve their choice from the full à la carte menu there, or to set up a table for two in a private suite. This wouldn't do. The man spent the next ten minutes in the sedan-chair telephone booth at the entrance to the Malmaison ringing round the city's best restaurants for a table, while I made conversation with the lady. I would have made the calls for him, but he was in such a rage, he wouldn't listen. He returned angrier than before – not one restaurant could offer them a table.

On the Tuesday the newspaper featured a double-page spread with a series of photographs of the woman – a ballet dancer appearing at the Kings Theatre – posing on a traffic island in Sauchiehall Street first in the pants suit, then minus the top with just trousers and a white chiffon blouse, then minus the trousers but clad in the black velvet jacket – every bit as long as any newly fashionable miniskirt and perfectly decent. The story of the Malmaison escapade was recounted in detail. The reporter had rung me to ask for my comment, and I explained that while I was extremely sorry to have to turn away two clients and even sorrier for any embarrassment they had suffered, rules were rules and I believed we had done the right thing by the head waiter and by the other guests who conformed with those rules.

The following Saturday evening, the couple returned to the Malmaison, the ballerina in long evening skirt, her escort charm itself; clearly all was forgiven.

* * *

In just over two years at the Central Hotel we suffered a series of set-backs that diminished the satisfactions of the job. Jean was becoming increasingly disabled and was confined to a wheelchair for much of the time. We had been fortunate in having Graham accepted as a pupil at the marvellous Allen Glen Academy, but Russell at seven was too young. We enrolled him instead at a highly recommended and very expensive preparatory school, St Ronan's, run by two spinster sisters. They were imperious in the extreme when we took Russell for interview, and he had to pass what seemed an unusually stiff test before they agreed to take him. Russell was a bright boy and very keen on sport, but St Ronan's was academically oriented, operating almost as a 'crammer's' and boasting about its record of pupils who went on to top public schools. There was virtually no sport except when a schools inspector was due, when games and handicrafts sessions were hastily arranged.

Russell was very unhappy and did not respond to the teaching at St Ronan's. Either I or Jack Maguire, a good friend who was manager of the North British Hotel, had to meet him from school every day and he was often depressed. On one occasion I had to wait for nearly an hour before he was released, having been kept behind as punishment for a small misdemeanour. At my wit's end, with an important meeting looming, I went into the school and asked if I could collect my son. I was met by the senior sister, who said she had kept him in because he was 'naughty' and 'not responsive'. She went on: 'We know all about your wife, you know. You must realise that your son is mentally retarded.' That was the only time in my life that I nearly struck a woman. Her arrogance and impertinence had driven me beyond endurance.

Russell never returned to St Ronan's. I knew full well there was nothing wrong with his IQ, and immediately he took the entrance examination for the top academic school in the city, Glasgow Academy. He passed with ease, but we were on the move again before there was a vacancy. In London he distinguished himself at City of London School, picked up creditable bachelor's and master's degrees at Bristol, and is a senior international economist based in Tokyo. The sad thing is that while to me Glasgow was in many ways a great city, and I was proud many years later to marry a Glaswegian, he recalls his schooldays there as the unhappiest time of his life.

The other event that complicated our lives was that I was accepted on an advanced management course at the British Transport Staff College at Woking just three weeks after I took over at the Central Hotel. I had applied while at the Queens Hotel in Leeds when I learned that Frank Hole believed hotel managers who showed promise should go there, and looked more favourably upon those who did, when it came to promotion. Two of my colleagues, Ian Jack and Bill Currie, were 'graduates', had thoroughly enjoyed the experience – and done well as a result, Bill becoming head of rail catering and Ian promoted to Southern Area Hotels Manager. A place was offered to me just three weeks after I took over at the Central Hotel.

I would be residential at Woking for 14 weeks, returning to Glasgow at weekends. My wife was ill, my job was new, my family not yet established in Glasgow. I talked it over with Sam, and contemplated turning down the place. We both felt sure I would not be offered another. Sam thought I should accept before Jean's condition deteriorated further, and while Ellen, her mother, could look after her and the boys.

The college, a beautiful Lutyens house in extensive grounds, trained the high-flyers of the transport world in modern business methods.

I found the going extremely tough, though the other 31 participants seemed to take it in their stride. We were subjected to endless lectures, syndicate work, report writing and such a vast amount of reading and studying that I could only keep pace by reading far into the night – every night.

The sporting challenges were almost as gruelling as the academic. I had barely seen a squash court, had only played tennis as a teenager, yet found myself expected to play both. Golf and billiards I could manage, although I was disconcerted to find I would be the billiards partner of Frank Hole on his end-of-course visit. It had been so long since I played, I went out and bought a book of rules the day before so I wouldn't make an utter ninny of myself. Every Friday evening I flew back to Glasgow to see Jean and the family, and caught the sleeper back to London on Sunday night. I found it impossible to sleep, and Mondays were always a strain trying to keep awake on hot days in the lecture room.

Our group spent a week in Germany and Belgium studying the forthcoming Common Market, and once again I recall endless hours of listening to very long lectures, simultaneously translated, in very hot lecture halls.

We were allowed one day off to take a trip on the river Rhine, with ample supplies of German lager and wine on board. The night was spent at the Hotel Dreissen in Bad Godesberg, where Hitler met Chamberlain in 1938, and as I was the only hotelier in the party I was given the Presidential Suite. Whose bed, I wondered, was I sleeping in?

I confess to a certain satisfaction when our small syndicate team won the National Computer Business Game and our conclusion – 'when business is in decline, invest more, not less, in marketing' – was one that I found very relevant during the recessionary period of 20 years later.

I will always be grateful for that opportunity to study investment planning and all the facets of modern management at a level I never experienced before that gruelling three and a half months. I have benefited for years from the knowledge I gleaned at Woking. Before I retired from Claridge's we had a 25-year reunion of the 'class of '67', and although it was shocking to discover so many of my fellow delegates had died or become seriously ill, and that some of those who attended looked so *old* (which they might well have thought about me!), we were able to look back with satisfaction and great good humour at time well spent.

I wonder how the curricula of such colleges has changed. Between the 1940s and the 1960s practical training for hotel management was everything: a manager was expected to have trained in every hotel department, a chef in every corner of the kitchen. By the 1970s that gave way to the accountancy age, when managers were sent back to school to learn to count beans. In the 1980s sales and marketing became the twin deliverers which would save the civilised hotel world as we know it. In the 1990s they, too, began taking a back seat as hotels and their owners discovered that everybody else is out there hustling, too – and it costs! And now? The asset-strippers, the property men, the merchant bankers and the City takeover specialists are moving in for the kill. As one hotel group after another either merges or is taken over, it's déjà vu for me to observe other fine hotel companies in grave danger of being snapped up and sold off piecemeal, going through the decline that those once-great railway hotels suffered two decades ago.

Staff college might have made me better equipped to be an executive, but it also left me more convinced than ever that the truly important aspects of hotel management are those they cannot teach you in college, and those that do not change with the changing times.

I believe the manager of even the grandest hotel should be like mine host of an inn. His presence is required. He ought to be around to make sure everyone feels welcome and at home – and everyone should *know* he is the innkeeper. However palatial the 'inn', it should not be impersonal; guests should feel as if they are in the home of friends.

The hotelier runs two hotels: one for the guests and one for the staff. Especially where staff live on the premises, they, too, are at home. They eat, sleep and live their leisure hours there just as the guests do. When the students I speak to ask: which is more important, the guests or the staff? I'm inclined to point out that while the guests are the reason why you are there – and provide the wherewithal for you to be there – they come and they go. Your staff are with you all the time, night and day, 365 days a year. A genuine interest in the welfare of both guests and staff is a prerequisite of good management; the ability to put oneself in the shoes of the other person, to have an enquiring mind, to listen before you judge, to be open to ideas and suggestions.

He should be able to lead by example, not be afraid to get his hands dirty, and never give an order which he himself would find distasteful, to offer constructive criticism and not destroy the personal pride that we all have, never to dampen enthusiasm – and never to lose his own enthusiasm. He – and for 'he' read 'she', too – thinks about the knock-on effect of any decisions. In remembering that 'the buck stops here', he takes the ultimate responsibility – and the blame – when things go wrong, passes compliments and news of success down the line when they go well.

Too many hoteliers leave their staff thinking nobody out there is listening to them, and believe they alone know what is best for the guests, forgetting every guest and every member of the workforce is different and their requirements cover a wide range and need many different skills and talents. The same hoteliers – and I could name a few – are satisfied if everything looks well front-of-house, content to leave the non-public areas to be supervised by assistants. They delegate then abdicate by blaming mistakes on their staff, and spend time with only the most influential, wealthy or titled visitors.

It's easy to recognise these people in their own establishments: they will have the best table in the restaurant at peak periods, and the best service, and ignore the paying guests who complain to the waiters of neglect. You will never find them in the kitchen, especially on a hot day, or inspecting the staff quarters, or having lunch in the staff cafeteria.

He's the one whose breath smells suspiciously of peppermint and who sways a little as he greets you with slightly slurred speech and beatific expression. He will have his favourites among the staff and cultivate the ones who fawn over him, but won't hesitate to tell them off in front of others should they do something wrong. He cultivates favoured guests, too, appearing as if by magic when the rich and titled walk through the door, trips over his well-polished shoes to get to directors and their families when they visit – and ignores those he considers unworthy of his attention.

He is easy to spot on the night of an important banquet because he will be there in the front line bowing low to the arriving VIPs. But you won't find him in the kitchen, where they especially appreciate encouragement when under pressure. He might wait until the first course is on the table before going off for his own supper, leaving the party to more junior managers who will, of course, carry the can should anything go amiss.

A hotelier worth his salt, on the other hand, sleeps in his own beds, never visits the kitchen without a tasting spoon, and looks at the building inside and out with the eyes of a first-time guest. He surrounds himself with talented young people – the hungrier and the more ambitious the better – and gets rid of yes-men. He delights in new ideas, visiting and learning from other hotels wherever he travels, and studies the latest techniques so that even in his advancing years he is not overtaken by the young and their new technology. And he never imagines he has learned it all. Every day brings new experience, and if he is lucky enough to move around a lot, so much the better. Fifteen years' experience in anyone's book beats one year's experience fifteen times over. He never achieves his ambitions, always has a goal to strive for, and cultivates the gentle art of making the difficult look easy.

Were the christening fairy to offer just one gift, let the aspiring hotelier choose the ability to rejoice in the good fortune of others, for if he grows up to be resentful of wealth and privilege, he cannot cultivate the art of hospitality or enjoy being at the sharp end of the happiness business.

7

London at Last

Towards the end of 1969 Frank Hole, Chairman and latterly Managing Director of British Transport Hotels, was about to retire. Etienne Vacher had already retired as Chief Hotels Manager, and with promotions and restructuring this meant two area manager vacancies within BTH, one for the 12 Scottish hotels, which included Gleneagles and Turnberry as well as the Central Hotel, and the other to supervise the 19 hotels in England. I was invited to St Pancras Chambers for what would be my last interview with Frank Hole, and this time I faced the outcome with some anxiety.

I had discussed with Sam, my wise father-in-law, the likelihood of being offered one of these two jobs, and had decided that if an offer was made I should accept, knowing that to refuse promotion would adversely affect my prospects. The problem was, although I was ambitious, I was honest enough to admit to myself that I did not want to be an area manager. I loved running hotels. Management at the sharp end is what appeals to me, making a hotel the best of its kind, pitting my skills against the market. Administrative management, I felt sure, would leave me frustrated and longing to be back at the helm, just as a sea captain feels most at home on the bridge of his ship, not running the line.

Then there were the facilities I needed for my wife, by this time confined to a wheelchair. While we lived in I knew she had company and care, and hotel staff to look after the domestic chores. My salary as a living-in manager was much less than those living out, but having Jean comfortable and secure was more important than money in the bank. Would an area manager's salary be sufficient for me to buy or rent a house for a family of four and pay for a living-in nurse or companion? I suspected not.

Then again, I could see what lay ahead for British Transport Hotels.

Money was tight, profits were down, capital investment almost non-existent by now. Following the demise of the railways under Dr Beeching, the high standards which had been maintained by the company were slipping inch by inch. Anyone with an eye to the future should have been wondering whether to stay on and wait for the index-linked pension, as most of my contemporaries did, or to strike out and take a chance elsewhere.

As I left St Pancras Chambers after my interview, I felt sure an offer would be made and for the first time in 27 years I did not look forward to promotion.

When I walked back into the Central Hotel I learned that Michael de Marco had checked in. He had worked with me at Gleneagles as reception manager. A bright young man hell-bent on a brilliant career, he was now general manager of Oddenino's Hotels and Restaurants in London. The group, owned by Instone Bloomfield, included the Royal Garden, the White House and the Athenaeum Hotels. Over a drink Michael told me he was looking for a general manager for the five-star Royal Garden Hotel in Kensington, which he had been overseeing with the help of an assistant. Would I be interested?

He gave me a little time to think about his proposition, but the package he offered was a generous one, with a much higher salary and the promise of an apartment in a mansion block a few minutes' walk from the hotel in Wynnstay Gardens. The company would furnish the apartment and provide a maid to service our flat and act as companion to my wife.

I was concerned that a move at such a time would not be the right thing for Jean, but her father insisted I seize the opportunity to go to London. Wise and loving man that he was, he knew that a demanding job was vital to me, and that I would always be a better husband to his daughter if I was fulfilled in my work. Jean was equally happy for me to accept this new challenge.

I told the company immediately and arranged our move to London. I never did discover whether or not I might have been made area manager, but was happy to hear that one of the two jobs had gone to Ian Jack, my predecessor at the Queens Hotel in Leeds, and the other to Dennis Aldridge, son-in-law of Etienne Vacher.

I had worked in 15 of the 32 railway hotels, counting acting and relief manager positions. Now my only link with them would be a pension paid from the Pearl Assurance Company, which took over the LMS superannuation fund, the day I reached 65. I receive the handsome sum of £115.98 a month after tax, the rewards of 27 years of service. My consolation is that I witnessed the hotels at their grandest and proudest, and was spared the bitter experience of being present during their decline.

The whole family was excited about moving to London, even though for the boys it meant yet another change of school, friends, home and environment. I managed to secure a place for Russell at the Pembridge Villas Prep School in Notting Hill Gate before he 'graduated' to City of London School. After taking advice we enrolled Graham, then aged 14, at Holland Park Comprehensive, then the fashionable habitat of Wedgwood Bennites and a breeding ground for champagne socialists. The school was 'unstructured' and to us resembled a seat of learning about as much as a monkey house resembled a country-house dining room. Discipline seemed non-existent, Graham's academic prowess came to a dead stop. But he was happy there and refused to consider any other school. He was in his element as a teenager of the 1970s, his world one of loud music, leather jackets, long hair and loathsome habits. He has a happy nature, generous, well-adjusted and outgoing, and people have loved him all his life.

Russell was the more studious of the two and City of London School suited him perfectly. Although he devoted as much time to sport as to academic pursuits, he emerged with some creditable O and A levels that would take him through two economics degrees.

* * *

The Royal Garden Hotel had opened in 1963 to a fanfare of publicity. The architect Richard Seifert had designed hospitals, but this was his first hotel, and it showed. The bedrooms were too small, and although most of them had balconies, those overlooking Kensington High Street were too noisy, and those with views across Kensington Gardens too narrow to be used. The hotel had five kitchens on five different levels – convenient for the four restaurants and the banqueting suites, but absolutely impossible to staff, as any hotelier could have told him. By the time I arrived in 1969 there were cracks on the front of the building, the decorative mosaic was falling off, and our neighbours in the grace and favour residences in Kensington Palace Gardens still hadn't forgiven being evacuated when the excavations for the car park had gone too deep and their homes were in danger of subsiding.

If the hotel had too many kitchens, it also had too many fire-escape

100

doors. On my first walk-round I counted 32, none of them alarmed. I subsequently counted nearly as many prostitutes patrolling the corridors offering room service that was not on the menu. It was easy as pie for one to come into the hotel through the front door, then open the fire escape doors to admit her sisters for the night shift. I think the staff were appalled when I frogmarched one hooker out through the revolving door and escorted another in a half nelson after she declined to leave of her own accord. Not as appalled as I was, however, when I encountered the same girl in court, this time sans false eyelashes, make-up or beehive hairdo, hot pants replaced by a calf-length pleated skirt, white blouse buttoned up to the neck – and looking every inch of 15 years of age.

At six years old, the Royal Garden desperately needed investment for upgrading bedrooms and public areas. The owner, Instone Bloomfield, a property and banking millionaire who used to start each day by barking into a telephone 'What's the price of money today?', was reluctant to put up the money. He had been assured when the hotel opened that everything in it would last at least ten years. With 500 bedrooms, most of them identically furnished and decorated, and four restaurants, the hotel seemed to me, after the grandeur of the railway hotels, like a cardboard cut-out of a five-star hotel. César Ritz had invented at the beginning of the century the ingenious device of click-on switches, similar to those in refrigerators today, which automatically operated a light inside closets and cupboards. At the Royal Garden these had been installed to activate a strip light in even the smallest wardrobes. When a guest crammed her fur coats into the cupboard and left the door ajar, the smell of burning fur attracted the attention of the hotel security staff. Inside they found the strip light had burned a patch on the shoulder of a mink coat.

The guests could not be described as five-star either. Many of the rooms and suites were reserved for airline crews until I was able to replace their contract with individual guests. Roger Moore was married from the hotel and the Michael Caines and Charlie Drake were regular visitors, but the Royal Garden was at heart a hotel that attracted the *nouveau riche*. We thought we were doing well if the guests simply behaved themselves.

Michael de Marco continued to oversee the four London hotels owned by Odenino's; the Royal Garden, Athenaeum Court, the White House and the Alexandra National. He enjoyed the boxing matches staged in the hotel ballroom when thugs in black tie would work themselves into a frenzy of excitement over other thugs bashing the living daylights out of each other. I never got used to the sight of elegantly gowned 'ladies' in the front rows shrieking with laughter as blood spattered their designer dresses.

Marjorie de Marco was described as being 'burdened by a bosom like a bolster' and Michael in his cups (if you'll pardon the expression) was more than once heard to tell a waiter serving their meals: 'How dare you look at my wife's breasts?' How the poor chaps were supposed not to, when Mrs de Marco seldom bothered to more than half cover them, I can't imagine.

The French chef was a professional award-winner; he excelled in cooking competitions at home and abroad and spent more time travelling to those than he did supervising or cooking in his own hotel. When he did appear, he had so many medals and medallions his shoulders seemed bowed under the weight.

The first time the prestigious male dining club the Reunion des Gastronomes (the Gastrobores, as my wife christened them) came to the Royal Garden, I was invited as a guest and seated next to the President. Chef returned midway through the proceedings flushed with success and hospitality from Hotelympia. He had a bee in his bonnet about the British liking their meat overcooked and insisted the Gastronomes should have their lamb *comme il faut, mes braves, comme il faut*. To a chorus of protestations from the sous-chefs he made them take the lamb out of the oven. The meat had just gone into the oven a few minutes before, but out it came – the fat still white, the meat so underdone that a good vet could have revived it. It was many years – and another chef later – before the Gastronomes returned to the Royal Garden.

I also inherited a few great people whose skills far outshone their surroundings. Head housekeeper Rosemary Zander went on to the same position at the Savoy Hotel. A young management trainee, Jean-Jacques Pergant, became general manager of the Berkeley in 1995. Rod Walker and David Webster were first-rate assistant managers; Rod came to work with me at the Athenaeum Hotel and is now general manager of a five-star property in South Africa.

One of the world's great hall porters, Alex Serra, also followed me to the Athenaeum Hotel, and Ronald Crompton, the credit controller, remained a dear friend into retirement.

The hotel's Royal Roof Restaurant was noted not only for its views over Kensington Gardens and the cuisine of Guy de Laurent, our new chef. It was also a Mecca for music-lovers and incurable romantics who came to be serenaded at the table-side by Joe Stein and his Royal Roof Strings – 12 violinists who turned schmaltz into an art form.

There were one or two hair-raising parties during my tenure in Kensington. The most important was the second international congress of the World Wildlife Fund. Among the 750 delegates under the chairmanship of Prince Bernhard of the Netherlands were HRH the Duke of Edinburgh, the ex-King and Queen of Greece, Prince William of Gloucester, the Grand Duke and Duchess of Luxembourg, Prince Albert of Belgium, Prince Henrik and Princess Margrethe of Denmark. To balance the regiment of royals we had the Earl of Harewood, Group Captain Douglas Bader, Sir John Betjeman, Sir Vivian Fuchs and Lord Hunt; and astronaut Neil Armstrong, Sir Peter Scott, David Attenborough, Jacques Cousteau, Thor Heyerdahl, Sir Julian Huxley and John Aspinall.

Even with such a star-studded guest list, there was no way we could provide a seated or even a buffet luncheon for so many. In the end we devised picnic boxes – long before they were issued to the Institute of Directors conference at the Royal Albert Hall – and Prince Philip could be seen squatting on his haunches like Little Jack Horner as he 'put in his thumb' to pull out smoked salmon and chicken salad, strawberries and cream, cheese and biscuits, and a small bottle of wine. The lunch boxes in fact helped the congress retain a relaxed and convivial atmosphere often lacking at such a major event.

One of the most unforgettable conferences I was involved in had been booked into the Royal Garden Hotel several years before I arrived. The hotel was exclusively reserved for the 600 delegates of the American Women in Radio and Television, their nineteenth convention and the first held outside the United States. What nobody had mentioned was that they would all arrive together. Planes and buses had been chartered, and as one coach after another bowled into traffic-jammed Kensington High Street during the early evening rush hour, I would despatch it, with our compliments, on a sight-seeing tour of London to give the coachloads in front a chance to register.

The four-day event went like clockwork, with visits from the Archbishop of Canterbury, Lord Mancroft, Mary Quant and Simon Dee. On the evening of the final banquet, after a rousing and inspirational speech by Margery Hurst, founder of Brook Street Bureau and a champion of women's causes, the lady chairman of the AWRT got to her feet. She graciously thanked the Royal Garden Hotel and the staff for the splendid way they had been looked after then announced to the assembly: 'Mr Jones will now make a speech.' First I'd heard! I am by no means a natural when it comes to performing – rather the type who needs a script, rehearsal and time to prepare. I can only imagine the utter relief that this major event had gone smoothly and was now all but over lent silver wings to my tongue. (Well, at least I didn't make a fool of myself.) In fact I spoke the truth when I said it had been a pleasure to look after the 600 ladies and their guests.

The Royal Garden Hotel overlooked Kensington Palace Gardens, known as 'Embassy Row' because most of the major embassies or ambassadorial residences were there. We were excited when the Russian Ambassador asked us to cater for a dinner at the embassy, Harrington House, to be hosted by the visiting Minister of Foreign Affairs Mr Andrei Gromyko and Mrs Gromyko on 28 October 1970. Edward Heath, then Prime Minister, and other government ministers, including Sir Alec Douglas Home, later Lord Home, would be attending.

This was in the midst of the Cold War, and the Russians were paranoid about security. They insisted on having, weeks in advance, the names and pedigrees of every one of the 50 or so staff who would cook, serve or wash up at the dinner. They were all security-cleared, and it was agreed that the food – bortsch, lobster thermidor, blinis, caviar and smoked salmon; then roast pheasant; and for dessert white peaches, woodland strawberries and vanilla ice cream – would be cooked in the hotel and heated or finished in the embassy's very limited kitchen space.

On the day of the dinner I had to travel up to Hull for a medical check-up. I had waited weeks for an appointment with the specialist and the check-up was long overdue. Everything was well under control, and I would be back in good time for the evening's events.

When I returned to the hotel, the Russian Embassy had decreed that the staff must be cut by two-thirds. Only 17 people, including myself, would be allowed into the embassy, to cater for 150 guests. Everybody would have to do at least two jobs. My assistant manager would be both bartender and wine waiter. The banqueting head waiter became a waiter and plate-clearer. And I, instead of supervising, bussed tables, transported dirty dishes in the rope-driven lift to the kitchen three floors below, where there was a single sink, and helped with the washing-up. Was this my first taste of Communism, I wondered, where everybody was equal?

There was one compensation. After dinner, which was declared a great success with warm speeches from the top table, the Russians invited us poor workers to eat our fill of the best Beluga caviar and slake our thirst with unlimited quantities of imported vodka, to fulsome toasts from the embassy chef. For a few minutes at least the Cold War thawed. We extended a heart-felt invitation to the Russian chef to visit our hotel, but he explained with tears in his eyes that while he would dearly love to visit his new friends, he would not be allowed to.

* * *

In 1971 Instone Bloomfield decided he would make the Athenaeum Court Hotel, a 1930s building then being used as a London hotel base for PanAm airline crews, the flagship of his company. The hotel overlooks Green Park from Piccadilly, with views across to Buckingham Palace; it is close to Park Lane, in the middle of Mayfair, and only a credit-card swipe from Bond Street.

When he asked me to oversee the total refurbishment and partial rebuilding, I was elated. The hotel's potential was obvious. Adjacent to it, in Down Street, was a sister block of 32 Edwardian apartments. The family would to all intents and purposes be living in again, but with the advantage of a separate entrance so the boys wouldn't need to change football kit for smart clothes every time they entered and left the premises. This had been a bone of contention ever since they were small, and although their mother and I had got used to carrying damp cloths to wipe dirty hands and faces, and a change of clothes at the end of every day out before they could walk through the hotel, Graham and Russell never did. They have rebelled against formality all their lives. Even as an adult with two daughters of his own, Russell looks back on a kind of perverse 'deprived childhood' under the constraints of living in five-star hotels. Graham, happily ensconced with his own wife and two daughters in laid-back Los Angeles, discarded jackets and ties for life when he left London – though he still appreciates five-star food and service when he has the chance.

The re-named Athenaeum Hotel was smaller than most of the hotels I had managed, with only 150 rooms including the apartment suites, but I was determined to make it the most fashionable hotel in London. By the time I left 12 years later in 1984, it had fulfilled every iota of its early promise. It had one of the happiest ambiences I had ever worked in, a string of awards for the staff, and an international clientele.

Not, however, achieved without a fight or two.

During the year of the hotel's reconstruction, I shared an office with the accountant in Down Street. As well as recruiting staff, I operated, with the help of the existing personnel, 30 of the apartments as a mini-hotel, and worked closely with the designer. Instone Bloomfield and his wife had spent a holiday on a yacht designed by Jon Bannenberg, the fashionable Australian, and had chosen him to design the interior of the Athenaeum Hotel. His schemes were in perfect harmony with the building and with the period, bright without being garish, restful, dignified but with no hint of stuffiness. Above all, every piece of furniture suited the purpose for which it was intended. People take this for granted, but how many restaurant chairs are comfortable and the right height? How often do you get a good night's sleep in a hotel bed? How many times is there a lack of drawer space in a bedroom, nowhere to plug in a hairdryer close to a mirror, no shelves in a bathroom, or a desk and chair the wrong height for each other, the telephone out of reach, the desk lamp not bright enough?

The Athenaeum Hotel looked terrific and it felt terrific to stay there. I know. I slept in virtually every room, as I did in most of the hotels I have managed. I would make it compulsory for every hotelier to do this, because it is the only way to judge the comfort of a bedroom, sitting room or, especially, a bathroom. It's only from the bathtub you can observe dirty pipework behind a washbasin, or sitting on the loo that you realise the toilet paper is on the wrong side or out of reach! There's nothing like having to clamber out of bed in the middle of the night to bring it home that furniture is badly positioned, light switches too far from the bed, rugs liable to slip on a polished floor. The venerable Stanley Marcus, whose family founded the Texas department store Neiman Marcus, always travelled with his own light bulbs in his luggage, because no hotel provided bulbs with sufficiently high wattage for him to read in bed.

Before the opening of the Athenaeum I had Claudio Guarnori as assistant manager, a young Italian of great charm who had worked at the Hyde Park. Together we hand-picked a team that was the envy of many West End hotels. I selected the china, the silver, the glassware, and some of the carpets and furnishings, which few hotel managers get the chance to do. Everything had to be approved by Mr Bloomfield, but we agreed on most things.

I hadn't been more excited or more enthused since Turnberry. I would go to bed in the early hours planning the day ahead. By 5 a.m. I'd be wide awake, striding through Green Park to clear my head and longing to get on with the day's work. I could look in on Jean frequently, and the maid we had in Kensington came to be with her during the day. This lady, devoted in her way, was permanently tired or unwell. Most days she had a headache, an upset stomach, a cold, or was just exhausted. She would lie back and regale poor Jean, who could do little but listen patiently, with her tales of an ungrateful husband and family.

Something, I suppose, had to bring me down to earth. One morning shortly before the opening I arrived at the office to find there had been a break-in. The safe had been jemmied and the thief, presumably disappointed at not finding much money inside, had made off with an equally valuable commodity: all the new hotel keys. When I reported this to Instone Bloomfield he hit the roof. If I couldn't be trusted with his keys, he shouted, how could he possibly trust me with his flagship hotel? He would have to reconsider his decision to appoint me general manager.

In the meantime, he announced, just like a headmaster doling out a hundred lines to a recalcitrant pupil, I was to prepare a 'document' setting out in detail my plans and intentions for the new hotel, and present it to him in a week's time. That was one of the most anxious weeks of my life: if I lost this job, how would I support the family? Jean needed constant care by now, and if I couldn't provide it by working in hotels, what were the alternatives? I had already spoken to Sam about investing our meagre savings in a small shop-cum-post office, which I thought would provide the security the family needed and a flat over the shop. He told me not to be so bloody ridiculous: I was a hotelier, I had worked for what I had since the age of 14 and if I contemplated giving up now I was a bigger bloody fool than he had imagined. Sam wasn't one to waste a good expletive!

Like an obedient schoolboy, I duly prepared the document as instructed and, had he but known it, Instone Bloomfield did me a great service, because having to set out clearly on paper exactly what I planned for the Athenaeum Hotel was to prove a great asset later on when I was briefing the staff, talking to the media and writing to the guests.

A week from the date of the burglary I approached Instone Bloomfield to hear what he had decided about my future. I presented the document to him and he tossed it, without a glance, into his out-tray. His desk was always clear. He filed nothing, so far as I knew. When he read a letter he either scribbled a hand-written response under the signature and sent it back, or crumpled it into the wastepaper basket. So it would be, I guessed, with the document which I had worked on late into the night, imagining my future might depend on it.

The matter of the stolen keys was never referred to again. Bloomfield was basically a kind man but not always the soundest judge of character, and surrounded himself with ill-chosen advisers. My successor at the Royal Garden Hotel left after 11 months, protesting he couldn't stand it a moment longer. Mr Bloomfield sent for me and said he now realised what an enormous effort I had put into looking after the Royal Garden, although he hadn't at the time. He knew the circumstances surrounding my wife's illness and told me he wanted to send me away on a holiday anywhere in the world for two weeks. On one condition: that I must go alone, in order to have a break from the combined pressure of overseeing the pre-opening of the hotel and coping with Jean's illness and two teenage boys. I went into Thomas Cook in Berkeley Square and chose a holiday in Gran Canaria – the cheapest package I could find – grateful for the chance to soak up the sun and rest. Jean's parents came to stay while I was away, and I came back to London revitalised and ready for anything.

*   *   *

Before the year was out, Instone Bloomfield announced he had sold his hotels to the Rank Organisation. My new boss was Tom Sawyer, former general manager of Grosvenor House and the Hyde Park Hotel, now managing director of Rank Hotels. The Athenaeum Hotel opened under the Rank umbrella, after a dummy run when all our friends and business contacts came to stay and write a critique. Some new clients, like former US Marine Coastguard officer Robert Lakey from Texas, came to us because they had walked along Piccadilly during the months of refurbishment and thought how inviting the hotel looked. Bob remained a guest up to the time I left in 1984.

The publicity surrounding the opening was tremendous. Judy Tarlo, one of the all-time great – and surely one of the most down-to-earth – PR people, ensured we were in every newspaper, on every radio talk show, on television shows all over America. Judy, whose mother Nora was a director of Oddenino's, worked for Rogers and Cowan, and had been retained for two spells of six months before and after the opening. She was brimful of ideas that worked: monogrammed Athenaeum bathrobes were sent to dozens of Hollywood stars, and most of them

108

came to stay. The Athenaeum's own star was in the ascendant and the staff – me included – were on a permanent high. Nothing was too good for our guests, and they were, surely, the best guests any hotel ever had!

I used to say the Athenaeum was a hotelier's dream, just the right size in just the right place and full of the right people.

I briefed the staff on the principle of the 'home away from home'. Nobody was allowed to say no except me: if a guest asked for something a member of staff couldn't provide or didn't know, he or she was under strict instructions to pass on the request to somebody who could help. I also introduced the 'link system'; each member of staff would try to introduce a new guest to another member of staff, using the guest's name, so that soon after their arrival every guest would be called by name. This started with the doorman or luggage porter, who learned quickly to decipher names on luggage labels as the guests emerged from their car.

Our philosophy was: Imagine this is the town house of wealthy friends. You tell them you are coming to London and they say, 'We are so sorry we will be away, but do come. The staff are here and they will look after you and see you have everything you need.' This was the atmosphere I was trying to create, the kind of quiet attention that always thinks ahead, and it seemed to work from the outset. Reservations came in faster than we could deal with them. Forecasts were good.

Imagine my astonishment, then, when Tom Sawyer asked me to come to his office one Friday about a month after the official opening. He was surrounded by seven or eight Rank executives. 'You seem to be the only one who hasn't heard,' he informed me without preamble. 'We're going to sell the Athenaeum Hotel.' The directors – Sir John Davis was Chairman at that time, Graham Dowson, now a neighbour at the Barbican, Chief Executive and Ed Chilton in charge of the hotels – had decided that the hotel was 'too small to be viable'.

'You can't do that!' I shouted. 'Haven't you seen the figures for the first four weeks? Haven't the directors seen the forecasts for the year? And what about me?'

'You'll be all right for six months,' was Sawyer's reply. I still couldn't take this in. 'Just tell me you're not going to sell it to those awful bankers from Paris I had to show around the other day.' 'Yes,' he came back. 'They're the ones who are going to buy it.'

'You can't!' I yelled, not caring now. 'You cannot let them have it.'

'If you don't like it,' said Sawyer, 'then get us a higher bid.'

'I'll do it,' I yelled back. 'And I'll do it today.'

Little did Sawyer know that I had had a call that morning from the Barclay Brothers, who owned the Londonderry Hotel on Hyde Park Corner, and who many years later bought The Ritz, asking if I would manage their property. I wouldn't, but agreed to have lunch with them to discuss the matter and perhaps make some suggestions. I felt I might be able to persuade them to make a bid for the Athenaeum Hotel.

At the same time, I put in a call to my old friend and staunch supporter from Turnberry days, Niall Hodge, former chairman of Blackwood Hodge. He promised he would speak to a couple of influential business friends and encourage them to put in a bid.

The ploy worked. Tom Sawyer marched into my office a few days later and said: 'Repel all boarders. We've decided to keep the hotel.'

Those of us who were involved at the beginning of the project felt part of something very special, and have remained friends – staff and guests. Sally Bulloch, a pretty redhead who came to work as a reservations clerk and longed to go into public relations, not only became my PR manager but went on to manage the hotel, which she still does at the time of writing, though no longer for Rank Hotels. The two hall porters, Alex Serra and Donald Birrane, were a double act unequalled in my hotel experience, Alex a compact and dignified, beautifully mannered Spaniard, as kind as he was smart; Donald a leprechaun of an Irishman with huge blue eyes that mesmerised guests of all genders. 'This is the world's most exciting hotel here,' he would announce to anybody he called on the phone. And would expect them to know, as they always did, who was speaking.

Felipe, our immaculately groomed lounge waiter, who died of Aids a few years ago, knew everything about the current musical theatre. Having enjoyed the movie *La Cage aux Folles*, I asked Felipe what he thought of the musical which had just opened at the Palladium. 'She no great,' he said in his heavily accented English. 'But the frocks they are lovely.'

Felipe was the most unpopular man in the hotel when Dolly Parton came to stay. She ordered room service one afternoon when Felipe was on duty. He knocked on her door, silver tray held aloft, and dashed back downstairs complaining indignantly: 'Miss Parton. She having a dress fitting and she naked. She *naked*! It is *disgusting*!' The other waiters nearly lynched him. There were no difficulties rostering overtime for the rest of her stay . . .

110

Stephen Gresham, one of the best piano players I ever heard in a hotel died, too, after several years of entertaining our guests in the restaurant, sometimes with his own compositions. He had played for me at the Royal Garden Hotel, and I hadn't seen or heard from him for years until one evening sitting over dinner in the Hyde Park Hotel I heard the introduction to *Falling in Love Again*. Nobody, but nobody, ever plays the haunting introduction to that Marlene Dietrich song. I looked across the room to find Stephen smiling over a grand piano, knowing I would recognise that somebody was playing this especially for me. He had just returned from working in the Philippines. We were able to bring him to the Athenaeum Hotel a few months later, where he married one of our cashiers, and gave enormous pleasure to countless guests before his untimely death. He also produced a cassette featuring some of our favourite songs, and one or two of his own compositions, including *Rainbird*, a piece he composed specially for my wife.

Because music plays such an important part in my own life, I have introduced it into every hotel I worked in. As with so many aspects of hotel-keeping, César Ritz had done it first, when Johann Strauss and an orchestra were performing for a season in London. He introduced them to the Savoy Hotel, where he hoped they would persuade patrons to linger over dinner. 'Just ask the sommelier what that would mean,' he pointed out. Ritz had noticed that while the French, the Swiss and the Italians considered an amiable buzz of conversation an appropriate accompaniment to fine cuisine, the English dined in virtual silence.

Where music already existed in the hotels, I extended it. More important, I *listened* to it, which is something hoteliers who are not fond of music never do. They don't really listen. Musicians are performing artists and need to be appreciated. They respond when you encourage them, and will take criticism, too, if they know you care about what they do. You can always tell a hotel or restaurant where *le patron* is not musically aware. These are the places where the piped music sounds as if it could be a tape – any tape – played backwards, or vocal music played just too soft to be heard, too loud to be ignored. Worse, a guitarist or a harpist sunk in their own reverie playing soft, mournful music that puts a dampener on the happiest of evenings. Usually, I'm convinced, it's because they assume nobody's listening, and it takes only seconds for a switched-on manager to convince them that *he* is.

The Hungarian Quartet at Claridge's; Joe Stein and his 12 violinists, who serenaded guests at the Royal Roof Restaurant; Stephen Gresham at the Athenaeum Hotel; Ian Gomez, who played the piano at Claridge's and the Savoy; and wonderful Mike Mackenzie at The Dorchester then the Savoy – these men brought joy into the hotels, and our lives.

The register of Athenaeum guests was filled with the names of just those people any hotelier would have chosen to be there. English county folk in town for shopping or the season; business people from Europe and the United States; theatre people and film people, most of them on the personal recommendation of their friends. It became known as: The Athenaeum Hotel – Where Your Friends Are! Hollywood embraced us, and for them we were an intrinsically English hotel where American film people felt at home.

Cary Grant married his fourth wife Barbara while staying in an Athenaeum apartment next to ours in Down Street. The couple had met while Barbara was a PR girl at Rank's Royal Lancaster Hotel. John Wayne stayed for several weeks while filming *Brannigan*. He was so tall that even our generous-sized beds could not accommodate his long legs, and we had a two-foot extension, which screwed to the head of the bed beneath the pillows, specially made for him. He missed 'his' bed so badly when he left to stay with friends in Cheyne Walk, we had to lend it to him for the duration of his stay in London *and* each time he visited.

The divine Kim Novak, in town to film *The Mirror Crack'd* with Elizabeth Taylor, arrived with her own masseuse. (So that was the secret of her unbelievable figure – possibly the best I have ever seen!) Shirley MacLaine brought her own astrologer, who forbade any of the entourage to sleep in any room with the number seven.

Rex Harrison was based at the hotel for six months after moving out of the Connaught when his German-born ex-wife Lilli Palmer stayed there while she promoted her book *Change Lobsters and Dance*. There were always surprises when stars either let us down or impressed us in spite of ourselves: Charlton Heston with the worst toupee ever seen; Mick Jagger disarmingly patient and well-mannered with the press; and Harrison Ford, who made the female staff swoon when they watched him on screen, turning out to be a short, sparse little man who crept in and out of the hotel in trilby hat and raincoat. The amiable Hume Cronyn and Jessica Tandy always stayed when they were in London, and Richard Crenna at the height of his Hollywood fame.

Angela Lansbury paid a special visit after we had been introduced via the press. She complained in an interview that while she always got the best tables in New York restaurants, she was never recognised in

London, even though she was starring in the musical *Gypsy*. I wrote to the newspaper to say I was a great admirer of Angela Lansbury; I had even had her photograph pinned up on the bulkhead of the battleship *King George V* towards the end of the war. I made it clear that 'table five – the best in the room' would be permanently reserved for Miss Lansbury any time she cared to come in for luncheon or dinner.

A few days later she did come in, with her husband, and told me that if I had pinned up her picture in 1945 'you must really have liked big girls . . .' I truly liked this 'big girl', and tossed a bouquet on to the stage when I went to see her later that week in *Gypsy*.

My connections with that show went back to the day I met Gypsy Rose Lee herself at the Midland Hotel in Manchester. She was there to promote her book *Gypsy* and, rather than the seductive siren I had imagined, was a nice middle-aged lady with hair pulled severely back from her face, hardly any make-up but an astonishingly good figure. Since then I have seen every stage production in the UK and every film, the last with Bette Midler in the part played by Angela Lansbury.

Composer Jule Styne and lyricist Sammy Cahn were regular visitors, Robert Wagner and Stephanie Power made it their base in London, and equally revered people from behind the scenes in Hollywood, like Bud and Frank Westmore, the legendary make-up artists, were our frequent guests.

The Hollywood character actress Maureen Stapleton stayed for several weeks while making a film in London. When she came down to pay her bill I cravenly hid behind a pillar, having learned to keep out of her way when she had been drinking.

'Jeez-us!' she shrieked. 'Three thousand dollars. And I didn't even get to — the manager . . .'

The stars knew that when they stayed with us, if they wanted peace and quiet, we would do all in our power to ensure it. If, on the other hand, their visit was a public one, we would help with press interviews and appoint Sally Bulloch, herself a child actress who had appeared in the St Trinian's films, as their personal public relations and media representative in London.

With such a guest list, there were some great parties! Some we attended, some we hosted, some produced a surprise or two. John Wayne regaled us with cowboy songs around the piano at the end-of-film party for *Brannigan*. When I arranged for Blossom Dearie to perform in cabaret in the Windsor Lounge there was a party after the first night. Two of the guests were Adelaide Hall and Elisabeth Welch, both in their eighties, both of whom had starred in the Broadway musical *Blackbirds of 1928*. These two great ladies of jazz could not resist a duet, then another – and another. Separately and together they entertained us late into the night.

Not all our visitors were quite so welcome. One couple stayed in the hotel for several weeks, the lady enjoying leisurely shopping forays to Bond Street and Knightsbridge, her husband leaving for business each morning. At the end of their first week, and their second, an account was rendered as is usual, and settled promptly. At the beginning of week three the husband explained to me that his wife was going into a Harley Street clinic for a hysterectomy and when she came out would spend another three or four weeks convalescing and generally taking things easy at the Athenaeum. He had business overseas but would join her when time permitted. I naturally felt sympathy for the woman when she was released from hospital, though she seemed fit and in good spirits, and when the husband failed to reappear over the next two weeks, was not overly concerned. When two weeks later he still had not shown up, I had to take action. We had given the account each week to his wife, but had received no payment since their second week's stay.

The lady could tell me nothing about her husband's return, nor where he was. She did give us a telephone number somewhere in Europe, but we could get no response from it. I invited her into my office and asked an assistant manager and the hotel security officer to join us. Still she insisted she could not pay, but her husband would eventually settle all the outstanding accounts. My two colleagues were a little taken aback when I told the woman I would take her jewellery as security against the bill. I had noticed she wore what appeared to be very good pearls, several diamond rings and an expensive gold watch. She refused to remove them but I told her I would not let her leave my office until she did. After a few minutes she gave in and handed me the jewellery. I made a swift telephone call to a jeweller in Burlington Arcade, outlined the situation and asked if he could send an assessor right away. The jeweller came himself and carried out the valuation in the lady's presence. The pearls and two rings were sufficient to settle the account; I returned the watch, and told her I would hold the other items for three days. If the money due to us was paid by then, she would have her jewels back.

The woman left the hotel that day and we learned she had checked into another at Heathrow airport, but we managed to alert them about the unpaid bills. Some days later we had a visit from a rather shifty man who claimed to be her solicitor and demanded her jewels be returned. We refused, and it was another three months before the account was eventually paid and the jewellery could be returned. I'm convinced some of the staff thought I was a monster for stripping a lady of her jewels, but to me it's quite simple: there is no shame in paying your bills.

Every year we staged a Scotch Whisky Festival around Burns Night. This had been the natural follow-on to the Passport to Malt that I had introduced to the Athenaeum Bar, where we featured 100 brands of single malt whisky. Regular visitors were encouraged to sample the malts one by one and have their passport stamped. When they had sampled all 100, they were presented with a bottle of their favourite.

During the two or three evenings of festivities, I was happy to appear in the kilt. My mother had been a Scot and I am entitled to wear the Mackenzie tartan. The management team were sometimes less eager than I to dress the part, even though they were younger and often better endowed in the calf department. Hollywood guests were encouraged to don full Highland dress, sometimes to dramatic effect. When Billy Dee Williams, the black, six-foot-seven hero of *Star Wars II* posed for press pictures in full Campbell regalia he caused a sensation.

I'm thankful I appreciated those Athenaeum years while they were happening. Had I but known it, they were to prove the saddest as well as the happiest of my life.

* * *

Since Jean was diagnosed as having multiple sclerosis in 1963, while we were at the Queens Hotel in Leeds, every decision I made was governed by her condition and based on what was best for her. In a way, it had been a relief to know the worst. Her increasing weakness, loss of the use of her limbs, her deteriorating eyesight and speech, had caused tremendous anxiety. In those days doctors were reluctant to commit themselves or to break bad news. They tended to fob you off with 'let's wait and see what happens'. I had been trying for so long to get a straight answer as to what exactly was wrong with my wife that the point came when I could stand it no longer. I stormed into the office of the specialist at the Leeds Royal Infirmary and demanded to know what was wrong and what the prognosis might be. The consultant – and only years later did I acknowledge how uncomfortable he must

115

have felt at the interview – was in a frightful temper and shouted at me: 'Your wife has multiple sclerosis. There is no cure.'

Now I knew. There was no reason to tell Jean. She didn't ask, and she was as cheerful, good-natured and patient as she had always been. She did wonder aloud what was wrong with her, but seemed satisfied to be assured that we didn't know. Had she insisted on knowing the truth at any time, I believe I would have told her. As it was, I felt I was reacting as she needed.

As her condition worsened, she gradually lost the use of her limbs. The boys were too young to really appreciate how ill she was or what needed to be done. We were fortunate to be living in. Opening the new hotel was exciting but made enormous demands on my time and energy. All sorts of people had suggested over the years that Jean should go into a nursing home, but that was never an option. She was my wife; her place was with me, and mine with her, and neither of us would have considered any alternative.

I learned to dress Jean, to feed her, wash and bathe her – do all the things in fact that no woman would choose even her husband to do for her. It seemed a small service in return for the years of happy marriage and stable family background that she had provided.

She remained confined to a wheelchair for the last ten years of her life, but we never stopped getting dressed up and enjoying as active a social life as these restrictions would allow. Jean would have her hair done by Malcolm Brown at his salon in Fulham, which he later moved to the lower ground floor of the Athenaeum Hotel. Every week Malcolm would help me carry the wheelchair downstairs to his basement premises. We continued to enjoy the theatre and to attend receptions and dinners just as we always had. I was determined she would live as full a life as possible.

True friends like the late Ben and Ivy Chapman in Hull, and Bill and Margaret Andrews from Windsor, still an important part of our lives, rallied round magnificently, organising outings and holidays. And Jean's parents were wonderful. They helped and supported and encouraged, as they had always done, despite my mother-in-law being handicapped by profound deafness. They would stay with Jean if I had to be away, and were always happy to look after the boys during school holidays, or have them up to stay in their bright house by the Mersey near Southport.

I took up the cause of wheelchair access in public places, reading the

Liverpool, 1930

Newly arrived in Sydney, Australia, 1945

'My' battleship HMS *King George V* entering Tokyo Bay, 20 August, 1945

'… the right size in the right place, full of the right people …

…an hotelier's dream.' The Athenaeum Hotel, 1978. (Photograph, top, by Thistle Photography, bottom, by Ray Brown)

'One small step…' Welcoming astronaut Colonel Neil Armstrong, centre, to the Royal Garden Hotel, 1970. Right, assistant manager David Webster. (Photograph by Jalmar Photography)

With co-director and proprietor Ingrid Sorenson, Dormy House Hotel, Broadway

Mother- and father-in-law, Sam and Ellen Wood

Jean, Graham and Russell, Turnberry 1960

First management – Dornoch Hotel, Sutherland, 1956. (Photograph by Tom Naismith)

Gleneagles, 1954. (Photograph by Tom Naismith)

'Class of '67'! British Transport Staff College, Woking, 1967. (Photograph by British Railways, Southern Region)

Management and kitchen brigade, Central Hotel, Glasgow, 1968. Jean-Maurice Cottet centre front. (Photograph by W. Ralston Ltd)

Great-grandfather John Ban
Mackenzie, 'King of Pipers'

Mother and father, Harry and
Margaret Jones

'Waiting for the off!' Official starter at Gleneagles staff sports day, 1954.
(Photograph by Tom Naismith)

Grand finale of the Christian Dior fashion show, Entente Cordiale Ball, Gleneagles, 1955. (Photograph by *Courier and Advertiser*, People's Journal, Dundee)

As a young assistant manager (standing centre) keeping an eye on the top table. Gleneagles 1955. (Photograph by Tom Naismith)

Glorious Turnberry! The Open Golf Championship 1994. (Photograph by Turnberry Hotel)

At long last – completion of the new kitchen at Claridge's, a marathon project for the Slovenian, Maitre Chef des Cuisines Marjan Lesnik; the Austrian, Senior Assistant Manager Rudi Jagersbacher; and the Englishman! (Photograph by Thistle Photography)

Celebrating another award for Claridge's with Eve, definitely 'best of the best', 1992. (Photograph by pic Photos)

With the Rt. Hon. John Lee, Undersecretary of State for Tourism, at Claridge's

The uniformed staff at Claridge's including Head Linkman Mario Utilini and Head Chef John Williams, take time out to walk for Cadbury's Strollerthon for charity, 1993. (Photograph by Alex Lentati, Evening Standard)

Sharing a joke with US former President Nixon, Claridge's 1993. (Photograph by Antonia Reeve Photography)

With President and Mrs Reagan the same year. (Photograph by Harold Baruch, Cameo)

'Welcome, Prime Minister!' The Rt. Hon. Margaret (now Lady) Thatcher on one of her many visits to Claridge's. (Photograph by Professional Photographic Services)

HRH Princess Margaret in sparkling form at Claridge's. (Photograph by Professional Photographic Services)

HRH the Duke of Edinburgh arrives for the World Wildlife Fund Congress at the Royal Garden Hotel, London, 1971. Sir Peter Scott is on the left. (Photograph by Jalmar Photography)

Welcoming the Princess of Wales, a regular visitor to Claridge's. (Photograph by Professional Photographic Services)

Prime Minister Harold Wilson at the Royal Garden Hotel, 1970

And the Rt. Hon. Edward Heath MP visits the hotel a year later with Peter Chandler, Oddenino's area manager, in attendance. (Photograph by Jalmar Photography)

The backbone of any good hotel, the food and beverage team at Claridge's, 1993. (Photograph by Harold Baruch, Cameo)

The newest OBE! Buckingham Palace, November 1989. (Photograph by Herald Photography)

Her Majesty the Queen arrives at Claridge's for the party following the marriage of Prince Andrew to Sarah Ferguson. Just 650 close family and friends! (Photograph by Professional Photographic Services)

Welcoming Her Majesty Queen Elizabeth the Queen Mother for luncheon at Claridge's

The Duchess of York arrives at Claridge's for the State Banquet of King Fahd. (Photograph by Professional Photographic Services)

HM King Hassan of Morocco, host to Her Majesty the Queen, at the State Banquet held at Claridge's, 1987. (Photograph by Professional Photographic Services)

riot act to anybody who tried to deny access. In hotels, theatres, restaurants, I was quite shameless in asking staff to clear other people out of the ladies' cloakroom so that I could take Jean in.

She died in 1975 as a result of severe septicaemia, caused after she dropped a lighted cigarette on to her leg and was, mercifully, unable to feel the injury it inflicted. This happened one Saturday when I succumbed to perfectly understandable pressure from my younger son, who complained that I never went to watch him play football for City of London School. I knew it meant a lot to him, so when Bill and Margaret Andrews volunteered to come and sit with his mother, I gratefully accepted. The Andrews called to say they would be delayed by 15 minutes. I saw that Jean was properly settled and comfortable and decided it wouldn't do any harm to leave her for just that short time. During the period alone she managed, God alone knows how, to pick up cigarettes and matches and light one – something I always had to do for her. She dropped the lighted cigarette and by the time our friends arrived it had already burned a deep hole in her leg. The wound, despite daily dressing by a nurse and by me, never healed.

She had suffered so much, and when the doctors at St George's Hospital said the only hope of saving her life was to amputate a leg, I declined permission. She had been through enough. Right up to the end I believed, against all the odds and all the facts, that she would recover. Her death came as a ghastly shock. I suppose it always does.

After Jean died I thought my life was over. It wasn't a self-pitying complaint, just an assumption that I had been married, had brought up a family, had worked hard – and that was it. I could look forward only to the boys leaving home to make their own lives, then hopefully not-too-early retirement and a solitary old age. I was 51.

8

The Art from the Heart

Just over a year later I was flattered to be approached by the weekly magazine *Caterer & Hotelkeeper*, which wanted to feature me in a series of articles on 'Great British Hoteliers'.

The journalist assigned to the story was Eve Macpherson, a name familiar to me from reading the trade press but whom I had never met. She called and asked for an hour of my time. I said I could spare half an hour and got together a sheaf of press clippings and information to save time.

We talked for two and a half hours. We had lunch and I said I must get some work done. Could she come back that evening and we'd have supper and talk some more?

My version of what followed is that she asked so many questions I had to marry her to keep her quiet: hers is that it didn't work!

The attraction was obvious from the start. However, it was too early for me to contemplate another relationship, and she was in the midst of a difficult separation and divorce. For well over a year we remained 'just good friends'. We saw each other at hotel receptions and sometimes had a drink together afterwards. We even danced together on the brand-new carpet of the Hilton on Park Lane – because the band playing to honour hotelier Louis Bluet on his retirement was too good to resist. Other couples joined in, and a rather staid and formal reception turned into a great party, while the giant ice carving in the middle of the room melted away.

We both adored dancing, music, the theatre, travel – we had so much in common, including many hotel friends, and when we were together we could have danced *or* talked all night. The vital spark was there all right, but I didn't dare fan it into the flame it was to become.

At the beginning of 1978 Eve went to America for several weeks on a work assignment with John Tovey, the fashionable chef-patron of

Miller Howe in the Lake District, who had been instrumental in introducing us (it was John who told Eve that I ought to be the first subject in her series about top hoteliers). So enthralled was she by the United States that she came home in March for just a few weeks to pack her bags and return there to live, in either Dallas or New Orleans. When she told me all this, bubbling over with enthusiasm for the opportunities she could foresee in the US, it worried me, and I wasn't quite sure why.

A couple of weeks after her return Eve rang me. 'I wanted you to know,' she said, 'that I'm going sailing in the Solent. If I drown and you hadn't said goodbye, you'd be sorry, wouldn't you?' My severe secretary Jeanette Parkinson's horn-rimmed spectacles glinted at me from across the desk. I stammered a response and found myself asking Eve to dinner the following evening. She seemed unsurprised. Fine, she said, would 7.30 be all right? Much later I found out she'd arrived in her little mustard-coloured Mini well before seven and sat in the car listening to *The Archers* to calm her nerves until she felt she could decently make an appearance without seeming too eager!

I put a bottle of Chablis on ice in the apartment. Champagne seemed ostentatious, and I remembered that John Tovey, whom I admired, always had Chablis as an apéritif – and that Eve liked it. We had dinner in the hotel: asparagus, poached salmon, crème brûlée, and returned to the apartment to finish off the Chablis.

That was it. Starbursts, sunbursts, coloured lights. We were in love. Eve couldn't stay the night. Graham, my elder son, was due home from his manager's job at the Hard Rock Café around midnight. (Russell was in Europe taking time out before university.) The maids would be in the building before eight in the morning. A scandal was simply not an option, and the general manager having a woman in his apartment would certainly cause a scandal.

I drove back to Richmond with Eve – we didn't want to be apart a moment longer than was absolutely necessary – in my car, leaving hers to be collected next day. Driving through Hyde Park, we stopped by the Serpentine, walked to the water's edge and danced in each other's arms while we sang songs from our favourite shows. We could have been a thousand miles away from a chilly London spring night. Until, that is, a torch beam caught us amidships and a deep voice intoned: 'Aye, aye. What 'ave we 'ere, then?' or words to that effect. We parted and gawped at the two policemen, speechless.

119

'Is that your car, sir?' said one.

'Yes.'

'And where do you live, sir?'

'In Down Street, just off Piccadilly, officer.'

'And where are you going, sir?'

'Just seeing this young lady home, officer, and it was such a lovely night and we just got carried away and we didn't think there was anybody around and . . .' I started gabbling but the police officer cut me short.

'Been drinking have you, sir?'

'Well, officer, only a glass of wine several hours ago.'

He must have realised my speech was not slurred, I was not unsteady on my feet and my breath didn't smell of intoxicating liquor, as they say in court. He clicked off the torch, said, 'Very well, sir, but I'd be on my way if I were you.'

That was 27 April. Three weeks later on a beautiful spring Saturday, I asked Eve to marry me. I had driven over to Richmond just after lunch, bringing a bathrobe and toothbrush with me, which somewhat surprised Eve. We held hands walking through the lovely old town with its handsome Green and Georgian houses. We sauntered up Richmond Hill and brought out drinks from the Roebuck pub to enjoy overlooking the flowered terraces that slope down to the river below. I felt happier than I'd ever imagined.

'You know what I want for us, don't you?' I said, rather tentatively. 'I want us to get married.' Eve put up quite a strenuous resistance – for all of five minutes. She told me I shouldn't ask, she wouldn't make me happy. She didn't want children. She was evil-tempered. Reclusive. Couldn't cook. Hated housework. Was selfish and self-willed. Having got that off her chest (always two of her best features) and seeing I either didn't believe her or didn't care, she capitulated and we were engaged.

On the Monday, a bank holiday, I shamelessly rang the Reverend Canon Edwyn Young, CVO, Queen's Chaplain and the Bishop of London's Chaplain to the hotel industry, at his home in Kingston. We both knew Edwyn. He had once told Eve after a particularly good luncheon at the Westbury Hotel as guests of its ebullient general manager Alan Fairbrass, that if ever she decided to remarry, she must let him do the honours. Eve thanked him but assured him she didn't believe she would be calling on his services.

120

Edwyn insisted we come over straight away. Mary, his wife, would give us tea in the garden. A couple of 'their girls' would also be there. We knew this was likely to mean a pair of striptease artistes from Soho; Edwyn was also Chaplain to the West End theatres and clubs and he and Mary often entertained one or two girls whom the Canon had persuaded to be baptised or confirmed.

Our wedding was planned for 29 September 1978. The Queen's Chapel of the Savoy, the Chapel of the Royal Victorian Order, remains closed during August while the Queen visits Balmoral, and September, on the return of the Royal Family, was always a busy month. The date gave us enough time to prepare but not enough to despair of ever becoming husband and wife. First there would be a register office ceremony in Richmond, opposite Eve's flat in Paradise Road. Then a formal blessing in the chapel adjoining the Savoy Hotel.

The chapel was filled to overflowing – mainly with hotel friends on both sides – with standing room only at the back. The Athenaeum Hotel florist, the aptly named Dorothy Kew, had bedecked the chapel with garlands of cream roses. It was what Canon Young called an 'OMB' wedding – organ, men and boys. The full works, musically speaking. We had Albinoni and Bach and Purcell as well as our favourite hymns; Eve wore cream chiffon trimmed with bands of satin; my two sons as ushers were ten times more nervous than I was; and Edwyn had warned Eve that if she cried, as she predicted, he would look at her most severely.

They both did just what they said. As we were about to exchange our vows, I could see Eve's chin tremble dangerously and her eyes fill with tears. Edwyn's brows drew together in a deep frown over his black-framed spectacles – and a loud bleep-bleep reverberated around the walls and ornate ceiling of the Queen's Chapel. Typical hotelier's wedding: a colleague manager, Graham Tomlinson from the Chesterfield Hotel in Mayfair, had slipped out in a hurry and brought his pocket pager. Now he was being paged in the middle of our wedding. The congregation – including Eve and me – could barely suppress a giggle. From that moment, the ceremony was utterly joyful, and when it was time to walk back up the aisle I had to restrain Eve from fairly skipping at a rate that would have prevented our guests from catching a glimpse of us on our way out.

The staff of the Athenaeum Hotel formed a guard of honour for our return, and each one wanted to congratulate us and shake our hands

121

before we took our places by the door of the Windsor Lounge to receive our guests. The receiving line took over an hour. Our bridesmaid Jane Baker looked after 140 guests who had come from all over the world to be with us. My two sons took it in turn to read 86 telegrams from friends and colleagues worldwide who could not be present. Eve's brother David made a hilarious speech which left her red-faced and the guests hysterical with mirth. He hadn't enjoyed himself so much, he said, since her coming-out party. And the prison governor and her probation officer had agreed that that was quite a party. And . . . 'Our late mother's maiden name was Helen Black,' he told us. 'Everybody says my sister is her double. "Doesn't she look like Helen Black?" they say. "But," I tell them, "you should see her in green . . ."'

At last we were persuaded to join the poor chauffeur who had been waiting to drive us around Hyde Park Corner to the Hyde Park Hotel, where we were to spend the first two nights of our honeymoon.

We were shown up to the Royal Suite, which the general manager Willy Bauer had arranged for us. Eve counted 13 flower arrangements, 12 telephones, and a glorious view across Hyde Park. The sitting room was so grand we decided we must share it with our friends. Next day we telephoned all the guests who had flown in from overseas and invited them for yet another glass of champagne in our suite: Simone Berbion, Eve's dear friend from Bordeaux, Norman Knight from Boston, Robert and Sylvia Huth from Los Angeles, and half a dozen others. Later that night we and the Huths, whom Eve had met at Miller Howe while they were on their own honeymoon, dined and danced together in the Vintage Room at the Inn on the Park before they flew back to LA the following day.

We took off for Amalfi and Venice early on Sunday morning, and not even hangovers and Luton Airport could dull our sense of excitement. The Cipriani Hotel on Giudecca island was simply the perfect honeymoon destination and the finest hotel in the world. It was then, as it is now, managed with charisma and efficiency by Natale Rusconi; it radiates style and understated good taste, cossets guests shamelessly and, if Conrad Hilton is to be believed, it is the hotel with everything that matters – location, location and location – in spades!

One of the conditions Eve had put on agreeing to marry me was that, since it put paid to her plans to live and work in America, I must promise to take her there every year – and I have.

Marrying Eve was the beginning of a new life. Everything changed.

We were soulmates, 'complete unto each other'. We live together, love together, and work together, never tire of each other's company and hate to be parted. We're a good team and neither of us dares contemplate a life without the other.

* * *

As luck would have it, my appetite for the New World was as keen as Eve's. A sales promotion trip to New York for the Athenaeum Hotel and an earlier visit to Canada had opened doors to professional and business opportunities and to friendships that were to play an important role in my life. I'd like to think that together, hand in hand, in true Hollywood fashion, my new wife and I set out to conquer the United States of America, but in truth it was the US that conquered us and turned us into two of its most devoted fans.

We have revelled in the opportunity over two decades to experience North American hotels, compare the styles and examine the differences and the similarities between them and their European counterparts.

Not all have been five-star or de luxe. We in the UK still have a lot to learn from American budget hotels and motels, their pricing, service and standards of cleanliness. Also, the way the United States has encompassed the 'bed and breakfast' concept and made it uniquely their own has impressed us across the country. Americans are hospitable by nature, and when they open their homes to you, whether as friends or as paid hosts, they put their hearts and souls into making you feel comfortable and cared for.

In my own sphere of operation, I discovered that the best US hotels are 'grand' in quite a different way from their European counterparts. Less formal, more relaxed. Less bowing, more smiling. It is a *different* experience, but one from which any European hotelier can learn.

Usually when people ask 'What do you think are the best hotels in the US?' I do my best to get out of giving a straight answer. It's like being asked 'what's your favourite restaurant?' It depends: on the occasion, on who you're with, on your budget, and on your expectations. It's great to dine in the hottest spot in town or in the most elegant hotel dining room. But sometimes what you want is to go out for pizza. Same with hotels. If I'm part of a conference for 400 people then what I want from the hotel is state-of-the-art facilities, swift response, efficiency, arrangements that go like clockwork and courteous, well-trained personnel used to dealing with the requirements of large-scale meetings. Quite different from what I look for when I take my wife for a romantic weekend in the sun: comfort, good food and a leisurely atmosphere. And that is different again when I'm staying in an unfamiliar city on business, making calls or hosting receptions. Then, it's attention to details, good business and in-room facilities, great concierges, and reliability. The only thing I don't easily forgive in *any* kind of hotel is the lack of a warm, sincere welcome.

The welcome can be as homely as the lady of the house, still in her apron, appearing on the porch to greet you with a smile when you check into the family bed-and-breakfast. It can be the manager of a motel coming out from behind the desk to help get your bags out of the car. Or it can be, for the really fortunate traveller, Frank Bowling at the Bel Air in Los Angeles or Jeff Trigger at The Mansion on Turtle Creek in Dallas appearing as if by magic as soon as you arrive to shake you warmly by the hand and tell you how good it is to see you.

The prize for our most royal welcome, however, would go to the Windsor Court Hotel in New Orleans back in 1989. The hotel was still under the control of James Coleman Jnr., whose father had built it. A regular visitor to Claridge's and a close friend of Princess Margaret, Jimmy Coleman and his wife Minnie had often talked about their New Orleans property and we were keen, as hoteliers always are, to see how it shaped up.

The Windsor Court limousine was there to meet us at the airport, which was just as well because Eve tripped on the shiny floor surface and slightly twisted her ankle. It wasn't bad enough to accept the offer of first aid, just a minor but painful wrench that left her limping slightly. The driver witnessed the incident and seemed concerned.

As the car pulled up to the hotel entrance the doorman, a concierge, two bellmen, a manager and a first-aider standing behind a wheelchair came out to greet us. 'How's your ankle, Miz Jones?' the manager enquired. We assured him the ankle was just fine, though when she saw the trouble they'd taken, Eve said she felt the least she could do was continue to limp a little.

We were shown up to the largest hotel suite we'd ever seen. A library – lined floor to ceiling with books ranging from Condensed Readers' Digest to a series of textbooks on Modern Obstetrics and Gynaecology – housed a concert grand piano. The sitting-room had two walls of windows looking out over the city. The bedrooms, one large enough to sleep an entire family, the other big enough for four, were sumptuous. In the fully equipped and stocked kitchen were two uniformed maids

124

with basins of hot and iced water, armfuls of snowy white towels, and an assortment of creams, lotions and liniments.

'We'll take care of that ankle for you, Ma'am,' they fussed. 'You-all just sit right down.' A waiter poured champagne from a silver cooler into crystal flutes. That, we insisted, was all the medication she required.

A somewhat different reception lay in wait for us some years before at the erstwhile Houston Grand, then a new and self-consciously hi-tech hotel owned by a consortium of doctors. We arrived, as we had specified, around 9pm. The receptionist, barely looking up to acknowledge our presence, tapped our name into a computer. Head down, he said: 'I'm sorry sir, we do not appear to have a reservation for you.' He checked again, confirmed our initials, shook his head again – and clearly hoped we'd go away and stop bothering him. I told him we had a confirmed reservation and what's more, I would dig out of my briefcase a telex I had received from the company president. He gave it a cursory glance, then solemnly bowed his head once more, 'eyes down' time at the VDU. Another combination was fed in, still nothing remotely useful came out.

Losing patience, I said: 'Look, it's nearly 9.30 We've had a long flight, a long day and we're tired. Do you have a room?'

'Oh yes,' said the young man. 'No problem, sir . . . we have *plenty* of rooms.'

Honestly. An old boss of mine once accused an assistant manager of 'living in an inkwell'. I suppose the modern equivalent would be hiding behind a VDU. Computerised front desk systems always remind me of the cartoon showing St.Peter at a desk with a VDU. He is saying to a new arrival at the Pearly Gates: 'You're not coming up on my computer. How long did you say you've been dead?'

We enjoyed some great hotel experiences – and some amusing ones – with Ritz Carlton, a group I always admired for getting it right so much of the time. Joe Freni, their dynamic President at that time, outlined the company philosophy and training policies to me. Not only were they sound and forward-thinking, but they worked.

We stayed at the Ritz Carlton in Naples, Florida, for the first time in 1990. It was one of those hotel experiences that soothed the soul as well as rested the tired body and brain, though it didn't start out that way.

The American Eagle commuter plane that was to fly us from Miami to Naples was a 12-seater. I let Eve board first and she took the first

125

single seat behind the curtain that screened off the flight deck. The curtain was pinned back, and on the floor sat the captain's black flight bag. From it protruded a dirty, greyish and very dead-looking hand. On the bag itself a yellow sticker over-printed in large red letters: 'With care. Human remains.' I managed to restrain my wife who was by now trying to 'de-plane' and refusing to fly. Even when we realised the 'hand' was a fake, she wasn't at all sure about flying in the care of somebody with such a bleak sense of humour.

The pilot came on board, rearranged his bag, made the flight safety announcements in a laconic tone, and serenely picked his nose for the entire taxi-ing procedure.

It was late by the time we checked into the Ritz Carlton and we were unable to sleep in our seventh floor bedroom because of the incessant mechanical noise from, we guessed, the air conditioning or ventilation plant. I called down to ask what could be done, but was assured by a bewildered night manager that there *was* no engineering plant of any description anywhere near our room, and nothing he could suggest that might be causing the racket.

We slept the best we could, and next morning set out to investigate. And to prove the power of mind over matter. They offered to move us to another room, but clearly nobody understood what we were complaining about. That night, we were standing on our balcony when the noise began again just after dusk. *Frogs*. In the pool way below our window. Dozens. Hundreds. Probably thousands of them. As darkness fell the mating ritual began, gradually building up to the metallic, reverberating crescendo we'd heard the night before. We decided we loved the sound and slept through the night! As for the people who lived there – they had got so used to it they didn't even hear it.

The hotel was superb. Public rooms spacious, elegantly furnished – some said too elegantly for a beachfront property. We had a beautiful suite, the guest amenities were exceptional, service as near perfect as could be. When we neglected for the second evening running to open our (second) complimentary bottle of wine, there was a call from the food and beverage department asking if perhaps the wine was not to our taste and would we care to choose something else.

There were 700 staff – not one, it seemed to me, ugly, over-weight or over 30. They had elevated wholesomeness to an art form (although humour had been adjourned *sine die* . . .). In the Club Lounge a bevy of beautiful female concierges bombarded you with kindness. Nothing

126

was too much trouble, everything achieved with an orthodontically unchallenged smile and a positive, outgoing attitude. On her knees, bent almost double as she tried to crumb down a coffee table after our breakfast service, the tall blonde concierge beamed and said: 'This table surely is the most challenging to buss . . . ' We learned she was part-Swedish and told her how much we had enjoyed a recent visit to Sweden. Full-frontal high beam flashed again. 'Well, thank you all for sharing that with me.' She didn't bat an eyelid when, in all innocence, I said: 'No more, thanks, but those buns of yours are wonderful . . . ' How was I to know they were called blueberry muffins here? In fact, I'm pretty sure if somebody had asked if she was wearing a black lace garter belt and peek-a-boo bra she'd have smiled and retorted: 'Sir, have you tried our house cocktail tonight? I know you'd just love it . . . '

The in-company training programme and philosophy were impressive: personnel are 'ladies and gentlemen looking after ladies and gentlemen.' There was a 20-point Credo that included being knowledgeable of hotel information (hours of operation, guest facilities, and food and beverage outlets for example) to answer guest inquiries. And 'knowing the needs of internal and external customers (guests and employees) so that we may deliver the products and services they expect.' There was also, on the laminated booklet staff carry around with them, a three-point Steps of Service plan to ensure a guest's guarantee of unparalleled comfort and care.

We were delighted when we learned that Rainer Burkle, one of the best young trainee managers who worked with me at Claridge's, and his wife Irene, had joined Ritz Carlton, even more so when he was promoted to food and beverage executive appointments, and worked with the teams that won the coveted Baldridge Award, the hotel industry 'Oscar' in 1993.

Even Ritz Carlton doesn't get it right all the time, and not all Ritz Carlton hotels get it right even most of the time, but of all the groups we've experienced, they achieve the most consistency in the quality of product and service they deliver.

I can cite examples of other, individual, hotels that get it right. I certainly count these among my favourites, and they couldn't be more different from each other.

The Mansion on Turtle Creek in Dallas gets it right. The property is beautiful, the location is good, it has a great dining room. More important, from the minute you arrive, you know that the staff are totally committed to the guests' comfort and welfare. You get a warm welcome when you arrive, and a smiling acknowledgement each time you walk through the lobby. The bellmen and valet parking attendants are always alert and eager to assist. Nobody lounges or slouches. Nobody looks bored. Nobody lets you walk past without a greeting.

The Bel Air in Los Angeles gets it right. The cottages, apartments and suites are immaculate. The grounds are a sub-tropical delight. Even the snow-white swans gliding serenely under the hump-backed bridge seem to encourage tranquillity. Service is crisp and attentive. It's the kind of hotel that throws its arms around you so that you really don't want to leave once you've checked in. Everything you need is right there. The fact that you might, as I have, lunch at a table next to Nancy Reagan, lie on a poolside lounger a few feet away from Lauren Bacall (and no – for those old enough to remember – she didn't holler and I didn't whistle) or shamelessly listened-in on a movie mogul's multi-million dollar deal over the mobile phone network, is merely added value so far as I'm concerned.

What these two have in common is a couple of extraordinary general managers. Frank Bowling, custodian of the Bel Air, is a Yorkshireman with a Savoy Hotels training in the finest European tradition. He came first to New York, where he made the Carlyle the only place to stay. He then brought his inimitable style and elan to the Bel Air. Frank is one of those managers who makes everything look easy. Nothing is too much trouble, you never see him flustered, and he can make things happen as if by magic. He takes the strain of a Hollywood producer's power breakfast, a VIPs wedding or a visiting potentate's entourage in his well-shod stride. One of the things that concerned him when he first arrived at the Bel Air was the way many of the hotel's Hispanic personnel averted their eyes as they walked past the guests. Putting himself in their shoes and projecting *them* into the guests' shoes – he got the hotel to provide free English lessons. Now, you can't pass a Bel Air staff member without a friendly greeting. Frank Bowling is an exponent of my kind of hotel management: 'the art from the heart'.

The Mansion has Jeff Trigger, an energetic all-rounder who didn't even intend to be a hotelier. Jeff began his career as an accountant, but once he came into the hotel business and got the bug, he wasn't afraid to take lessons! While he was manager of The Adolphus in Dallas, Queen Elizabeth II and the Duke of Edinburgh came to visit. Jeff's PR team at the time admitted, 'We were worried. Jeff was a finance man. All he seemed interested in was the bottom line. He seldom made contact with the guests, and now here he was, catapulted into the front line as the highest profile hotel manager in Dallas!'

David Davis, one of the best hotel PRs in the business, called me in London and asked if I would talk Jeff through the protocol of a Royal visit. Jeff and I had several lengthy sessions by transatlantic telephone, and even Her Majesty remarked that the royal visit to The Adolphus had been one of the best organised in the US.

Jeff Trigger wasn't afraid to learn, and he is still learning – as are all the best hoteliers. He is still a finance man, too, but overlaying the business acumen is a real understanding of how it feels to be a guest in his hotel. Like Frank Bowling, Jeff seems to be always there. Around the property. Greeting Guests. Overseeing staff. And still finding time to be the corporate player that today's hotel-keeping demands.

They understand that being a manager means more than the application of management skills. This is a mistake made by mediocre hoteliers who hide behind paper qualifications. Academic and business qualifications are essential – of course they are – but they are not enough for the hospitality business. You need to understand people, too, to genuinely care about them, and to make them realise they are important to you, as guests or staff or suppliers of goods and services. A hotel manager is like an actor on the stage. He is in the spotlight most of the time and he – or she – must believe in the role and be word perfect in the script, able to project so that the 'audience' gets exactly the message he intends to put across.

Every great hotelier I've known has been a little paranoid! You can tell by the way they sweep a restaurant or a banqueting room with their eyes and immediately home in on the table or the waiter service where there's a potential problem. They bend down to pick up any piece of litter they detect on the lobby floor. It drives them mad when they see not just a dead light bulb but one that has been replaced by another of the wrong power or wattage. I've even seen them discreetly run their fingers behind their back along the hand-rails in elevators to check for chewing gum! They are sticklers for attention to that kind of small detail however much they may be preoccupied with financial projections and manning levels and the five-year strategic plan.

9

What d'You Say After 'Have a Nice Day'?

One of the questions I'm most often asked in the US is: 'What are the biggest differences between European and American hotel style – and which is better?' Neither is *better*. The best US hotels are great in a quite different way from their European counterparts. The training of hospitality managers from the outset is a little different on each side of the Atlantic. In America they train *managers*. In Europe, we train *hoteliers*. Who's right? Is it better in today's climate – and I can only speak for the de luxe hotel end of the market – that we should be training people who may be responsible for administering millions of dollars worth of business, in the arcane art of flambée work? Or is it smarter to turn out executive wizards who don't know pastillage from patisserie? One of the wisest and wiliest hotel men I know, Janos Damon, who lives and works in Israel, believes that in a perfect world, 'The best hoteliers would go to hotel school in the US and get work experience in Europe.'

Pick out the best hotels you know and I'll bet they have one thing in common wherever they are and however large they are: a general manager, or at least one senior member of a management team, who maintains a visible, tangible and accessible presence for his guests and his staff. They don't pass the buck by indiscriminate empowerment of staff. 'Empowerment' along with 'downsizing', 'outsourcing', 'yield management' and 'fast tracking' were some of the great buzz-words of the 1990s. Great, that is, while they last, and I've no doubt they made a fortune for the academics who dreamed them up. I like to think they write their books and retire to Hawaii on the proceeds. Trouble is, too often that's all they are – different words for the same old maladies. 'Fast track' has come to mean 'normally we're too damn slow', 'downsizing' that 'we're top-heavy' and 'outsourcing' that 'we're too damn

130

slow, top-heavy and nobody can get the job done.' It's all very well empowering staff but only if they have the experience and the training and are given the support and back-up they need. And only if they know to whom they – and the guests – can turn when they're short of any of those. I see too many cases of empowerment leading to abdication of responsibility by the people who should be responsible. Besides which, it takes the power away from those who should have it – the paying guests.

If it is to work effectively, empowerment has to be achieved in a seamless, unselfconscious fashion. If staff are given the authority to compensate or reward for lapses in service, for example, management needs to make sure the individuals also have the intelligence and the sensitivity to know when to take action.

In a five diamond US hotel that should have known better, we ordered a simple dinner and a glass of red wine each in the coffee shop. After bringing the wine, nobody came near us for 15 minutes. Then we heard an almighty crash from the direction of the service door. Ten minutes after *that* I called our waiter over and said if our food was still not ready, we'd go out on the terrace to gaze at the sunset for a while. He grinned and said: 'No, it's not ready yet. That crash you heard? That was your dinner.' Now with a policy of empowerment in place – and I knew there was – who could have been more deserving of another glass of wine than we were? Or at the very least, a visit to our table to explain and apologise for the delay?

Another problem which hotels fail to take on board is that the bully always wins. One hotel group boasted that since its receptionists were empowered to give away free rooms, the free room allocation had decreased dramatically. Well of course it did! Because non-managerial staff are understandably reluctant to take that big step of giving away a room *unless* confronted with an angry client who makes a noise and *demands* compensation for things gone wrong. The silent majority who feel they've had a raw deal and are not offered something in return simply never come back. And what's more, they tell their friends and their business associates to stay away, too.

I wonder if instead hotels should be teaching staff – all staff, from bell-boys to maîtres d' to managers – to put themselves in the guests' shoes. Instruct them, or let them visualise, how it feels to be away from home, late for a business meeting, tired after a long journey. More important, what it's like to sleep in the hotel room, dine in the food

131

outlets, and be reliant on 'the kindness of strangers' – even when those strangers are being well paid or well tipped.

Maybe then you wouldn't have so many situations where minor details are neglected and build up into a major annoyance for the customer. A complimentary fruit plate with kiwi fruit and prickly pears – but only a knife to eat them with. Used plates and glasses left to attract flies instead of being cleared away by any member of staff who comes into the room with no excuse that 'it's not my job'. No central lighting switch so that guests have to go around switching off an assortment of floor and table lamps before they go to bed. An ice bowl never refilled unless the guest calls to ask.

Even in hotels with a five-star reputation guests can be left floundering because the people in charge are so busy with corporate strategy they forget about the microcosm of comfort, customer care and hospitality that should be a hotel's stock in trade. In other words, they don't put themselves in the customers' shoes. In one of these quite recently, we were assigned a great suite with no wastebasket in the sitting-room; no proper desk, just a slimline table not big enough to work at; no telephone within reach of that; not enough pencils and notepads for the number of telephones. They brought continental breakfast for two on a small plastic tray with no side plates, no butter, and no mats so it could be laid out on the polished dining table. We sent for a trolley, but the chairs we sat on to eat breakfast were left standing in the middle of the room after the trolley was removed, for the rest of the day.

The finest hotels in the US understand and practise the art of anticipation, responding to the needs of the guest with as much sensitivity and style as any in Europe. When the example comes from the top, the rest of the team seldom let the side down.

Arriving at DFW airport for our first visit to The Mansion, we were met by an embarrassingly elongated stretch limo. In conversation the driver found out my wife had always wanted to see a rodeo. When we arrived at the hotel, the general manager was at the door to greet us. Within minutes the concierge, unasked, had sent up a hand-written note, a newspaper and information on all the rodeos around town over the weekend, offering to book whatever we wanted.

We left the suite for a two-hour meeting. When we got back, the ice had been refreshed, there were clean glasses, clean napkins, and our messages as well as flowers from friends and wellwishers, had been placed on desk and tables around the room. In a less good hotel they'd have waited for us to be in the room and delivered these goodies one at a time. Not for The Mansion the hounding of guests so aptly described in one of his *Dallas Morning News* columns by Dave Barry, surely one of the funniest writers in America.

His experience encapsulates the diligent hotelier's (and the diffident guest's) nightmare when he complained that after

'thrusting money at everything in my path including floral arrangements I made it to my room, and . . . thought I was safe. But immediately there was a knock at the door, and it was yet another hotel person, announcing that he had brought me some ice. I didn't need ice, but here was this tuxedo-wearing person holding a silver ice bucket that cost more than my car, and I didn't want to look cheap, so I pulled out my wallet and gave him the smallest bill I had left, which was a five. Moments after he left, *another* hotel person came around, and this one, for some reason, had strawberries.

'I happen to hate strawberries, but this person had a tastefully arranged plate of them on a rolling cart, and I felt I had no choice but to give her what was now the smallest bill in my wallet, a twenty. So now I had spent $25 for ice, which was melting, and strawberries, which were being eaten by small, tuxedo-wearing flies; and of course word was spreading like wildfire among the hotel staff that if you wanted to make big money, you could take virtually any random object up to the luxury suite . . .'

On our frequent visits to New York we liked to try out different hotels. We had several favourites including the Carlyle and the Mayfair Regent, but we'd also enjoyed some of the city's larger properties – the Peninsular when it first opened, the Pierre, the Regency. When our friend Donald Smith was producing class cabaret acts like Steve Ross and Michael Feinstein at The Algonquin back in the eighties, we were happy there, too. Our tastes are eclectic and it's hard not to be happy as a visitor to New York City. We loved having cocktails or afternoon tea at the Plaza or the Waldorf Astoria. But we drew the line at the Helmsley Palace. When I heard that's what the New York Palace used to be, I wondered what I had let myself in for. A reception was being hosted for us jointly by the New York Palace and the Athenaeum Hotel in London. With some misgivings we agreed to stay overnight in what we envisioned as a 900-room monster with fairy lights over the canopy and a lobby more ostentatious than Imelda Marcos's shoe cupboard.

What we found was a hotel that after a change of ownership, two-year refurbishment, and close attention to staff motivation and training, could give lessons to its smaller counterparts in the Fats Waller principle of 'Find out what they like and how they like it – and give it to 'em just that way . . . '

Our arrival at the Madison Avenue entrance was inauspicious. A surly cab driver who spoke no English was gibbering with fury after a relatively short and very slow ride to find a line of two or three other cabs waiting to disgorge passengers at the kerbside. He climbed out of the cab waving his fists and without bothering to open our doors or close his, he hauled our bags out of the trunk and deposited them in the middle of the road. The New York Palace doorman, busy as he was with several guests arriving at once, rescued the situation with charm and good humour, apologising to us and doing his best to defuse the driver. We put the incident behind us and crossed the marbled entrance hall to a curving, elegant front desk staffed by smiling receptionists. The one who welcomed us seemed genuinely disappointed that our reservation was for the adjacent Towers block, and accompanied us through the lobby to the separate reception area.

It's not the spacious suites overlooking the spires of St. Patrick's Cathedral, or the fine furnishings that impress. It's the extra thoughtful touches provided: irons and ironing boards – though there's an all-day valet service, too; beautifully equipped kitchens in addition to a 'service hotline' (and isn't *that* good psychology . . .); private fax machines as well as a state-of-the-art business centre; even notepaper, envelopes and business cards embossed with the guest's name and 'in residence until . . . '. Now those who agree that life's too short to stuff a mushroom will no doubt also turn up their noses at personalised notepaper but all I know is – it impressed the hell out of me! We branded it 'the hotel that thinks of everything – so you don't have to!'

Even more important is that this hotel with 900 bedrooms had more *heart* than a farmer's-market lettuce. That's because the staff were so good. From the doormen and bell captains to the duty managers and the room maids – they all seemed to have been recruited for their charm and their genuine desire to care for their guests. When I learned the New York Palace spends a million dollars a year on staff training I was surprised but – it showed. Coincidentally – or not – the general manager is one of the few female GMs in the city, and the manager of the Towers is a woman, too.

Despite its size, they managed to avoid the formula approach. This is one of the major irritations I find in US hotels, even those where staff training is a priority. Young people are taught to deal with guests by rote, so that while they are well versed in the hotel's facilities and services, while they smile beautifully and offer sunny personalities and instant friendship, they are completely flummoxed if you ask a question or have a problem they haven't been programmed to deal with. Great training, like great systems and great theories, needs great back-up and great follow-through.

It's no use proclaiming yourself a client's instant best friend if there's nothing behind the full-frontal smile. If the eyes glaze over and the face drops when the customer asks a question to which you haven't got a ready-prepared answer. What somebody needs to teach them is: What do you say *after* Have a Nice Day?

It's just as annoying in a British five-star hotel when you have to break through a wall of frigidity, formality and politeness. But things do get done. A friendly greeting is great, but in a hotel or restaurant what I – and I suspect most guests – want is that friendly greeting backed up by some action and genuine care. I really despaired when I took over the reins at Claridge's when American guests said of a senior assistant manager: 'He gives a great welcome, but it's no good asking for anything – he always forgets.'

I see examples all the time of hotel personnel who are in danger of losing initiative and the ability to be themselves and to sound sincere. You hear them recite the pitch, observe them rely on the formula responses. They tend to look without seeing, to hear without listening, to react without responding. Take the waiter. Why do I get the feeling, when he asks 'Everything OK?' that he's just daring me to challenge him with 'No. Actually it's not OK.' If he looked he might see I wasn't eating. Or that I appeared less than OK. If he *listened* to the tone of my voice, he might sense I wasn't happy. Rather than invite me to interrupt his polished performance with a complaint, why not ask: 'Mr. Jones, is there something I can do for you?' In one hotel I counted six times in a morning being asked by staff. 'How are you today?' I don't think any one of them wanted to know. But even a stock question demands a response – and some effort from the client. If you don't want to know, don't ask! A simple 'Good morning' will do just fine.

I have found at all levels, the best hotels prove that really – it isn't size that counts. And that the best hoteliers surround themselves with the finest people. Caroline Rose Hunt, a hotelier with the Midas touch, picks the best and most motivated managers and lets them in turn surround themselves with the best teams, then leaves them to run the properties. She should be formidable, but she retained the common touch while building and running hotels that are the envy of the world – The Mansion on Turtle Creek and the Crescent Court in Dallas, and The Lanesborough in London are examples.

Los Angeles has more than its fair share of fine hotels, and we enjoyed consumer-testing a number of those we had heard about as movie-mad teenagers. Eve's work as a journalist allowed her to research articles for the hotel and travel press on our US trips, at the same time as assisting me in 'cold-calling', organising and hosting receptions. Until we 'came home' to the Bel Air and formed an allegiance we hope will last for as long as we do, we explored Tinseltown's favourites, like the Beverly Wilshire in the days of Hernando Courtwright, doyen of US hoteliers. Hotels inevitably suffer from major reconstruction, but just as Shakespeare decreed that the play's the thing, to a hotel groupie like me, the hotel's the thing. If a hotel is good enough, it can stand any amount of changes of ownership and renovation and still be something special. The main lobby of the now-Regent Beverly Wilshire is superb – not least, my wife assures me, because it is a mere precious stone's throw from Rodeo Drive. It probably also has one of the most impressive Presidential Suites I've seen in the US. At the time of writing it costs $4,000 a night to stay there – which works out at a dollar per square foot per night!

While staying at the Beverly Wilshire I unwittingly committed my first breach of dress code. It was one of our first visits to L.A. and Barry Mirkin, a Century City impresario we knew from London, invited us to Sunday brunch at the Hillcrest Club. This was described as a country club which, to me, implied a casual sort of place where people played golf in open-necked shirts then lounged at the bar and drank beer. We dressed accordingly, I in a new navy polo shirt which I thought quite smart, Eve in a white cotton dress. Barry appeared in carefully pressed linen slacks, navy blazer, Gucci tie and pearl pin. We quickly offered to go up and change but felt worse still when our host said: 'No don't worry, I'll fix it. We have to go. We're meeting George Burns for lunch at his table.'

At the Hillcrest Club we crept past 'la crème' of Beverly Hills society dressed up to the nines as we were shown by the maître d' to a corner table behind a pillar where George Burns joined *us*. Our discomfiture was soon forgotten as George, then in his eighties, regaled us with stories and one-liners, tales of his latest girlfriend, and most of all – how much he still missed Gracie. He puffed all the while on a huge cigar – the only Club member allowed to do so in the dining room.

The Beverly Hills Hotel – the Pink Palace – which has also been restored to the way the movie stars of our youth would remember it, was also an other-worldly experience. We stayed one year in one of their famous bungalows, and another in a hotel apartment and enjoyed both. But the whole point of the Pink Palace is to see and be seen.

It was Mother's Day in Beverly Hills. Everybody who was anybody – and their mother – formed a line that snaked its way from the patio of the Polo Lounge back through the hotel lobby and outside. Lunch had been sold out months in advance and by 11.15 everybody waited for the best table. Before noon matrons in full evening dress, starlets in backless sequined gowns, escorts in white tuxedos and spoiled, hyper-active grand-children in velvet breeches or puffed organza frocks, tucked into lobster soufflé. Accustomed as we were to a sedate English Mothering Sunday lunch around 1pm with roast beef and claret, we relished the spectacle of the Hollywood movers and shakers paying court to their mothers while still managing to negotiate contracts, do deals, shout news across the room, and table-hop. All the time showering Mom and Grandmom with lavishly giftwrapped presents, balloons and compliments.

The sight of so much conspicuous consumption encouraged us to keep up our gentle jogging routine, and next morning we set out along the conveniently flat mile-long stretch of boulevard opposite the hotel. It was about 7am and we were surprised to see all the other joggers running on the hard sidewalks, ignoring the empty broad strip of lush green grass and trees down the centre of the highway. We chose the grass and soon discovered why we were alone. Promptly at 7.30 the sprinkler system burst into action along the entire length of the boulevard. Unable to cross to the sidewalk in the rush-hour traffic and with traffic signals hundreds of yards ahead, we arrived back at the hotel drenched. From that day we learned to follow the locals.

The Beverly Hills Hotel was the venue for our first business breakfast, which we hosted for Los Angeles and Beverly Hills travel professionals. We had learned not to mix the travel industry and the media. Each demands total concentration, and the speech or presentation hasn't been invented that is truly dual purpose. We had heard that Americans had this odd habit of doing business over breakfast but approached it with some suspicion, not really believing people could be social – in my wife and hostess's case, barely even awake – at 7.30 or eight in the morning. I once confessed I couldn't wake my wife in the morning for love nor money. Her reply was, 'But darling, you've never tried money . . .'

The hotel dining room had been up and running for an hour before our party was arranged – it was business as usual for them – the weather was warm enough for us to have a long table set up on the patio, and as we welcomed our guests fresh and unsullied by a frantic day's work (them as well as us!) we found it an ideal way to entertain and do business. People could enjoy as light or as substantial a meal as they wished, nobody felt unsocial for refusing a cocktail, we didn't feel mean for not providing them, and conversation flowed.

After that we tried to host at least one business breakfast wherever we stayed.

The Westwood Marquis also became a favourite hotel in L.A., surrounded on two sides by the UCLA campus and medical faculty and close to one of LA's most fun 'villages'. We loved Westwood, not only for its proximity to Beverly Hills but also because it was one of the few places you could walk everywhere without being thought odd – or stopped by the police as we were once in Beverly Hills on suspicion of not being in possession of an automobile.

The hotel was a surprising one, a tall, thin building with an outside glass elevator (for luggage, not guests), frontage smothered in greenery and a forest of shrubs, its pool and health spa hidden from public view and facing inwards around a pretty courtyard. The building had served time as student accommodation and an old people's home – now, I believe, it's an apartment block – but during the 1980s it was managed with European elan by Jacques Camus, an elegant Belgian famous in the UK for being the shortest-lived g.m. of The Dorchester in London. During the 1970s The Dorchester was nicknamed the managers' graveyard after it suffered continual changes of management – something like seven general managers in five or six years. Nobody stayed for long, but Jacques Camus came, he saw, and he left. Two weeks was all it took. Now he was comfortably ensconced at the Westwood Marquis, running it in the manner of a country house in the middle of town. His philosophy was much like mine; he lived on the premises and was very much in evidence to his guests and staff. 'A lot of businesses do not work,' he told me, 'because the owner or manager is not being seen to be there, taking care of his property or his product.'

Suites at the Westwood Marquis were spacious and opulently furnished in Oriental style, with antique armoires and polished wood floors covered with Chinese rugs. Ours was big enough to accommodate 30 guests at our business cocktail party, and gave the whole occasion a more intimate, personal feel. A day or two before, we received the most stylish turn-down ever. The late Sammy Cahn and his glamorous wife Tita couldn't come to our reception and had their RSVP hand-delivered. It was an extravagantly presented block of hand-made Swiss chocolate. Piped in coloured frosting: 'So sorry. Sammy and Tita are in New York this week. Please call us . . . '

Just before our first guests were due I almost literally bumped into Paul Newman in the car park. We exchanged polite greetings and apologies and my wife, one of his greatest fans, nearly divorced me for not at least asking him to join us!

Los Angeles provided a good launch pad for exploring southern California and Mexico. We'd rent a car and enjoy a leisurely drive down to San Diego, stopping a night or two en route at some of the Beach resorts, staying at decent motels, which we enjoyed immensely, rather than in de luxe hotels. This way we discovered Carlsbad, an easy drive from L.A., and San Clemente, which had a great little dinner-theatre. This was something new to us, and we stood in line for salad, roast beef and baked potatoes, and waited like a couple of teenagers for the show to begin. We saw Li'l Abner one year, Oklahoma another, great little productions both.

I had longed to visit the Hotel Del Coronado near San Diego ever since I learned that Some Like it Hot was filmed there. With its red-roofed, white pavilions by the beach, it looked like the perfect California resort. Besides, legend had it that it was under the chandelier of the rotunda restaurant that the Duke of Windsor was first introduced to Mrs. Simpson.

While staying there I would have liked to present, had such a thing existed, the most positive PR person award. We had noticed – or rather my wife had noticed – numerous handsome, fit and friendly individuals jogging on the beach. None failed to wave and bid us a cheerful good morning. We had also noticed the constant ear-splitting din of jet planes close overhead. In conversation with the hotel's PR lady we asked about these interruptions to our rigorous sunbathing routine. 'Oh!' she gushed. 'Doesn't it just make you feel so *secure*? Those are the fighter planes from the US naval base right next door, and I always feel *so safe* just knowing they're there . . . '

From San Diego we drove south into Mexico, planning to stay a couple of days in Ensenada. We had reservations at the 'best' hotel there, a low-rise built around a fountained courtyard. Late afternoon our room wasn't ready but, said the desk-clerk, we were very welcome to go up anyway. We went upstairs to leave our bags to find no sign of a maid, the bed not stripped from the night before and a shower stall so ingrained with dirt neither of us would use it. It reminded me of one of our American guests, a physician and a household name in his own country though less well known in ours, who came regularly to London. Every time, he brought a supply of toothpicks – 'I'm just like Johnny Appleseed,' he'd beam. Instead of scattering apple seeds, he would use his toothpicks to clean the immaculate hotel shower-heads. 'None of you guys ever get these things clean enough,' he said. And that was despite giving the shower in his bathroom special attention before his arrival every year.

We elected to move on from Ensenada the following day, but that night went to dinner in a nearby restaurant with mariachi music, which had been highly recommended. Rightly so; the restaurant was clean and attractive, and the food very good. We arrived early and in the empty bar four musicians soon finished a set, then lounged about and sourly contemplated their instruments. Feeling sorry for them with nobody to appreciate their music, we made a list of all the Mexican songs we knew, from La Paloma to Cielito Lindo. I handed the list to the leader with a couple of dollars and waited. The four went into a huddle, talking and gesticulating, pointing to the paper, looking menacingly towards me. I wondered if inadvertently I had written something obscene in Spanish. After a minute or two the leader approached our table, faced me squarely, waved the note and accused: 'Seven tune. Seven dollar.'

We grew to like Mexico more as time went on, and decided to 'blitz' the travel trade in Mexico City. Nothing had prepared us for the pollution in this overcrowded metropolis. It was the only place either of us ever recalled being car-sick. The day we arrived Argentina had just invaded the Falklands, and we were nervous lest the Mexicans felt more inclined to sympathise with Argentina than with us Thatcherites.

This wasn't helped when, after checking into the hotel Eve paid a visit to the beauty salon. She was under the hairdrier when she received a telephone call. 'We have your husband,' a man's voice announced without preamble. He repeated it just so she'd be sure. 'We have your husband.' When she finally found her voice Eve said: 'If this is a joke I do *not* find it amusing. Who are you and what do you want?' That was her first acquaintance with Jimmy Dubin, hotelier and practical joker, patron of the Hotel La Reforma – and our host! He had invited me for a welcoming cocktail in his suite and called Eve from there. It *was* a daft thing to do, and he deserved the dressing-down my wife administered when they met face to face.

A hotel doesn't have to be grand to be good, but it does need what I call the 'wow' factor before it can be great. Assuming Conrad Hilton's key three of location, location and location, it then needs that extra special something that takes your breath away. The hotels that have it include the Cipriani in Venice – and that has location in spades, too. Turnberry Hotel in Scotland has it. Our three favourite US hotels, already mentioned, have it.

I believe, though I haven't yet visited it, that the Oriental in Bangkok has it, too. The reason I believe it, sight unseen, is that any hotel whose mission statement is 'To satisfy and *delight* our guests' gets my vote. Another Mexican hotel, Las Brisas in Acapulco, supplied all the satisfaction and delight we could have wished for.

The vital ingredient that elevated it to the ranks of great hotels for us was *romance*. Some might call it kitsch – and they'd be right – but my wife and I were suckers for this pink and white paradise. We spent two of our many honeymoons there, tucked up in one of the 300 private casitas and apartments set into a hill overlooking the Bay and one of the world's most spectacular panoramas. These 'little houses' are strictly for incurable romantics, each with its own pool (though we were warned to make sure ours was near the top of the hill, since those on the lower slopes were overlooked). Breakfast is delivered – in little pink jeeps – through a flap in the wall into a 'magic box', just fresh tropical fruit, juice, croissants and coffee in a vacuum jug. At dawn a silent gardener floats hibiscus blossoms on your private pool. (Ours did alarm us when he called back to repair the pool light, said 'Scusa, Senora', removed his sombrero, stripped off his shirt, took a deep breath – and submerged himself from the top of his head to his waist, holding tools in one hand and disconnecting the underwater lamp with the other . . .) In the evening a maid strews more hibiscus or 'tulipani' petals on the bed while you dine under the stars in the outdoor restaurant on Fetuccini Alfredo, drinking in the scent of the gardens, the ocean and the warm night air along with the chilled champagne.

Our work in the US provided a springboard to experiences we might otherwise have missed. At the end of each business visit to Florida, for instance, Eve and I would hop on a Chalk's seaplane – the 70-year-old airline that boasted the best safety record in the US – and make the short journey across to the Bahamas. The plane glided on to a silver-sanded beach lapped by turquoise waters. After passing through a corrugated one-man customs shed we just laid back and enjoyed the tranquillity of a hotel we both loved, the Ocean Club on Paradise Island. The colonial-style mansion had been the retreat of Huntingdon Hartford, and it retained the intimacy and exclusivity of a private home even with 70 rooms in the house and five cottages and a dozen cabanas around the tropical gardens and tennis courts. If we were lucky, our good friend Joel Grossman would join us, and he and George Myers, larger-than-life head at that time of Resorts International and supremo of Bahamas tourism, would insist we leave the padded womb of the Ocean Club for long enough to check out the Casino, the Las Vegas-style shows, and a few of the high-style restaurants around the island. If we were luckier still, they'd let us sneak off for peas 'n rice or conch fritters at the Poop Deck just across the bridge in Nassau.

One year we tried one of the Family Islands, Eleuthera, but the hotel was too basic, the weather too hot, the mosquitoes too militant – Eve counted about 60 bites on me at one stage, she swears, and 20 on herself, proof if nothing else that there wasn't enough to do on Eleuthera. We agreed that Paradise Island was quiet enough for us and flew back several days early to the ministrations of Stephen Sawyer, the congenial young general manager, and his staff.

If we didn't go to the Bahamas we were happy to stay for our few days r&r in Florida, making our base the Boca Raton Hotel, another vast property that most of the time manages to retain a very human face. For us, it was a dual-purpose hotel. Located midway between Miami and Palm Beach, the sources of much of our East coast business, all of our best travel agents found it within striking distance and vice versa if we visited them. The hotel had everything we needed, from small banqueting and reception rooms alongside the huge convention and conference facilities, to penthouse suites that proved perfect venues for our cocktail receptions for 30 or 40 people or a luncheon or dinner for half that number. After our business was completed, the president Michael Glennie would have our luggage transferred to the Boca Beach Club, a short boat ride across the waterway, where we could relax in an ocean-front room and enjoy the hotel's sports and leisure facilities. It was the ideal place to wind down after a six- or sometimes ten-city tour. Without going 'off-property' we could play tennis, swim, sun-bathe, cycle, go for boat rides, dine in a half-dozen different restaurants, and shop in a mini-mall where our favourite store was called 'Knickers: a great shop to poke about in . . . ' Had we been golfers or deep-sea fishermen we could have enjoyed those, too.

While staying there we were interviewed by Rise 'Ginger' Jackson, energetic social editor of the *Palm Beach Daily News*. Determined to launch us into Palm Beach society, Rise had us invited for cocktails by her friend socialite Celia Lipton, to her Palm Beach mansion. The Lipton limousine fetched us from the hotel, and after we were warmly welcomed by Celia I walked into the drawing room to the surprise of my life: staying with her was her father Sidney Lipton, whose famous dance orchestra played at the Royal Garden Hotel in London while I was manager there. I thought the world of Sidney, who had also been musical director at Grosvenor House, recalled the wonderful 'big band' radio broadcasts, and played his records frequently. To come across him again and find him in such good form after so many years and well into his eighties was a great treat.

Eve was eager to show me New Orleans, which was one of the two cities she had fallen in love with in 1978. We finally added it to our itinerary in 1982 and I was hooked. Within two years we were back, staying at the Hotel Pontchartrain on St. Charles Avenue. Owned and run by three generations of the Aschaffenburg family, this was one of America's special hotels, dignified and traditional, with fine suites, lots of chinoiserie, and a legendary restaurant, the Caribbean Room. Eve had been befriended by Albert Aschaffenburg and his English wife Nancy during her first solo visit. Albert's father Lyle had founded the hotel, and his son Honoré was following in his father's and grandfather's footsteps as a graduate of Cornell, planning to make his career at the Pontchartrain.

The Aschaffenburgs took us under their wing and introduced us to some of the wonderful eccentricities of New Orleans life besides Mardi Gras and the debutante season; the start of the crawfish season at the

Bon Ton, breakfast at Brennan's, the 'inherited waiter' system at Antoine's. Albert allowed us to 'borrow' Sidney, the waiter who had looked after him and his father for decades. This meant we could avoid standing in line with the tourists at Antoine's on a Saturday night and enter by the side door into a gaslit passageway where Sidney would be waiting for us.

On a later visit after I became manager of Claridge's we were presented ceremoniously with the keys of the city and made Honorary Citizens by the Mayor of New Orleans, and Albert Aschaffenburg arranged for our visit to be reported by the New Orleans Times Picayune's glamorous social editor Nell Nolan. Nell must have thought we were good copy because she told a colleague, Millie Ball, now the paper's travel editor but at that time a feature writer, that she ought to meet us. Millie Ball had only returned from a trip overseas on the Friday and we were leaving for the UK on the Sunday afternoon. However, she pressed us to see her for half an hour. Conveniently forgetting what happened when my journalist wife first asked me for a 'brief interview' and keen for the right kind of publicity for Claridge's, we invited her to our suite for coffee after we finished packing.

That interview, with Millie probing and pressing, my dodging and weaving and trying to remain as discreet as Claridge's expected its manager to be, and Eve's journalistic background overcoming my propinquity to say nowt, was tricky. Millie Ball wanted disclosures and tales of the rich and famous. I wanted her to have the history of Claridge's. Eve wanted me to appear in a good light. Time and again I had to refuse details of the royals, the righteous – and the rest. The feature that eventually appeared carried the sub-headline 'You can talk about the *dead* guests, darling . . . '

The following year Millie Ball visited us at Claridge's with her husband Dr. Keith Marshall, a Rhodes scholar at Oxford with Bill Clinton. She sent her mother Mildred, a Louisiana matron just born to hold court in Claridge's Foyer and who visited us regularly with her friend Gladys Jurgens. She sent her mother-in-law Naomi Marshall, who with her son had transformed their beautiful Louisiana plantation house, Madewood, into a delightful small hotel. And she sent journalists, friends and business visitors to Claridge's after enthusing them with her own experiences of London and the hotel. Busy as we all four have been with our own lives and careers these past dozen years, the friendship is picked up, however infrequently, as though we had been

144

'visiting' only yesterday. I help out with advice or suggestions at Madewood whenever I'm invited, and Eve writes travel features from time to time for Millie's paper. Both Marshalls came to Marlborough College Summer School to take Eve's wine course, and we are already plotting a Madewood celebration for New Year's Eve 1999!

A warm and treasured friendship developed, too, with the Ashaffenburgs. It was sad for New Orleans and sad for us – far more than just sad for the Aschaffenburg family – when they lost control of the Hotel Pontchartrain in 1987. The hotel was no longer the special place it had been under the family's stewardship and for us, the city would be a different place.

Nowadays the Windsor Court Hotel continues to take good care of us, however, and as Albert Aschaffenburg is fond of telling people, 'A funny thing happened on the way to retirement.' He now has a brilliant new career teaching classes in public speaking and presentation at the University of New Orleans and at Tulane, and at seminars around the US.

Much as I love New Orleans, I'm a good ol' down-home boy at heart – and that belongs to Texas! Maybe it's the contrasts. This vast, flat State that could accommodate our entire country in one corner yet with major cities where people know each other as well as they do in an English village. The larger-than-life people whose generosity and hospitality overwhelm us, whose old-fashioned courtesy and politeness barely conceal a toughness and invincibility and the conviction that Texas Rules – OK? Our characteristically surly waiter at the Stage Deli in New York one year, as he chucked their bill on the table, remarked to our neighbours 'You from Texas? I was there for a week. I got to be so goldarned polite I couldn't stand myself . . . '

We love it and we laugh at it and with it. How could it be otherwise in a State where in one day you can see a car sticker saying 'Happiness is a warm gun' and another (supporting the Fort Worth Symphony) 'Fill the Hall, y'all'? I was hooked the first time we stopped at a diner for breakfast en route from Houston to Dallas. The lady behind the counter was tall, slim, blonde, of indeterminate age – and tough as cowboy boots with spurs on. I didn't dare tell her how let down I felt at my first taste of grits. Why, they weren't 'gritty' at all! As we left, she shouted: 'Y'all come back now, y'hear?' and I wanted somebody to say that to me every day for the rest of my life. Some comedian in Las Vegas once said: 'Have you noticed how many syllables they can give a word with only one vowel sound? When a Texas gal says "Y'all go to hell" – you really want to go!' I take a perverse pleasure when somebody says, as they often do, 'I jest luhrve y'all's accent' in retorting 'But my dear, I don't have an accent . . . *You* do!' The fact that they seldom get it just adds to the fun. Yes, Texans are brash and xenophobic, but I love 'em. I'll bet we were the only couple in the Cotswolds who sent out invitations hand-lettered on parchment in 1986 inviting our friends and neighbours ' . . . as Moreton-in-Marsh's only naturalised Texans' to help us celebrate the Sesquicentennial of this Great State. 'Come have a ball y'all!' And we did!

Although my wife was made an Honorary Citizen of Houston in 1978, Dallas is our spiritual home, the place where our American adventure all began nearly two decades ago and the place where they make us feel we belong. It's always had great hotels, some of them larger-than-life as the Texans who built them.

For years after it first opened as Loewe's Anatole Hotel, now The Anatole, developer Trammell Crow's red stone landmark towering over Stemmons Freeway was one of the most exciting hotels in the world. We loved it for its sheer scale and the fact that we could be totally anonymous after a week's high-profile business and social entertaining in the city. The vast twin atria hung with batik banners; indoor gardens forested with growing trees; works of art, paintings, sculpture and treasures from the Orient, South America, India and Africa greeted the visitor at every turn. The hotel had seven restaurants from the Plum Blossom, which served gourmet Chinese food, to casual Mexican and upscale French; even a deli from which guests could 'brown-bag' in their rooms, a clever 'if you can't beat 'em, join 'em' marketing ploy. There was a shopping mall where you could buy anything from Texas Chewies through Mayan artifacts to designer clothes. An additional building was added across the way, with one of the most extensive, state-of-the-art health facilities in the US and still more lavish guest accommodation. The Anatole can accommodate conferences for thousands, and as time went by, suffered the consequences of providing too many facilities for too many people. In its youth, however, we enjoyed it as a city-centre resort in its own right. It could only have worked in Dallas.

I'm a sucker for new hotels, and especially love to be part of an opening, either as a guest or, better still, as manager. There is nothing to beat the 'rush' of building, equipping, designing and furnishing a new hotel – except, perhaps, the even greater rush that comes from recruiting and training a new team of personnel. I guarantee instant election to the Hoteliers Hall of Fame to the man or woman who finds the answer to one of the toughest conundrums in the hospitality business: how to maintain or constantly renew the enthusiasm, commitment and freshness of approach that radiates from all the team during the first year of a hotel's operation. The approach may be different from one manager or owner to another and from one hotel group to another, but I have seldom observed five years into an operation the crispness and enthusiasm of that first year or two. I wonder how many hoteliers actually ask their staff, during brain-storming sessions, what *they* think about this? I suppose it's a little like asking a married couple to reintroduce the honeymoon factor into their marriage after three kids and a mortgage. It can be done, a few manage it, most just make the best of things. But in those hotels where apathy sets in among the personnel, it soon infects the guests.

Team-building is an essential part of it: let the personnel feel they 'belong' to each other and they'll work better for the organisation. But hotels need to monitor how team-building works for the guests. The process is seldom as seamless as it should be. You end up with a situation where the staff are committed all right – but to each other instead of the guests or customers. They are friendly and cosy with each other at all times, speak cheerfully as they pass, maybe exchange weekend plans or family news. They converse across a corridor or share a private joke. And the guest whose bags they are carrying, or the customer who is waiting for service, ends up feeling left out of a family conference.

When Caroline Hunt's company opened the Crescent Court Hotel in Dallas at the end of 1986 we looked forward to trying it out. I was a great admirer of Mrs. Hunt's entrepreneurial ability and style, nowhere more apparent than at The Mansion on Turtle Creek, and I was curious to see how she would handle a much larger property.

We were allocated a fine suite with parquet floors, elegant, understated furnishings and fabrics and sumptuous marbled bathrooms. We loved it. Until, that is, we started unpacking for our five-day stay and found there was not one single drawer in our three-room suite. Not one. Clearly another case of the management not sleeping in its own rooms! A call was made to the duty manager, and a couple of fine chests of drawers installed the same evening. We later discovered these belonged to the hotel's general manager and had been hastily emptied and removed from his private quarters after our call.

147

While staying at the Crescent Court our reception for travel and media people happened to coincide with the official visit of the Deputy Prime Minister of China. Arriving back at the hotel that afternoon after shopping, our taxi had to double back and around the road blocks erected for the Chinese delegation's motorcade. The lobby was swarming with security men, several of whom accompanied us up in the elevator where they waited until they saw us enter our suite.

An hour or two later, our guests began arriving at the same time as the Chinese dignitaries. Most of our people were allowed up to the reception room in the strictly guarded elevators. However, a couple of journalists who had stopped off at the ladies' cloakroom were locked in, security guards posted outside to prevent them exiting, and kept there for ten minutes while the Chinese PM processed through the lobby and up to his suite.

Our friends Margie and Rick Thompson had arranged to collect us in front of the hotel after the party. We had asked them to take us 'somewhere Texan' and we were anticipating a good home-style dinner and a bit of a knees-up at Billy-Bob's honky-tonk some distance away. Rick had even promised to teach us to dance the Cotton-Eyed Joe. However, deprived of the chance to show off some of Dallas's fine dining, Rick had generously tucked a bottle of Moet into an ice bucket in the trunk of the car, with crystal champagne flutes. As we got into the car, Rick opened the trunk, lifted out the champagne bottle and with a flourish that would have done credit to a Grand Prix winner, removed the cork. It shot out with a bang and landed twenty feet away. A score of jittery armed security guards positioned around the lobby and the hotel entrance drew their guns and wheeled round in our direction. We swiftly drew our heads and legs into the car, making ourselves as small as possible while poor Rick did his best to explain the 'shot' before driving away pale with relief.

Today the Crescent Court has a new neighbour in the Hotel St. Germain right across the street. A tiny perfect diamond in a sea of rhinestones, this tiny property is the brainchild of glamorous Claire Heymann. Was it courage, confidence or chutzpa that made the doll-like and sophisticated Ms Heymann believe she could open a seven-room ultra-de-luxe property right opposite the Crescent Court and minutes away from The Mansion on Turtle Creek?

The original 1906 mansion was refurbished, designed and furnished throughout by Ms Heymann. It is a startling contrast to its skyscraper neighbours, with pickled wood panelling, French antique furniture and sumptuous fabrics. No concierge here, no reservations desk, no wait-staff! Discreet butlers glide in and out of the dining room without as much as a rustle of starched napery. Such was her reputation after just a year or two of operation that three major chefs working in the US 'auditioned' on site for the job of head chef at St. Germain. In the dining room chamber music plays softly in the background, and guests look out over a New Orleans style walled courtyard with wrought-iron balconies all around.

It is the sort of property that even a seasoned hotelier can learn from. Claire Heymann had no hotel background, but she knew what she had enjoyed over the years as a businesswoman visiting European and US hotels. The St. Germain is a good example of a clever entrepreneur sensing a gap in the market and filling it, living proof that in the hotel business there is always room for the offbeat provided you follow that Fats Waller principle – 'find out what they like . . . '

Dallas has always had fine hotels. The Adolphus has been a landmark since 1912 when it was built by Budweiser beer baron Adolphus Busch. At that time Dallas was a city of 100,000 people and described as having 'more vitality than polish'. The Adolphus was re-opened in 1982 after a 12-year closure. Our friend, the late Betty Holloway, opened the hotel as Director of Press and Public Relations, a post filled today by Betty's protégé from that time, David Davis. The revival of a fine old building and the provision of 450 de luxe rooms to the Downtown area was long overdue. We were enchanted by the mahogany-panelled lobby, elegant 'high tea' (which I hope I persuaded them to change to its correct description of afternoon tea) served under Murano glass chandeliers in the upstairs lounge, and the exquisite French Room restaurant, which soon won accolades from just about every food writer in the US. In an article Eve wrote at the time she remarked 'This is not a lobby one would walk through in jeans.' *Oh tempora, oh mores* . . . Today The Adolphus has a plaintive appeal in its guest information booklet: 'Please help us maintain the tradition of grand hotels' by observing the dress code. Sadly, the attire and sometimes the demeanour of guests milling around the lobby of this fine property completely ignores the request: shorts, tee-shirts, athletic shoes and baseball caps. Accessorised, here and there, by a can or a bottle of beer – not, surely, in deference to the hotel's founder. The culprits are often conference delegates. Time and again we saw them refuse help with luggage. Though the hotel rates are high, these guys would rather stagger to or from their rooms laden down with bags than give a couple of dollars to a bellman for helping them out.

The Adolphus has been assiduous in 'reading' what most of its guests really want from a hotel. The French Room remains a Mecca for formal dining. There is an adequate coffee shop for informal meals throughout the day. And a clever addition in the form of the Walt Garrison Bar & Grill, a thoroughly Texan restaurant alongside the hotel where jeans and checked shirts are de rigeur. Even the barstools and dining chairs are upholstered in used Levis! Floors are unpolished wood, music country-style and artifacts pure Wild West. Customers are encouraged to shuck peanut shells on the floor, and you're disappointed when the bartender fails to slide your beer or your shot glass all the way along the bar.

If the hotel gods always looked kindly upon us in Dallas, they seemed never to be on our side in Houston. We stayed three years running at one of the best hotels in the city, they were kind to us, we held some good business receptions there, there was complimentary champagne from the management – but we never met or even saw the manager. Now in my view, when there is no visible manager, nobody truly in charge, the hotel inevitably lacks personality. The front desk had reserved not one but three rooms in our name. We worked out that one room must be for our reception, scheduled to last for two hours in two days time, and another for our US representatives, also due to stay in two days time, for one night. We untangled it and took our pick of the three rooms. When our colleagues arrived on the day of the party – there was no room reserved for them.

My wife asked the concierge to make a hair appointment for her at a nearby beauty salon. 'At 2pm if possible,' she specified, 'but definitely no later than 3pm. Our reception is at 5.30.' It was fixed for three o'clock. The hotel limo was in use, so she took the first of the taxis lined up out front. 'Please make sure,' she asked the doorman, 'the driver knows exactly where the address is.' (We had learned the hard way that cab drivers in Dallas and Houston hardly ever do.) The doorman assured her the driver would know. Eve leaned into the cab and asked, but the driver stared straight ahead.

Again the doorman said, 'Don't worry ma'am, he knows,' and shut the door. The moment the cab cleared the hotel entrance, the driver let loose a torrent of near-abuse, opening his window and yelling to the cabs still in the driveway, 'Man, I'm sittin' here for two hours an' she

150

asks me to go to X Street. They think this is a livin'? What they think I am?' Eve tried politely to explain that it wasn't exactly her fault. 'Lady, that is the *wrong* answer.' By now thoroughly perturbed, my wife just prayed the beauty salon would be close by. As the driver was about to shoot a red light at an intersection Eve noticed the street name and yelled at him to make a right turn. Tires screeching he did just that, and his thoroughly scared passenger scoured the street numbers until she was able to tell him to stop. He slammed on his brakes, said, 'Ten dollars'. No meter running, but the fare should have been half that. He said. 'Pay or don't pay. Just get out. I don't want nobody bad-mouthing me to the hotel.'

In the beauty parlour they put a gown on her, said they'd start her manicure and the stylist would be along at four o'clock. 'Four?' she yelled, now beyond reason. 'I said three o'clock at the latest. I need to be *out* of here before four.' They shampooed her hair then brought along a stylist who did the worst job she'd ever experienced. It was four o'clock. Our guests were invited for 5.30. This being America and not England, where it's polite to arrive a few minutes late, the first guests would arrive at five.

Reluctant to risk another cab ride, Eve called the hotel to see if the limo was back. 'On its way' said the concierge. 'It'll be with you in five to ten.' Twenty minutes later she called again. At 4.30 she called our suite and I tackled the concierge. The limo arrived. It was the same bellman/driver who had brought us from the airport two days before wearing scuffed Nikes with his dark grey uniform suit and told us in a confiding tone 'When I have to meet really important guests I have black dress shoes, but they make my feet sweat . . . ' He opened the door with a disarming grin.

'Miz Jones. How y'all enjoying your stay?' Eve told him. 'I've just had the worst hairdo of my entire life. I waited over half an hour for the car. I was verbally abused and badly scared by a taxi driver on the way here. And now I'm late for the party we're hosting.'

'Uh-huh. And apart from that, Miz Jones, are y'all enjoyin' your stay . . .?'

Next morning I called the operator to say there were no water glasses, no small towels and two treadmills out of order in the fitness centre. The response was, 'Sir. This is an un-manned facility.' I asked could she perhaps locate a man – or a woman for that matter, this being an equal opportunity complaint – who might assist and she said doubtfully that she'd try. Before we finished our work-out, a man in a bow tie came to replace the flowers and the fruit in the glass bowl, but did nothing about the glasses or the towels.

At lunch that day our guest's 'Bloody Mary, no vodka' arrived literally fizzing. The waitress asked in all seriousness: 'Ma'am, did you want your Virgin Mary with Sprite?'

Our first visit to Kansas City in 1988 was no smoother. The main reason for our presence was Eve's being invited to speak at the International Food Media Conference on American influences on British food. I seized the opportunity to fly the Claridge's flag by visiting travel people in the city.

We flew in, by British Airways as always, via Chicago, with barely 40 minutes between flights. We made it by the skin of our teeth, but only two of our three checked suitcases appeared on the carousel. I had a hunch the Skycap transferring those to our connecting flight wasn't really taking in the instructions we gave him, and I had a sinking feeling we'd arrive before our bags.

As the plane circled Kansas City, the pilot announced there was a lot of fog around and we'd have to wait for permission to land. After 15 minutes there was another announcement. 'The fog is still pretty thick, folks, but we're hoping to land soon. *Five out of the last seven planes have made it . . . *' There was a clatter of dropping jaws in the passenger cabin. Somebody must have nudged the captain, because the PA snapped into life again. 'Sorry ladies and gentlemen. I should have said – five out of the last seven planes made it into *Kansas City*! The other two diverted to Chicago . . . '

None of our bags reappeared at the airport. At the Westin Crown Plaza Hotel we were shown up to a suite so vast and with so many rooms and corridors that we called two friends in Texas and invited them to share it with us for the weekend. Even then, we saw nothing of them except by prior arrangement! Apparently, Michael Jackson had stayed there with his entourage the week before and *they* had a dance floor put in.

Eve felt unwell during the night, and by next morning, due to address the conference of 350 food writers at noon – and still with no luggage – she knew it was more than a head cold. As she listened to an earlier speaker she almost fainted, something she had never done before. When her turn came to speak, dosed with aspirin and with a temperature of 102, she climbed on to the platform still wearing her travelling suit and boots, and declared how happy we were to be 'right in the very Heartland of the US – and I know our bags will feel the same if they ever get here . . . ' I felt so sorry for her but also very proud. She delivered a great presentation, and the conference organiser wrote: 'By far, you were the most polished speaker at the Conference. Both in terms of content and delivery . . . ' Eve remembers almost nothing about it.

The hotel doctor diagnosed acute bronchitis and prescribed medication which left her nauseous for a week. While my wife recuperated, I 'cold-called' – literally, since snow lay several inches deep in Kansas City – on travel companies and the corporate headquarters of Hallmark Cards, and experienced the city's famous barbecue restaurants with our friends from Texas.

We had some bad luck in Chicago, too, though we took to the city from the beginning. I had been unprepared for the stunning architecture, though I knew the city had been virtually rebuilt after the fire that almost destroyed it. It was autumn when we visited, cold and crisp with morning mist rising off the Lake.

The Ritz Carlton was as impressive and as well run as we had come to expect. Our reception there was beautifully catered, well attended and started out being fun. However, I broke my golden rule and had just one dry martini *before* the end of the party. When, during my short speech of welcome I referred for the third time to being in *Boston*, the listeners were less than amused and I resolved to stick to mineral water in future.

We stayed to enjoy the weekend in Chicago, and on Sunday morning took ourselves off to the art gallery. The lines there were so long and the morning so cool, we decided we'd go for option two – an exhibit we wanted to see at the Museum of Science and Industry. We looked at our little tourist map and deduced the museum must be two or three miles out. We would walk and make it our exercise for the day.

Eight-and-a-half miles and three and a half hours later we arrived, almost speechless with exhaustion, at the science museum – to find the exhibit closed.

We caught the bus back into town and got out at Walgreens to buy a few things we needed, like toiletries and gift-wrap. We picked up a couple of National Enquirers, mesmerised by the banner headlines. 'Granddad, 82, swaps 15-year-old bride for a goat!' screamed one. 'Musical baby born whistling Dixie' the other.

The long walk, lack of lunch and relief at being 'home' as we approached the Ritz Carlton must have made the Enquirers seem funnier than usual. We were helpless with laughter when two young women approached us. One asked politely if we knew the time. The other grabbed Eve's purse from under her arm. What followed was more Keystone Cops than NYPD Blue. You don't stop to think in situations like that. You just react.

My reaction, knowing Eve might be carrying our passports and money in her purse, was to drop the Walgreens bags and chase the two women now racing into an alleyway.

At that moment a beat-up old Jaguar car came screeching to a near-halt before turning into the alleyway, burning rubber. Eve thought it was chasing *me*. She now gave chase. In the alleyway she caught sight of me almost spreadeagled in a doorway, the Jaguar alongside. She was about to attack the car driver with her roll of giftwrap when I managed to blurt out that the man had been trying to help and meant me no harm!

Eve turned her wrath – and her giftwrap – on the two females, fast disappearing up the street. Brandishing the giftwrap like a weapon and screaming obscenities neither of us knew she knew, she gave chase, gaining on them all the while – until the thief clutching her purse tossed it back to Eve and ran for her life.

By the time she returned to the alleyway, the police had arrived and were taking statements. They were wasting their time, we knew, and they admonished us for being stupid enough to chase *anybody* in that situation. How were we to know, they pointed out quite rightly, that the assailants weren't armed with guns or knives, or high on drugs? Both of us were panting for breath and hoarse from yelling. It was another two days before Eve got her voice back – but we still liked Chicago and fully intend to return. Only this time I promise not to call the Windy City *Boston* . . .

10

Cold Calls and Warm Welcomes

When we started visiting the US on a regular basis in the late 1970s, I marvelled at how easy it was to do business in even America's 'hardest' cities. With the exception of Washington (and there were exceptions even there) we were received with enthusiasm and interest by even the top travel industry moguls – and not just when we hosted receptions to which they were invited.

'Cold calling', always a dreaded expression in our country, took on a different complexion in the US. We would arm ourselves with our portfolio of brochures and photographs and a list of upscale travel agents in specific areas of New York, Dallas, Los Angeles or wherever. We would rent a car or hire a taxi for the day and systematically work our way through our list. At reception we'd ask for the president or chief executive by name and say we'd be glad if he or she could see us for a few minutes. In the UK this would have been a foolhardy thing to do. The response would have been: 'Do you have an appointment?' If we didn't, we'd be told Mr. Big-Chief never sees anyone without an appointment and advised to call ahead and make one – which of course would take you through a battery of front-line troops including telephonist, receptionist, office clerk and finally, if you were really lucky, personal secretary. All of them would require details of why you wanted to see the important person. An appointment with Mr. or Ms. Big-Chief would have been a lot to hope for.

In the US we were greeted warmly and asked to wait. If the person we wanted to see was in the office, they either came to reception to see us, or we were taken in to their office. Without exception they listened patiently to what we had to say, showed interest in the photographs and the brochures. If they knew the hotel and already sent clients there, they were keen to be up-dated on refurbishment or developments, and

155

if the hotel was new to them, they were willing to send clients to try it out as the opportunity arose. If they were out, we were invited to speak to an assistant, leave details or call back. The whole process became hugely enjoyable – for a time.

Then, on a visit to New Orleans in the summer of 1986, my Hermes tie literally disintegrated at the knot by mid-day in the blistering heat and humidity as we emulated the 'mad dogs and Englishmen' and foolhardily *walked* from one appointment to another. I decided we had served our apprenticeship. After that, we confined ourselves to hosting receptions and let the travel people come to us.

Any manager of a de luxe hotel property in Europe would be a fool to overlook or underestimate the importance of upscale travel professionals in the US. Worldwide reservations systems like Leading Hotels of the World and Preferred Hotels, consortia such as Relais et Chateaux or Prestige, are nowadays essential for a de luxe hotel of any size to succeed in the international market. But even they do not go far enough with the non-business traveller, the individuals who travel for pleasure, sometimes for lack of anything more pressing to do, more often for the sheer fun of being in London for 'the Season' of the Chelsea Flower Show, Royal Ascot, Henley, Wimbledon and the Derby. These are the cream on top of the milk, the guests who make a hotel a grand hotel, who can afford and demand the best and who recognise it when they see it.

When you look at the structure of the fully individual travel or 'FIT' end of the industry within the US it's hardly surprising that it attracts some unforgettable characters. A large proportion of the upscale travel business in major cities is conducted by a few individuals working alone or with a small team. There are larger travel companies, but clients who can afford the best usually work through an exclusive representative. The top people's travel counsellors often have no need to work in order to support themselves. Work they do, however, usually harder than anybody around them, pampering, pandering, shepherding, organising and assisting a select band of clients who often become personal friends in the process. Lest anybody think these 'fixers' have an enviable lifestyle jetting first-class around the world, cruising on luxury liners and staying at the best hotels, let me sketch in a little of the reality.

For every firm reservation there are literally hours, days or weeks of painstaking discussion, winkling out the travel peccadilloes, the dietary requirements, the leisure interests, the state of health and preferences on everything from travel companions to the type of sand on the beach. These are the clients for whom the phrase 'package tour' might be written in hieroglyphs, so meaningless are the words, clients with the wherewithal to pick and choose their destinations, their mode and time of travel, the size of the bed and the fabric of the sheets they sleep in. They expect their travel adviser to be utterly familiar with the limo service that transfers them to and from airports, the general manager, reservations supremo and the concierge of every hotel they may stay in, not to mention which restaurants are 'hot' and which shows are playing in every major city.

They are expected to remember passport and documentation renewal dates, birthdays and anniversaries – not just of the clients but of clients' children and grand-children who may go along on the trip. To have small mementoes, flowers or champagne waiting in the suites or staterooms, and to know there are adequate medical facilities available at a moment's notice if the clients are elderly or infirm.

Many of the best travel professionals take the trips right along with their clients. Bill Fischer and his wife, whose New York agency is so exclusive their business cards don't even carry an office address, often accompany their small, exclusive groups on Concorde and ultra-de-luxe hotel and resort trips around the globe, acting as host and hostess as well as organisers. Prospective clients have to practically audition before they are accepted into the Fischer embrace, but once they are, they seldom allow anyone else to handle their travel arrangements.

Leonard Parrish, doyen of travel in New Orleans, teases, cajoles and bosses his groups of seasoned world travellers like a twinkling, mischievous gnome, his implacable good nature and puckish sense of humour side-stepping any incipient disaster. Like all the best travel people, Leonard makes it look easy, but if you've ever taken your own small party on an overseas trip and tried to be responsible for everything from getting people on to a tour bus on time, through organising bedroom allocations and overseeing safe delivery of luggage, you'll know it's like the serene swan gliding over the lake – all the while, it's paddling like hell beneath the surface.

The very nature of tourism, whether at the point of travel or the destination hotel, implies hospitality, warmth and pleasure. People have to genuinely like people and have an innate desire to please them in order to be successful in 'the happiness business'. And since much of our early days in the US were spent calling on travel professionals to promote first the Athenaeum Hotel then Claridge's it's natural that many of these people became personal friends.

After the days of cold-calling we hosted some memorable receptions, lunches, dinners – even breakfasts, that most un-English way of entertaining which we quickly became acclimatised to. Our friends in the US travel business returned our hospitality fourfold, welcoming us into their homes, introducing us to favourite restaurants, and sending us their most valued clients.

One even entrusted Eve with her wedding arrangements. Margie McCarter was an executive of T.H.E. Travel in Dallas. When she and Richard Thompson, with seven almost grown-up children between them, decided to marry, Margie confided that she longed to wed somewhere extraordinary and unforgettable in England – 'like Buckingham Palace . . . ' Eve tactfully explained that would not be possible, but she would see what alternatives she could come up with. Woburn Abbey, home of the Duke and Duchess of Bedford, proved possible; the Queen's Chapel of the Savoy would be difficult; however, when Westminster Abbey was suggested, Eve knew she need look no further. Margie and Rick were thrilled: a wedding ceremony on England's most hallowed ground, officiated by a Canon of Westminster Abbey, in the 15th century St. Faith's Chapel by Poet's Corner. Canon Sebastian Charles performed the ceremony on a perfect summer's day, Eve and I were witnesses, and the couple celebrated with a small party at the Athenaeum Hotel before leaving for a honeymoon in Switzerland.

Harold Rosenbluth, patriarch of America's largest and oldest-established travel company, now run by the fourth generation of the family, with his wife Franny became firm friends who share our love of the arts as well as hotels and travel. When we hosted a reception in Philadelphia for Rosenbluth's and other travel agencies, one of the guests rather shocked us when she introduced herself: 'I'm with Rosenbluth, King of Prussia.' A little disloyal to her boss, we thought, who in any case struck us as being a rather gentle and sensitive guy, to refer to Harold as 'King of Prussia'. It was an hour into the party before we learned King of Prussia was the name of the mall where the branch office was situated.

In Boca Raton, Dusty Aronsohn, a top people's travel adviser and her husband Ben welcome us warmly to their beachfront apartment and share their friends as well as their travels with us. Cruising on Royal Viking Queen a year or two back, they docked overnight near Tower

Pier and invited us to have dinner with them on board ship. We were sent conflicting instructions from the ship and from the shipping company's London office, and found ourselves, in evening dress, abandoned and alone on Hay's Wharf, watching as the ship's tender picked up the other guests from across the river. The cavalry came to the rescue in the form of the River Police, who ferried us aboard their launch down-river to the ship. There, we straddled the police launch and the ship's gangplank while the crew tried to prevent us from boarding because the documentation we'd been sent was not the right kind! After a ten-minute wrangle, our hostess Dusty Aronsohn looking on mortified as I argued with the junior officers, the chief purser appeared at my request and quickly relented. Our compensation came in the form of generous quantities of caviar, iced vodka, perfect roast lamb with a fine claret, and crêpes Suzette. We have been regular cruisers and guest lecturers ourselves on Royal Viking ships since then – and still good chums of the Aronsohns!

Los Angeles has its share of memorable travel advisers like James Rety, 'Monsieur le Vicomte', who survives illness with fortitude and the help of frequent visits to the Far East and its traditional practitioners of Chinese medicine. Many of our guests at both the Athenaeum Hotel and Claridge's were recommended by James and by another stalwart of the travel business in California, Miriam Rand with her specialist team of advisers like Elizabeth Sides, a world-class championship bridge player who accompanies her small exclusive parties on cruise liners in between competing in international bridge tournaments. In Dallas Rudi Steele, the city's 'Mr. Travel' and Marilou Sargent and Marjorie Purnell in their respective companies and partnerships look after the city's international jet-set.

If the hotels I have managed have been truly grand hotels, it is their clients who have helped make them so, for without 'grand' guests there is no grand hotel. Our friend Lucy Zimmerman at the age of 20 just after World War II was the first woman to own a travel agency in Dallas. She still looks after special clients and friends, manages to look 39 years old, and often hosts Eve and me on our annual pilgrimage to Texas, on our last visit inviting 35 friends and former guests to a reception for us at the Park Cities Club in Highland Park.

In Houston Connie Burke, who takes care of the top individual clients of American Express Travel, invited us to the lavish apartment she shares with her husband Leonard. Connie had said 'come casual – we're going to a little neighbourhood restaurant.' I had learned my lesson at the Hillcrest Club, so a blazer and silk tie was as casual as I was prepared to go. Even at that my wife felt under-dressed in a Guy Laroche pin-tucked cotton number when Connie arrived looking stunning in sequined cashmere. The 'little neighbourhood restaurant' was just that – right across from their apartment block – but what Connie had omitted to tell us was that it also happened to be the hottest dining spot in town! Before dinner we were treated to caviar and Dom Perignon in their apartment while we viewed their mind-boggling collection of the heads, bodies, skins and remains of the animals they'd shot in Africa. Connie is less than five feet tall, most of the animals that crossed her sights at least twice that height. Barely a section of wall, a floor or a flat surface was visible beneath the trophies, and in the master bedroom a full-grown male lion stood snarling convincingly at the foot of the bed, a testament that the art of the taxidermist at least was alive and well. Heaven help any burglar who breaks in there on a dark night . . .

So many of our regular guests came from Florida that in the difficult recession years of the late 1980s and early 90s I introduced a Claridge's Award for the travel agent who sent the most business over a specified number of room nights each year. With the help of British Airways we were able to offer the winner, along with an engraved silver trophy, a prize of return flight, either first-class or Concorde, to London and a week's accommodation at Claridge's. Almost predictably, the prize alternated year and year about between Miguel Riera, head of Royal Poinciana Travel in Palm Beach, and Susan Lehrman, president of Royal Palm Travel.

Travel professionals like these make demanding guests themselves, but they are often the best kind. They know what they want, they recognise quality, style and service, and they insist on all of those being absolutely guaranteed before entrusting a hotelier with their most favoured clients.

Our flag-flying goodwill visits to US travel agents also played a major role in keeping the hotel busy during quieter years. We never forgot these people had a choice of fine hotels in London, nor did we underestimate the importance of reminding and updating them on why ours were the right properties for their clients. In all this from the very outset we had two staunch allies who made everything seem possible. One was Joel Grossman, a hotel marketing man who had worked on both sides of the Atlantic, with outstanding abilities, great contacts, and unparalleled generosity of spirit. The other was the admirably laid-back Norman 'Lucky' Congdon, then senior sales manager for British Airways on the East Coast, now with Air France. Thanks to Joel's expertise, so freely given as one friend to another, to Lucky's and British Airways' generosity, and to the hospitality of the US hoteliers with whom we stayed, Eve and I were able to travel frequently to the US and put together an invitation list of top travel and media people without involving the hotels that employed me in anything but the most basic expenditure. I don't think my employers were ever aware of just how much work my wife put into organising our travel and hotel arrangements in up to ten cities a year, overseeing the design and printing of invitations and RSVP arrangements for half a dozen receptions, checking on attendances and non-responses when we arrived, and hosting our parties. Juggling this with her own career commitments was tough at times, but it was enormous fun for both of us and we would not have changed any of it. In the leanest years of recession it helped boost occupancy rates at the hotel.

And besides – it enabled me to fulfill my promise to my bride that I would take her back to America every year.

* * *

Our involvement with hotels and travel provided the wherewithal and the opportunity to indulge our appetite for new places, new hotels and new people. But rewarding as our business visits to the US were – and still are – the real enrichment has come from the friendships Eve and I have formed there.

It seems fitting that our US adventures began with hotels.

In 1978 Betty Holloway was Director of Press and Public Relations for the Fairmont Hotel in Dallas, renowned and loved by the city's media, business and social community. Part of her job was booking the shows for which the Venetian Room at the Fairmont was famous. When Sammy Cahn, Lena Horne or Billy Eckstein came to perform in cabaret, Betty looked after them like a mother hen brooding her chicks. No matter how difficult or temperamental a performer, Betty managed to charm them and they loved her, every one. It's no exaggeration to say that most of the best hotel public relations people working in Dallas today were Betty's protégés.

She took care of the arrangements for the Festival of English Country House Cooking that John Tovey brought to Dallas in 1978. Eve, whom

I knew only slightly at that time, was part of the British group and arrived at the Fairmont Hotel ahead of the others to check the arrangements and to research the articles she was writing on the Festival. Betty Holloway called her from home in the middle of that Saturday afternoon to welcome her, and arranged to come in and have dinner with Eve so she could see the cabaret. When Eve learned it was one of her long-time favourite performers Sammy Cahn, she was thrilled. She and Betty sat through both performances of the show with a small high-spirited group of Dallas media people. Betty introduced Eve to Sammy Cahn afterwards, the conversation turned to London hotels and they discovered they had a favourite hotel and a favourite hotelier in common – yours truly!

The John Tovey dinners the following week were lavish six-course affairs with 140 people sitting at round tables of eight or ten. The food was spectacular in John Tovey's inimitable style of plated service, daring combinations of ingredients, generous use of fresh herbs, and seven separate vegetables served with the main course. His small brigade of young people smart in dark green blazers and grey flannels or skirts charmed the Texans, the ambience was elegant, the guests relaxed. Eve was introduced to two couples well known in Dallas, Tav and Carolyn Lupton – Tav was the head of the Coca Cola company in Texas – and Eugene Smith and his actress wife Mary Ann. At table Eve was seated – by fate, she says now – next to a family from East Texas, Dr. & Mrs. Terry, their son and his wife Pat.

Before she left the city, Eve recalls standing by the vacant lot next to the Fairmont Hotel car park and thinking: 'I can feel this city growing around me, and I want to be a part of it.' Seven months later, we were married, and the following year we returned to Dallas together – we've been part of the city ever since. Eve's friends became my friends. We've been with them through marriages and divorces, the birth of children and grandchildren and the unutterable sadness of Betty Holloway's death.

I used to call her a 'Betty Grable blonde'. She once paid me the great compliment of asking my wife how on earth she could ever find a Ron Jones! Her laughter would start in her eyes with sparkle, then they'd crinkle and fix you with a puckish delight while she turned on the full beam of a gorgeous smile that few could resist.

Betty had introduced us to a young man she had trained to become another of Dallas's star public relations people, Michael Alexander, who in turn went on to become Director of Press and Public Relations for the Anatole, then the Kempinski hotels in the city. During our 1984 visit, we knew Betty had been ill for many months but, typically putting a trouper's face on it, she insisted she was just in the hospital in Fort Worth for 'a little surgery' and hoped to see us on our next trip. Mike Alexander, however, told us he thought we should visit Betty straight away. He would drive us over from Dallas. Betty was sitting up in bed, hair beautifully coiffed as always, in full make-up and dressed in a pretty lace peignoir. She didn't even look pale.

When the call came one evening in London a few months later to say she had died we knew we'd be grateful always to Mike for giving us this last happy meeting with her. Her death left us and so many other adoring friends truly bereft. We miss her still.

Betty Holloway's legacy to us has been the good times we had and are still having, and the friends we treasure in our beloved Big D. The people, like the city itself, are larger than life. It's the brashness and the culture and the way the two are juxtaposed that appeal to us. There aren't many places where the most sophisticated people you know, wealthy beyond our imagination, get as big a kick out of going to the symphony or to the newest exhibit at one of the outstanding museums and galleries, as they do at a rodeo or dancing the Cotton-Eyed Joe at Billy Bob's or the Traildust – or popping out for ribs at Sonny Bryan's Barbecue. Perhaps it's the same phenomenon that has them building multi-million dollar mansions in the best parts of town – cheek by jowl with other mansions just as imposing, only a garage and an alleyway or a strip of back-yard separating each property from its neighbours. The kind of houses that in our tiny country would be set in acres of garden and grounds, in Highland Park or Turtle Creek take up the entire 'lot' on which they're built. Next door's dogs and next door's children must be a constant encroachment on privacy but that, we're told, is the price you pay for building your house in the best part of town.

We still enjoy 'visiting with' the Luptons and the Smiths, and Pat – now Pat Chandler since her remarriage to a wonderful cowboy and horse-trainer in 1995 – is my wife's closest friend. Back then she was Pat Terry and lived in Jefferson, East Texas, in the beautiful century-old Terry home, with her lawyer husband and two small boys.

We first visited them when Seth was eight years old and his brother George four. The minute we stepped out of our car George had the situation sized up. While his older brother, mature in comparison despite his freckles, seized our bag and escorted us politely into the house,

George grabbed my hand and announced: 'Him and me's goin' to the library.' As soon as we were out of earshot he looked at me trustingly and said: 'We're not really going to the library, Ron. We're going to the drugstore. It's got a soda fountain.' He took me in the back way, saying: 'It's OK, they know me. My grand-pappy owns this place.' Later I discovered his grand-pappy, the town doctor, or one or other of his uncles seemed to own most of Jefferson. Right then, though, I was initiated into the delights of cherry lime soda and shown off to the townsfolk as 'Y'all, this here's my friend Ron. He lives in a big hotel but he's a good ol' down-home boy.'

Jefferson was a revelation to us. A prosperous wild west town on the Texas–Louisiana border that had 'died' when the river delta was damned in the last century, Jefferson had been lovingly restored by the townsfolk, especially the determined ladies of the Jessie Allen Wise Garden Club, which we christened JAWS. They had raised money from husbands and bank managers, rebuilt the Excelsior House Hotel, and extended the annual Pilgrimage in May when the blossoms are spectacular, to include visits to the restored homes. Tourists were welcomed by householders in costume and shown the beautiful rooms, with their original furnishings and artifacts, while the history of the house and of the town was unfolded.

As you strolled around the antique shops or revelled in the aromas wafting from the traditional bakery, you could wave to the visitors taking a tour of Jefferson in horse-drawn covered wagons. Lucille Terry, one of those larger-than-life Southern women, indomitably cheerful and with boundless energy, would pass by slowly or even stop her car in the middle of the street to bid a cheery 'Well, good mawnin' y'all!'. A former history teacher and school-fellow of Ladybird Johnson, 'Miz Terry' was the doctor's wife and a leading light in the town's restoration. She introduced us to the Excelsior House Hotel, which the ladies of the Garden Club had restored and run with little outside help for some seven years until it was self-sufficient. Now it was a superb property, with decorative wrought-iron balconies and a pretty, fountained courtyard. Guests enjoyed a southern breakfast of grits and sausages and eggs, served with little home-baked orange blossom muffins.

During Pilgrimage the Terry boys were dressed as children of the 19th century and expected to help entertain the visitors. Seth at the age of six had accompanied the docent as she described the rooms and the furnishings of the Terry home, and when the lady excused herself for a few moments, decided he'd go on with the tour, now in the master bedroom. 'This bed is walnut,' he explained, 'and is about 80 years old. And this . . . ' turning to a large oil painting opposite depicting a female reclining nude, 'This was the lady of the house . . . er . . . on a very, very hot day.'

The year George turned six, there were more Pilgrimage visitors to his home than usual, and the weather was unseasonably warm. Pat, his mother, made lemonade for the people waiting in the garden for the next tour. Gradually George's grandmother became aware of him listing slightly to starboard. On investigation she found one of his trouser pockets full of money. George, it seemed, had been politely taking glasses of lemonade to the visitors – and telling each one. 'That'll be one dime, please!'

Now we look at Seth aged 25 managing his own mega-store for farm equipment and George touring as manager of a rock band and remember those two cute boys in Jefferson quizzing Eve and me on what-all we did and didn't have in England. 'Y'all have schools in England?' Yes. 'And y'all have trees in England?' Eventually. 'What-all d'you guys not have in England?' Wracking our brains, we came up with 'Hershey bars. We don't have Hershey bars in England.' 'No Hershey bars? Wow-ee. You-all sure must be poor people . . . '

We were in Dallas during the Falklands war, and invited to an engagement party given by Tav and Carolyn Lupton for Gene and Mary Ann Smith's daughter. This was our first visit to a ranch and to us it was a Southfork setting. There was a barbecue around the pool, good music and good company. I helped myself to a Texas-sized steak from the grill, dipped into the real baked beans, skewered a baked Idaho potato and some soured cream and found a place to sit at a near-empty table. Soon I was joined by a burly, middle-aged man whose name I didn't catch. When the newcomer found out I was British, we were soon arguing hammer and tongs about our Prime Minister's handling of the crisis. The stranger was being pretty aggressive about Britain's tactics, and I took some pleasure in telling him how wrong he was. When he was formally introduced a few minutes later as Nelson Bunker Hunt, I was glad I'd taken the trouble.

Every year in Dallas we renewed our links with the media and the travel trade, and with our Texas friends and prospective hotel guests, through a series of receptions. We always greeted our guests together as they arrived, and we came to look forward to the moment when one of our favourite couples would arrive, hand in hand, Dr. Bob and Willie Sparkman. Dr. Bob – he was never called anything but Dr. Bob – was a prominent Dallas physician, author and benefactor and his wife Willie, already into her sixties when we met her, a true southern belle – a real steel magnolia. They were never apart if they could help it, and everybody knew they were soul-mates. We met after Willie's late sister Zelma Ramsay-Moore, wife of another Dallas doctor, stayed at the Athenaeum Hotel with our friends Dr. & Mrs. Terry from Jefferson.

I don't think I ever saw Willie Sparkman without flowers in her hair, carefully made up and clad in pretty dress and high-heeled, strappy sandals. And always clutching, beautifully gift-wrapped, our annual gift of Lammes Texas Chewie pralines!

It was only after Dr. Bob died in 1997 that I learned just what steel there was under that ultra-feminine exterior. 'I never did hold with all this women's lib,' confessed Willie. 'I like to be looked after and petted.' She and Dr. Bob had married more than half a century before, around the time America entered World War Two. Willie was 19 years old and he was her date at a ball. 'I walked into the room, took one look at him, and decided right then and there I was going to marry him,' she told us. He proposed formally six months later, and they planned 'a big, big wedding – six bridesmaids, six groomsmen – everything.' Then one Tuesday a few weeks later, Dr. Bob, by now an army medic on manouevres in North Carolina, told his fiancée he was being posted overseas the following week. They could either get married quietly right away, or else wait until after the war.

Without thinking twice, Willie decided they'd marry now – but not quietly! She had her heart set on a big wedding, and a big wedding she would have – even with only days to organise it. That was on a Tuesday. Next day she called the pastor at their Church and coerced him into marrying them that Saturday.

Next, Willie turned the force of her charm and determination on the dressmaker who had begun work on bride's and bridesmaid's dresses. She didn't know how, said the seamstress, but she'd see what could be done in the time available. She promised to do the very best she could. (Willie and her six bridesmaids were fitted and gowned with only hours to spare.)

She then phoned Dr. Bob's commanding officer and told him Bob wanted him to be best man and his medical colleagues to be groomsmen.

'Child,' retorted the General. 'You don't know what you're asking.

There's a war on! Saturday is three days away. And besides, if I let my men be groomsmen there wouldn't be a single medical officer left at Fort Sam Houston.'

'General,' Willie shot back. 'I don't plan to be married but this one time. Sir, I don't see how you can rightly refuse a girl something you know is so important to her. Especially when I don't know when I'll see him again after next week.'

The General turned up on Saturday to be best man. Dr. Bob's six fellow-officers were there too – delivered in an aircraft which stood by at a local airfield in case the men were summoned back in an emergency.

'We spent our honeymoon weekend,' recalled Mrs. Sparkman, 'at a hotel which is now the Park Plaza building in Highland Park Village. On the Sunday I modelled my entire trousseau for Bob, determined he should see me in it even if we couldn't have the honeymoon we planned.

'I bade him farewell on the Monday morning and I didn't see him again for three years and two months.'

They wrote to each other several times a week, but when Dr. Bob returned home as the youngest serving Eagle Colonel in the army medical corps, Willie was concerned they would be strangers to each other.

'I needn't have worried,' she recalls. 'The moment we set eyes on each other, it was as though we had never been apart. I wore the same outfit I wore when I bade him goodbye so that I'd look much as he remembered me. It worked.'

Half a century on, 'it' still worked. In 1997 Willie sustained a broken wrist, arm and leg which kept her in hospital for five weeks. Dr. Bob became ill, and just four weeks after Willie came home, she remembers. 'He sat on the edge of the bed on a lovely spring morning. He had been looking at his beloved azaleas which were like a glorious pink cloud in our garden. I said "Aren't the flowers pretty?" He just looked at me and said. "Flowers? I don't see any flowers. Just a bright, bright light." Then he took my hand, said "I love you, darlin" and just stopped breathing.'

* * *

Just after I retired from Claridge's in 1995 we were invited to join the 90th birthday celebrations of Stanley Marcus in Dallas. Eve and I flew over to spend a long weekend partying with the man who is the nearest thing the Texans have to royalty, and living proof that the next phase of our lives could be as fresh and exciting as any. Eve follows the credo 'retirement kills' and felt that 'Mr. Stanley's' good example in that direction was just what I needed.

Nonagenarian and venerable he may be, but Stanley reminded us that weekend that old friends, new projects and unquenchable enthusiasm for life social, cultural and professional, keep those around you in thrall. He had only recently formed a new company, and remained president or chairman of several others.

The first party of the weekend was a Friday evening champagne reception at the Downtown branch of Neiman Marcus, the department store founded by his family. Each of five retailing floors sported decorations, live music and elaborate hot and cold buffets with a different national theme. On the ground floor Stanley and his wife Linda, who had recently been awarded her Doctorate in Archaeology, received their several hundred guests. We arrived about 20 minutes into the party and already the store was packed. We made our way over to our hosts and from 15 feet away Stanley Marcus held out his arms: 'Ah! Here come the Joneses. And how was your visit to Malta?' *We* had almost forgotten the details of our business visit to Malta several weeks before, but here was this 90-year-old surrounded by acolytes and fans remembering this detail in the midst of his birthday party!

When we left around 9.15 the party was still in full swing and the guest of honour in the thick of it, good-humouredly parrying with radio and television reporters and a bevy of the most glamorous security people we'd ever seen.

Saturday morning we called into the store to buy a copy of Stanley Marcus's new book, which we heard he would be signing between 11 and noon. Admiring customers, many clutching birthday cards and gifts, were already lined up. A staff member told us Mr. Stanley had got there at 8am to have breakfast with some of the retired employees. He started signing at 10, and they hoped he'd take a break for lunch. As we were leaving the store restaurant around two o'clock, in came Stanley with a group of store personnel, having fitted in a half-hour photo session. Naïvely, we hoped he wouldn't tire himself out, for he was to meet all his overseas guests at five that afternoon to take them on a tour of his miniature book exhibition at the library of SMU. We needn't have worried. When we arrived Stanley was already waiting, and for an hour he walked and talked us through his tiny literary treasures.

From SMU the coach took us on to the Crescent Court Hotel for another champagne reception and dinner. We were entertained by the Dallas Chorale, who sang a song composed specially for the occasion, a close-harmony number which featured the names of every one of the 155 overseas guests by name.

Dinner was a down-home affair 'as it might have been served earlier in the century at a ranch in Texas', with Smoked Chicken Ranch Soup and Fried Rib-Eye Steak with Roasted Onion Spoonbread, Green Bean Casserole and Red Eye Gravy. As dessert arrived, Stanley's son took the stage and invited anybody who felt like it to 'come and say a few words about Stanley Marcus. But I warn you – I've got the hook, and anybody speaking for more than three minutes will be pulled off!'

One after another, guests took turns to sing Stanley's praises – as mentor, as friend, as grandfather, as colleague. My wife nudged me. 'Why don't you get up and tell the truth . . . ' I quickly caught on and got to my feet.

'The first time I met Stanley Marcus' I began, 'he handed me a seven-page letter of complaint.'

I then recounted how, within a week or two of my arrival at Claridge's, the doyen of style had come to stay, complete with the lightbulbs he always carried because no hotel provided lights bright enough to read in bed. Nothing pleased him. Everything that could be wrong, was wrong.

After I read his letter I asked to see him, looked him in the eye – and told him I agreed with every word. Would he, I asked, give us another chance and I promised that when next he visited I would have put right every point he had raised.

Stanley agreed, and the rest is history! Like everyone else whose path he crossed, Stanley won my admiration and my devoted friendship.

By the time the last speaker had raised a glass in honour of Stanley's 90th birthday and everybody volunteered to return for his 100th, we felt we'd enjoyed a full day. Outside, one of those torrential Texas rainstorms had started, and there wasn't a cab to be had. We made our way back to the hotel bar. Just in time to see Stanley, accompanied by a posse of grandchildren and looking as fresh as when we'd first seen him that morning, came in for a nightcap or – who knows – another round of partying!

While Dallas is like home to us, and New Orleans an old and trusted friend, New York remains a love affair. Approaching it like many a young lover the first few times, I was nervous and a little in awe. Familiarity, however, bred only content, and many of the city's charms were unveiled to Eve and me only after the pressure of work subsided a little and we could take time out to relax and enjoy ourselves. Contrary to most people's experience, the older we get the more we appreciate New York and all it has to offer.

Over the years it has produced an assortment of good friends, many of our favourite hotel guests, and a wealth of hotel experiences. Dorothy Sarnoff and her late husband Milton Raymond stayed frequently in London. Dorothy was a musical comedy singer and actress who played opposite Yul Bryner in the original Broadway production of The King and I. When she retired from the stage, she formed her own company, Speech Dynamics, through which she has groomed US Vice Presidents, Ambassadors, Congressmen and CEOs as well as thousands of ordinary people through her numerous books, on their presentation techniques for public performances. To Dorothy's book 'Never Be Nervous Again' Eve and I owe whatever skill and whatever confidence we have in lecturing and presenting to audiences as diverse as cruise liner passengers and hotel management students.

Lester Coleman, whose friendship began when he stayed with his late wife Felicia at the Athenaeum Hotel, looked after the tonsils and adenoids of the stars as one of Park Avenue's best-known and best-loved Ear Nose and Throat specialists. Lester and Felicia were the first people to share the news, back in the spring of 1978, that Eve and I were to be married.

Another Lester with special memories for me and whom I admire above all other bandleaders is Lester Lanin. Her Majesty the Queen and the Royal Family are among his greatest fans. On special family occasions it's Lester Lanin the Queen sends for to provide the music for dancing, usually non-stop from mid-evening until dawn. His music is toe-tapping, his energy in his 70s absolutely astonishing. I was somewhat taken by surprise – and so was she, I think – when our hotel public relations manager told me that Lester Lanin had said of me: 'Mr. Jones is so gentle and so kind – just like Jesus . . . ' I had been variously told that I bore a slight physical resemblance to the conductor Bernard Haitink and to His Holiness Pope John-Paul II, but this unexpected elevation to sanctity was something else again.

As we grew more familiar with New York and began to explore further than the Circle Line and the city's hottest new restaurants, we visited some of the legendary places we'd read about or seen in the movies. Greenwich Village and SoHo, Saturday markets and second-hand bookshops, a Broadway or Off-Broadway show on Sunday afternoon after lunch at the Stage Deli, with its gigantic portions and rude, funny waiters. Delmonico's for weekday lunch. And P.J. Clarke's bar. The bartenders are as brusque as the drinks are generous. Our special favourite was Frank Conefrey, a disgruntled-sounding Irish–American ex-boxer who for some reason took a shine to us and kept in touch between visits. Frank's Christmas card was always the same – a dollar bill signed with a seasonal greeting. His dry martinis, sloshed with apparent abandon until they overspilled the rim of a generous glass, were just the medicine we needed after a long flight or a hard day's cold-calling. When Frank died we were touched to be notified in a letter from his nephew, who had found my name in Frank's address book and recalled him talking about us.

The New York press was always supportive in keeping our hotels in front of the people who mattered. Pamela Fiori when editor-in-chief of Travel & Leisure magazine, Isla Stanger who became editor of Wine & Food magazine. And the impressively named Barbara-Lee Diamonstein-Spielvogel who wrote the first major feature to appear in the New York Times after my arrival at Claridge's. Other writers, too, helped spread the word of Claridge's ongoing transformation during the latter half of the 1980s, including Reader's Digest writer James Stewart-Gordon, one-time husband of Faith, proprietor of a favourite restaurant the Russian Tearoom.

An avid reader of contemporary fiction, Eve ceased to be surprised when she found Claridge's mentioned in just about every book she picked up, from Sidney Sheldon through Barbara-Taylor Bradford to Dominick Dunne. It was more surprising to find myself referred to by name in a novel published a few years ago by a New York friend Edward Hanna. Ed's book The Whitechapel Horrors began with 'Ronald Jones, newly appointed general manager of Claridge's', opening a safe behind his office to find a document containing mysterious information, the significance of which unfolds gradually in a Sherlock Holmes tale of murder and mayhem. Not, I hasten to add, within the confines of the hotel.

We always called Dominick Dunne 'the Marcel Proust of Claridge's', a soubriquet which he confessed he enjoys. Just as Proust used to sit of an afternoon sipping tea and making the occasional note in the lounge of the Ritz in Paris, so Dominick Dunne would sink into one of the antique armchairs in Claridge's elegant Foyer and quietly observe the comings and goings of hotel guests during the London Season.

A more eccentric first meeting with another couple of New York friends took place in the western highlands of Scotland. Staying with Eric and Betty Allen at Airds, their idyllic country hotel in Port Appin, we noticed this couple at dinner and again on our pre-bedtime stroll along the waterfront. They are not an easy couple to miss, since Michael Brooks is white and his wife Pat is black. I was on the verge of restraining Eve when she whispered: 'I *know* that couple.' She often said that and she very seldom *did* know, on closer inspection. Unable to resist, she caught up with them and said: 'I'm probably mistaken, but you do look very like two people I know. The man is Bryn Franks, who used to be editor of In Britain magazine, and the woman is Sheila Rule, the London bureau chief of a New York press agency.' The couple roared with amusement as they introduced themselves. 'There can't be too many couples who look like us,' said Pat. 'I didn't think we'd be that easy to confuse.' On their next visit to the UK they stayed with us at Claridge's, and we rely on them to introduce us to the best neighbourhood restaurants in New York and on Michael to comb his beloved second-hand bookstores on our behalf. A record producer by trade, he has also become the world's finest, most entertaining and literate pen-friend.

On one of our earliest visit to Los Angeles my wife had an assignment to write a magazine profile of the legendary Chasen's restaurant. Every movie star and, it seemed, every US president for half a century, had dined there and had their parties catered by Chasen's. Dave Chasen had founded it in 1936 and his widow Maude presided over the red leather booths and banquettes like a chatelaine. However, the man behind the business was managing director Ronnie Clint, an affable Liverpudlian who first sailed into L.A. on a merchant ship while still a teenager – and later returned to make the city his own.

Eve interviewed Ronnie at some length, and the two of us shared a lobster salad with him in his small office at the back of the restaurant, reminiscing about Liverpool, swapping stories about hotels, restaurants and famous clients we had in common. Ronnie, we discovered, although quite a shy character, had the great gift of recounting anecdotes about his rich and famous clients in a deadpan fashion that had us helpless with laughter. He told us about Frank Sinatra ordering Chasen's famous chili flown over to him during concert tours of Europe. About swapping stories with Alfred Hitchcock, catering in the homes of movie stars and at presidential parties. About Dean Martin, always a favourite at Chasen's, asked by a waiter: 'Would you like wine?' retorting 'Not while I'm drinking.' When Ronnie said: 'Dean, I hope you're not driving home after all that' Martin's reply was: 'What! Do you think I could *walk* in this condition?'

One of life's special friendships was born that day. Next time we saw Ronnie Clint was the first year he brought his beautiful wife Anita with their daughter and son-in-law to stay at the Athenaeum Hotel. Thereafter, they came to London or we visited them at their home in Santa Monica at least once a year. We have rejoiced in the birth of their three grand-children as they have in ours. Soon after I retired from Claridge's, Ronnie retired as m.d. of Chasen's when the restaurant closed its doors in 1995 after six decades of catering to the stars. Our lives have been immeasurably enriched by their friendship.

But then, one of the enduring joys of the 'happiness business' is the friends it brings. People whose paths you'd never cross were it not for their being hotel guests. Elsewhere in this book I described the pitfalls of imagining all the guests with whom you become friendly or with whom you socialise are truly your friends. The exceptions, though, are worth a hundred pleasant acquaintances.

Bill and Patsy Abell had been regular guests at Claridge's for 30 years before I arrived there. Bill's family owned the Baltimore Sun newspaper and Bill was actually in residence at the hotel when a cable came through from his son confirming the sale of the newspaper. Mischievously, Shep Abell had wired: 'Sun sold. Buy Claridge's.'

'Goodness knows how many of the staff got the wind up after they saw that,' Bill recalls, 'but we smoothed things down pretty quickly and assured the Concierge it was only a joke!'

When we first met them I was struck by the fact that even in her sixties Patsy Abell was an outstandingly beautiful and elegant woman – as she is today. Bill was dapper, moustached, with a quick, deadpan wit and a quirky sense of humour. Trained as a lawyer but by then retired, I found him one of the keenest listeners I ever met. He and Patsy share this gift of paying attention to everything you say and remembering it – a gift that isn't encountered too much by a hotelier whose job usually demands that he is the one who listens. Bill explains this by pointing out that in his profession you could do a great deal for a client and save them a lot of money besides, by offering a non-judgemental ear. Perhaps it was this that enabled him in retirement to write biographies of some of his eminent friends in the Catholic Church. He recorded, too, though mainly for the benefit of their seven children and innumerable grand-children, a historic two years spent travelling the world with his sister Margaret and their parents when they were children, being schooled by tutors and absorbing the cultural, historic and geographical experiences of a lifetime during the period between the two world wars.

We were very proud that during what proved to be their last visit to London we were able to take Bill and Patsy Abell to a Livery Company banquet at the Mansion House, with all the pomp and ceremony and tradition that entails. Resplendent in evening dress – white tie and tails for Bill and me – we processed up the grand staircase past Yeoman Warders and musicians of one of the Royal Regiments, to be presented to the ermine-robed Master of the Distillers Company and his guests of honour, then to sip champagne before a six-course banquet in the sumptuous Egyptian Room. The speakers that evening were on top form, the food and wine excellent, tables agleam with 17th and 18th century silver. The historic City rituals such as the Sung Grace and the passing of the silver finger-bowl filled with rosewater, and the Loving Cup, one of the City of London's most cherished traditions. As the ornate silver cup full of wine is passed from diner to diner, the guest on either side stands with the person drinking, back to back to protect them from danger while they drink. All the while, musicians played in the minstrels' gallery above.

After that, concern over Bill's health prevented the Abells from travelling overseas. Thankfully, we have been able to visit them in Chevy Chase, Maryland, every year since, to bask in their hospitality and friendship, take heed of their wise counsel, and enjoy the stimulating and entertaining company of two of the most Christian people I have ever known.

11

'When Dukes were Three a Penny'*

The dynamics of the hospitality industry, its ever-changing and constantly expanding role in the world at large, make it essential for those
at its heart to keep pace, embrace change, and grasp opportunities as
they arise. I had always encouraged young members of staff to gain
additional qualifications or to enter hospitality industry competitions
and I thought it only fair to swallow some of my own medicine when
the chance presented itself in 1979.

I had read in the trade press that the recently formed Master
Innholders were seeking recruits from among leading hoteliers. This was
a joint venture between the Worshipful Company of Innholders, one
of the ancient City livery companies, and the industry's professional
body, the Hotel, Catering and Institutional Management Association,
of which I am a Fellow. The aims and objectives of the Master
Innholders appeared wholly commendable, to uphold standards of
hospitality and professionalism and to promote our industry to the
world at large, lobbying in its interests, training young people and so
on. Applicants had to submit an essay on hospitality, outlining their
own philosophy and thinking about the development of the industry in
the future. If that passed muster with the 20 or so existing Master
Innholders, the Worshipful Company and the HCIMA, there would be
a panel interview.

Unaccustomed as I am to writing essays – in fact I couldn't recall
when I last wrote one – I nevertheless decided I should have a go. My
wife reminded me on a Saturday that Monday morning was the deadline
for the essay. Still I put it off, just jotting down the occasional note,
eventually settling down to write at eight o'clock on Sunday evening
and writing well into the small hours.

---

*Gilbert & Sullivan, *The Gondoliers*

A few weeks later I was invited for interview at the venerable Innholders Hall, whose charred beams survived the Fire of London. The panel had representatives from the HCIMA, the Worshipful Company of Innholders including the rather elderly and deaf Master, and existing Master Innholders. They asked me about everything including what I had done in the war. It was nerve-racking, especially when the deaf panellist kept asking me to repeat answers I had given several minutes before, when the rest of us had gone on to a quite different topic.

Much to my relief, I got through, was entitled to the letters MI after my name, awarded the Freedom of the City of London when I became Chairman two years later, and have enjoyed the privilege of belonging to an organisation whose members include the finest hoteliers in the UK.

I had been general manager of the Athenaeum Hotel for 12 years when in May 1984 I received a telephone call from Giles Shepard, Managing Director of Savoy Hotels. He'd like to see me, he said, as soon as possible. We decided on the next morning, and I invited him to the Athenaeum Hotel but Mr Shepard said he would prefer to meet at the Berkeley hotel in Knightsbridge at 11 a.m.

When I mentioned the appointment to Eve, we naturally wondered what he wanted and agreed the most likely explanation was that Shepard wanted to recruit Nicholas Rettie, my deputy manager, for the Savoy company. Nicholas is an able hotel man, Savoy trained and with an impeccable background that would suit that company perfectly. I would be sad to lose him, but I knew he was ready for a fresh challenge. I collected in my mind all the information I might pass on to Giles Shepard next day.

When we had taken a seat in a quiet corner he came straight to the point.

'Mr Lund Hansen, the general manager of Claridge's, will be retiring later this year after forty-seven years. We have been looking all over Europe for his successor, and now we realise the answer has been right under our noses. Would you be interested?'

I didn't hesitate. 'In a word, yes.'

'Good,' said Giles Shepard. 'That's settled then. I'll see to the paperwork and we'll discuss the details.'

Simple as that. It didn't cross my mind to refuse, or to think about it. I forgot to ask about salary, conditions, contract. Whatever the conditions and whatever the remuneration, this was the world's top job. I felt like the soldier who has walked around with a field marshal's baton in his kitbag, knowing that one day he would put it to its proper use. Or an athlete who has trained all his life and at last been selected for the Olympics.

Instead of going back to the hotel, I ran upstairs to find Eve at her typewriter – thank God, for I couldn't have kept this news to myself a moment longer.

We cracked open half a bottle of Veuve Cliquot. To hell with our strict rule of no drinking at lunchtime. We both shed a few tears, I because I couldn't help thinking about my late father-in-law Sam Wood, who had encouraged and pushed me to the limits. He would have been so proud. And I couldn't wait to tell John Turpie, my mentor from Midland Hotel days, living in retirement in Cornwall.

Rank Hotels followed my recommendation and appointed Nicholas Rettie my successor at the Athenaeum Hotel. He deserved no less; the staff liked and respected him, and I knew the hotel, which I had grown to love as much as if it were my own, would be in safe hands.

The next six months sped by in a haze of suppressed excitement. I wouldn't be required at Claridge's until 5 November and I had been asked to keep the appointment confidential until Mr Hansen's retirement could be announced to the staff.

On the slightest pretext we would drive past Claridge's, an imposing red-brick edifice enthroned on the corner of Brook Street and Davies Street, flags flying a visual fanfare over the canopy, top-hatted doormen opening the doors of Rollses and Bentleys as well as the more mundane London taxis. It was difficult to believe this was to be our home for the foreseeable future. We had only once been inside the hotel together, when Jacques Schneider, head of the Profile recruitment consultancy, took us there for champagne before dinner one evening. I remembered the pastel rose-strewn wall-covering of the Reading Room, the air of shabby gentility, the liveried footmen – never waiters – in velvet knee breeches, and the rather stuffy grandeur.

There had been a hotel on this site since 1812, the year of Napoleon's retreat from Moscow, when James Mivart opened his 'lodging house' amid strenuous objections from his neighbors to a hotel on their Mayfair doorsteps. Mivart dismissed their objections – and those of his hotel competitors – by claiming he was not operating a hotel, but 'a Private and distinct Lodging House only, the Apartments of which are always held by the Month . . . and not let by the Night to casual comers'.

Five years later Mivart acquired the house next door, and by 1838 owned five early Georgian houses along Brook Street. By the 1850s Mivart's was patronised by royalty and the aristocracy, including the King of the Netherlands and Grand Duke Alexander of Russia. It was known as one of 'just three first-class hotels in London'. When James Mivart retired in 1853, the property was bought by William and Marianne Claridge, who owned a hotel next door, and the combined property became known as 'Claridge's late Mivart's'.

During the 1860s Claridge's claimed the distinction of being the first hotel where ladies could visit or dine with propriety, after Queen Victoria had paid a visit to the Empress Eugénie during her stay there. Until then, hotels had not been considered respectable places for ladies to be seen.

When William Claridge died in 1882, his fortunes had declined and the hotel slid towards bankruptcy, unable at one stage even to pay its meat bill. The *Caterer & Hotel Proprietor's Gazette* reported in 1893: 'Happily, money has been forthcoming to satisfy Mr. James Ginger's meat-bill and costs, and Claridge's Hotel (Ltd.) still waves.'

That year the houses in Brook Street were sold to the owners of the Savoy Hotel, and the New Claridge's Hotel Limited was formed. The genius behind the Savoy Hotel was Richard D'Oyly Carte. He had introduced Gilbert to Sullivan, and on the proceeds of the comic operas conceived by this brilliant pair and staged by D'Oyly Carte, had built the Savoy, London's most luxurious hotel. The company was now in a position to expand, and acquiring Claridge's on its prime Mayfair site showed the great impressario's far-sightedness.

The existing houses were demolished and the new Claridge's opened in 1898, built 'in the style of the English Renaissance'. The architect was C.W. Stephens and the interior designer Ernest George. On the upper floors, suites of rooms with interconnecting corridors allowed visiting dignitaries to reserve any number of rooms for their entourage knowing that none would have to venture into the public corridors of the hotel. This feature remains one of Claridge's unique assets. Electric lifts or 'ascending rooms' and electric lighting, sumptuous Louis XVI and Adam décor and furnishings and a separate ladies entrance in Brook Street, helped make Claridge's one of London's most fashionable venues. The ground floor reception rooms, like those in country houses, 'divided themselves by sex', according to a *Country Life* report. 'The gentlemen could enjoy a smoking room and billiards room, the ladies a reading room and drawing room, while common to both were a top-lit winter garden behind the vestibule . . . a coffee room and a dining room.'

One of the advisers to the new hotel company was César Ritz, then manager of the Savoy, and his input and advice accounted for much of the hotel's initial success. His eye for décor, his feel for ambience and comfort, his gift for lighting a room to flatter the ladies, and his ability to attract the best staff, proved invaluable. Ritz was a Pied Piper and to 'his' hotels flocked the royal and the fashionable, the rich and the famous.

Soon after Claridge's opened, Ritz and his famous chef Escoffier – a trailblazing partnership if ever there was one – had their connections with the Savoy company abruptly severed. The reason remains shrouded in mystery. Savoy records claim it was because both men were taking 'backhanders' from suppliers while being paid generous salaries and commission by the company. (One source estimates Ritz's salary at the equivalent of £185,000 in today's money.) Ritz's wife Marie, in her biography of her husband, blames a malicious housekeeper who disliked Ritz and who was the mistress of one of the directors of the company. Other accounts claim that the 'malicious housekeeper' could have been D'Oyly Carte's second wife Helen, who had been responsible for the interior décor of the Savoy until her job was taken over – by Madame Ritz.

Whatever the reason, the pair were soon giving the benefit of their expertise to the new Carlton Hotel in London's Haymarket, opened in the same year as Claridge's. When César Ritz left the Savoy, the Prince of Wales moved with him to the Carlton, saying: 'Where Ritz goes, I follow', thereby ensuring the success of the new hotel. Ritz opened his eponymous Paris hotel and lent his name to the London Ritz and to others in cities throughout Europe and the United States. But he never quite recovered from the first of a series of nervous breakdowns he suffered while at the Carlton Hotel. He died in his sixties after being an invalid and unable to work for 20 years, bequeathing to the hotel world a legacy of practical and theoretical hotel-keeping which has never been equalled.

Even without Ritz's continuing expertise, Claridge's became truly a hotel of the new century, in the forefront of national events. A new wing, in pure art deco style and doubling the size of the hotel, was added in 1930. The hotel became a haven for royalty in exile during World War II. King George II of Greece stayed as plain Mr Brown; King Haakon of Norway spent the war years there, as did King Peter II of Yugoslavia and the Presidents of Poland and Czechoslovakia.

Queen Wilhelmina of the Netherlands was the bane of other guests' lives. She used to sleep in a curtained-off corner of the cellar used as an air raid shelter. And she snored so loudly that a member of staff had to go around at intervals with a feather to discreetly tickle the royal toes.

In the first general election after the war, Winston Churchill suffered a humiliating defeat and found himself without a London home. Hugh Wontner, who later became Chairman of the Savoy company, gave him the use of the penthouse suite at Claridge's. Winston was often to be seen pacing the rooftop garden and looking wistfully across to Big Ben and the Houses of Parliament.

While I was a young waiter at Gleneagles in 1953, Claridge's was at the centre of Coronation celebrations and the venue for state banquets and royal occasions. It was dubbed 'the annexe to Buckingham Palace' after it became customary for visiting heads of state, having stayed the prescribed three nights as guests of the Queen, to move with their entourage into Claridge's, where they would return Her Majesty's hospitality with an official banquet. 'Resort of Kings and Princes' was how one writer described it, and the story is not apocryphal that during the Coronation of Queen Elizabeth when someone rang Claridge's and asked to speak to the King, the telephone operator had to ask: 'To which King would you like to speak, sir?'

Taking over at Claridge's – on Guy Fawkes Day 1984 – was like stepping on to the stage of a Gilbert and Sullivan comic opera towards the end of a long, long run. The scenery was badly in need of refurbishing, the audience had aged in its seats, the stars were fading and the chorus in need of remotivating. A challenge any good director would rise to, given the inherent excellence and popularity of the play and the backing of an enthusiastic impresario.

Even the plot would have done credit to the operatic stage: wily old mandarin pitted against upstart Italianate villain intent upon seizing control of the palace riches. Lord High Everything-Else who never quite got his own way. Ageing female courtiers whose elegance might be confused with beauty 'in the dusk with a light behind them'. And all the machinations that normally accompany a fight for supremacy when the contenders pit profit against tradition.

Lead player in the drama was Sir Hugh Wontner, only the third chairman in the Savoy company's 100-year history, former Lord Mayor of London, Clerk of the Royal Kitchens, septuagenarian and bon viveur. Proud of his claim to have been born a gentleman (his father was an actor), which he felt gave him innate superiority over his arch-rival Lord

180

Forte. A dismisser of anyone 'not a gentleman', the most damning epithet he could bestow. A despiser of what he sneeringly termed 'self-aggrandisement' though himself a tireless exponent of the art. He hero-worshipped the late Sir George Reeves-Smith, who had chosen the young Hugh Wontner as his successor to the Savoy throne, and would lose no opportunity to regale me with the wit and wisdom of Sir George.

The second lead was played by Giles Shepard, Managing Director of the group, a dandy in a well-cut suit, shoes you could see your face in, striped shirt with white collar, wild silk tie with diamond or pearl pin, and bright yellow or pink socks. Shepard had considerable charm and enthusiasm and his appearance reminded me of Mr Toad in E.H. Shepard's illustrations for *The Wind in the Willows*. There the resemblance ended. Giles Shepard had been a King's Scholar at Eton and served in the Coldstream Guards before joining the liquor trade, and subsequently the hotel world as a director of the Dorchester before being appointed Managing Director of the Savoy group in 1979.

He may have had his eye on the chairmanship of the company because Sir Hugh was already well into his seventies and, on the surface at least, gave the impression of wanting to ease up on his responsibilities. However, he retained his power of veto until his death in 1992 aged 84, smoothly and craftily holding Shepard back from complete control.

The two kept up a polite battle of wits, their differences veneered over in public. Sir Hugh was fond of accusing Shepard of 'self-aggrandisement' – a clear case of the pot calling the kettle black. Meeting and being seen with the best people was mother's milk to both of them. At a party they would sweep the room with their eyes and make a beeline for the most important person.

Shepard was the right man in the right place at the right time. The company had lost its place in the league of grand hotels and was producing poor profits. The buildings were showing signs of their age and needed investment. Shepard had the kind of style and flair, the sense of drama, the company needed. Under his guidance the hotels took on a new lease of life as capital investment was directed towards the two that most needed it – the Savoy and Claridge's, both approaching their hundredth birthdays. He chose Willy Bauer as general manager of the Savoy Hotel, wresting him from under the nose of the Forte organisation, where Bauer had been general manager of the Grosvenor House and Hyde Park hotels. Bauer was followed as general manager of the Savoy by Herbert Striessnig, an Austrian who had been advising the hotel on food and beverage matters after being out of mainstream hotel management for a short time. Herbert was hard-working and knowledgeable, with a great feeling for the staff, who found his infectious charm a great motivator.

Giles Shepard's good qualities as a managing director far outweighed any deficiencies. He was fair and supportive, and he in no way deserved the night of the long knives which was his eventual reward from the Savoy board in 1994 when he was forced to resign – with, to be fair, a golden handshake reputed to be worth a quarter of a million pounds – amidst accusations of the group's underperformance. He had guided the company through several years of the worst recession in recent history without any of the UK hotels going into the red, and it seems tough on him that his replacement should come in and have seemingly unlimited funds thrown at him just as the hotel business was clearly on the upturn. The year before I retired from Claridge's in 1994, we had £500,000 to spend on improving the hotel. The year 1995–96 saw a capital investment of over £6 million, a total of £40 million by the end of 1997.

Cast in the minor roles in the production were a series of characters with walk-on parts, some of whom would like to have seen their roles expanded, and who needed careful direction.

The cast was assembled, the audience – without whom there would be no play – in their seats, and within weeks of my arrival at Claridge's the curtain came up on another act of an increasingly well-known Savoy operetta.

The latest Forte bid for the Savoy was in full swing by the early part of 1985. Knives were sharpened, dirty tricks rehearsed, and unguarded backs became increasingly vulnerable. I recalled the best piece of advice I had been given by my old friend Professor John Norman when I started my new job: 'Just make sure you have somebody to watch your back.'

Sir Hugh Wontner and his arch-rival Lord Forte were by this time like two old stags, antlers locked in battle. Whichever outlived the other, I was convinced, would see his company control the Savoy. Every Tuesday when Sir Hugh visited me in my office, he had a fresh dart to aim at 'the little chef' or 'that little man', as he called him. He would recount how he helped the former milk-bar owner in his early days by proposing him for membership of a small consultative or advisory committee at the Ministry of Food in 1946.

Lord Forte – and how that title must have rankled – had darts of his own to throw. He was frequently quoted on the subject of Sir Hugh and Lady Wontner's occupancy of one of the two penthouse suites at Claridge's. He had no sympathy for Sir Hugh's contention that it was 'traditional and essential' for the individual running of the Savoy's highly individual hotels that a director lived in 'to keep an eye on standards'. Forte declared that *he* lived in 'a house, a very nice house', his laundry was done there, his meals were prepared well and he lived very well *and* managed to keep control of his business. The Claridge's penthouse was a source of valuable revenue lost to the company. No, countered Sir Hugh, the penthouse was 'difficult to get at and hard to let. So inconveniently situated that visitors have to leave the lift, walk down a narrow corridor and climb a flight of stairs'. It was 'not air-conditioned, stifling hot in summer and freezing in winter'. Lord Forte might have been forgiven for wondering why the Wontners spent so much of their lives there, though they did have other homes in Buckinghamshire and Scotland.

And what about the Forte private jet, asked Sir Hugh, when he himself drove an ageing Mini? (No mention of the Rolls-Royce which he subsequently exchanged for a BMW convertible.)

Forte was not the first predator to set his sights on the Savoy, though he had an additional sentimental attachment to it. He had proposed to his wife at the Savoy Hotel, spent part of his honeymoon there, and apparently made himself a promise that one day he would own it.

Sir Hugh had successfully fought off takeover bids since the 1950s when two property magnates, Charles Clore and Harold Samuel, began buying up shares in sufficient quantities for him to be alarmed at the prospect of his beloved Savoy, Claridge's and the Berkeley being acquired by a company with no experience in the hotel business. The Savoy properties had been built to provide London with the finest hotels and restaurants in the world, and Wontner considered it in the national interest that establishments of such quality and style should not be gobbled up by property companies. Indeed at one stage Sir Winston Churchill, who had lived as a guest in the Wontner penthouse at Claridge's after his loss of the 1945 general election, ordered an investigation into the transactions in Savoy shares, which he called 'a profit-making ramp by speculators'. Peter, later Lord, Thorneycroft at the Board of Trade tried to refuse to order the investigation but was overruled. Coincidentally Thorneycroft was appointed a director of THF in the late 1960s.

Wontner was successful in fighting off the early predators, as he was at seeing off both Victor Matthews of Trafalgar House and Maxwell Joseph of Grand Metropolitan in 1970. Fifteen years earlier Wontner created a complex share arrangement to protect the company from takeover bids: one 'B' share for every 'A' share, voting power of each 'B' share to be between 20 and 40 times that of the 'A's.

Over the years THF went on buying up as many Savoy shares as they could get their hands on, and in 1981 made an unsuccessful takeover bid.

In September 1985 – 11 months after my appointment as general manager of Claridge's – the Savoy company announced higher profits for the first six months of the year, at £4.7 million a 40 per cent increase on the year before. 'All the hotels have done well,' said Managing Director Giles Shepard, 'especially Claridge's.'

THF was once again looking hungrily in our direction. By this time, thanks to the highly original structure of the shareholding, they held 68 per cent of the equity in the company, but only 42 per cent of the votes.

The shareholders' meeting at the Savoy on 1 July 1988 provided a platform for Sir Hugh's flair for the dramatic. Throughout the meeting he sat hidden behind a pillar at the back of the Abraham Lincoln Room. When he stood up he stepped to one side, into view of the 'audience' where a lectern and microphone had been strategically placed, and delivered a well-rehearsed speech worthy of the thespian traditions of his own family and the Savoy theatre. He admitted that the controversial parcel of shares (known as the Lancaster block) should have been disclosed, but asked rhetorically: 'Am I a thief and a blackguard who creeps around in the dead of night? I hope we hear no more of that! I have admitted it was wrong. That's the end of it.' He dismissed the suit as 'Lord Forte's latest manoeuvre taken not in the interest of you shareholders, but in his own interests by creeping in through the back door,' and sat down to thunderous applause.

Giles Shepard had taken his share of mud-slinging in the run-up to the meeting. Lord Forte had announced that if he acquired the Savoy he would make Shepard head porter. Shepard responded characteristically, 'I would make a very good hall porter. And an awful lot of money, too!' Meanwhile the two principals were damning each other with faint praise in the *Spectator*, where Dominic Lawson quoted Sir Hugh: 'He is a very little man and he is Italian. So you have a recipe for *folie de grandeur* . . . but I have no personal animus against him.' And Forte: 'He is a liar . . . he is a hypocrite . . . but I do not hate him.'

Sir Hugh retired from the Savoy board at the age of 79, having spent 47 years as a director, 37 as chairman. He remained Chairman of Claridge's, and Rocco Forte mused that it would be 'interesting to see whether he gives up his apartment at Claridge's. If he did, the company would benefit to the tune of £500,000 pounds a year'.

After years of bickering and costs amounting to well in excess of a million pounds on the Savoy side alone, the 'Lancaster affair' was fully and finally settled. THF undertook not to acquire any further shares and the Savoy not to issue any, for five years.

On a personal note, we breathed more easily. Forte had made no secret of the fact that if and when they gained control of the company, the hotel general managers would be asked to clear their desks. In preparation for such an event Eve and I bought a larger house in the north Cotswolds – a row of three cottages which had been knocked into one – with five bedrooms and five bathrooms. Roosters would serve as a weekend retreat, and perhaps be our eventual home. More important in the short term, if I did lose my new-found and much-loved job, we would open it to visitors as an elegant bed-and-breakfast!

We lived, during the latter half of the 1980s – not only the directors but the management and the staff of all the hotels – under the threat of a THF takeover. It was only when the hotel industry, like the rest of the country and most of the world, plunged deep into recession in 1990 that THF became less like a baying hound of the Baskervilles and more like a snapping Yorkshire terrier.

Sir Hugh Wontner died in 1992 and by 1993 the Savoy group showed a net profit of only £510,000 on a revenue of £83.3 million, and the dividend paid to shareholders was cut by half. The following year Sir Anthony Tuke, now 74, announced his intention to retire as Chairman of the group, and the search for his successor began. Suggestions and rejections were made by both sides. Sir Ewan Fergusson, a former Ambassador to Paris and Chairman of Coutts & Co, the Royal bankers, accepted the position and took up his appointment on 13 September 1994. The day before, Giles Shepard resigned, under mounting pressure from the board.

Before he left, Shepard had been urged by the board to persuade Lady Wontner to vacate the penthouse which she continued to occupy after Sir Hugh's death. She eventually agreed to move out on condition that she had the use of a smaller suite on the sixth floor, arguing that Sir George Reeves-Smith's widow had retained a home in the hotels as had the widows of several directors in the past.

I had told Giles Shepard in the early spring of 1994 that I intended to retire on 5 November – ten years to the day after I took up my appointment at Claridge's – which meant I would have worked three years beyond official retirement age, a total of 53 years in the hotel industry. I could see the kind of changes ahead that I knew I would find distasteful as the demand for profits in the short term outstripped the dedication to the standards of service and tradition that the Savoy group stood for. François Touzin, who had been my assistant manager for two years before being appointed general manager of the Savoy company's Hotel Lancaster in Paris, would replace me as general manager of Claridge's for the next three years.

Two days after I left Ramon Pajares, who had been general manager of the Inn on the Park Hotel and European vice-president of Four Seasons, became Managing Director of the Savoy group. He was to report to a chairman's committee.

Still there was to be no peace in the boardroom. There were inevitable changes; many of the senior staff and management left, departments were closed down or 'streamlined', enormous funds were found to invest in the hotels, and profitability increased at the same time. The year 1995 saw hotels emerge out of the depths of recession and into a period of recovery. London hotel profits rocketed – an exciting time for a new broom.

Just before the new Savoy Managing Director arrived, Forte won its nine-month battle for control of Meridian, the international chain of luxury hotels. A little over a year later Granada successfully bid £3.3 billion for Forte, Britain's largest hotel group. At the takeover Forte held 68 per cent of the total equity in the Savoy company, and 42 per cent of the votes. The balance of the shares are held by 'independent shareholders'.

The institution has always been greater than the sum of its parts. Like a Wagnerian opera or a Shakespeare play, this Savoy operetta could transcend even the most eccentric staging. Long may it be said that 'Claridge's Hotel (Ltd.) still waves'.

12

'When Every One is Somebodee, Then No One's Anybody'*

When Giles Shepard invited me to join Savoy Hotels in 1984, I told him that I was 58 and would therefore expect only a few years at the helm of Claridge's. He seemed satisfied that seven years would give me enough time to make my mark on the hotel and steer it through the remainder of the 1980s into a new decade. In the event, the seven years became ten.

While Shepard made the initial decision to hire me and my appointment was approved by the board of directors, there still remained an interview, albeit a formality, with Sir Hugh Wontner. I was summoned to luncheon in the penthouse with Sir Hugh and subjected to the first of many history lessons – on Claridge's, the Savoy, Sir George Reeves-Smith, who had chosen the young Hugh Wontner as his successor, and the background of the D'Oyly Carte and Savoy companies. Sir Hugh was only the third controller of the Savoy since the company was formed in 1889. Richard D'Oyly Carte had handed over the reins to George Reeves-Smith, having bought the Berkeley Hotel in order to obtain the young manager's services. Reeves-Smith was knighted for his contribution to the hotel industry, and chose as his own successor the young Hugh Wontner in 1941, the year I started work in the hotel industry at the age of 14. When Sir Hugh, himself knighted in 1972, handed over as Managing Director to Giles Shepard in 1979, Shepard became Managing Director of the company, while Sir Hugh was appointed Chairman.

I was concerned about having Sir Hugh and Lady Wontner living over our heads, so to speak. Resident directors have, in my experience, a habit of giving the benefit of their advice at all sorts of times of the

---

* Gilbert & Sullivan, *The Gondoliers*

day and night. But this was not the Savoy way. Sir Hugh visited only twice a week, always at the same time – Tuesday morning and Saturday morning if he stayed in town.

The routine with the Savoy company was that the four London hotel managers (Claridge's, the Savoy, Berkeley and Connaught) had a visit each day from a different director. I had Mr. Shepard on Mondays and Wednesdays, Sir Hugh Tuesday and Saturday, Victor Emery, then marketing director and Sir Hugh's son-in-law, on Thursday, and Martin Radcliffe, the director responsible for legal affairs, on Friday.

My years at British Transport Hotels had taught me that directors who made such frequent and regular visits could be mischief-makers if left without something on which to focus their attention. On my desk at Claridge's sat a little soapstone seal, a gift from a Canadian guest. I used 'Lionel', as he was dubbed, as a paperweight, and my method of dealing with the directorial visits was simple. I used to imagine the directors were seals in a zoo. To keep seals happy, what do you do? You throw them a fish! Seals catch fish, clap their flippers together and go: 'Ooh, ooh, ooh . . .'

I carefully collected fish for my seals, so that every morning at 10.00 or 10.30 I would have something ready to discuss with them, arising from recent events in the hotel, to keep them contented and well fed. The really important matters would be discussed at board level or at formal meetings convened for a particular purpose, but these were the opportunities for testing the water of new ideas. I learned long ago that what mattered, if there was something I wanted to do, was to get it done. It mattered not a jot whether I was given the credit, so long as I achieved the desired result. So I would always present an idea with an alternative, all the while pushing the main idea in a subtle way. Sir Hugh, for it was usually he who had the last word, could then choose from the two and take credit for the wisdom of his choice.

Dealing with the guests was an altogether more straightforward task.

True to its royal heritage, my first day at Claridge's had brought my first king and queen. After a gap of 15 years I was once again dressed in black tailcoat and pinstriped trousers, as were all the Claridge's management team.

Bob Lund Hansen was still in his office tying up loose ends before he finally retired. I had been perched all morning at a small table on a hard chair while he passed on nuggets of information. By lunchtime I was itching to be 'out front' meeting guests, taking the pulse of the hotel, observing how the staff dealt with day-to-day affairs. As I passed the small seating area outside the Causerie, the more informal of the two restaurants, I noticed an elderly man, round-faced and rather large, quietly reading a newspaper. He looked up and caught my eye, and as I always did, I said: 'Good morning, sir. Is there anything I can do for ·you?'

He smiled, said: 'No thank you' and went back to his paper.

A few minutes later one of the assistant managers remarked: 'Ah, I see you know the King of Norway.'

I remained, rather impressed, in the front hall, nodding to lunchtime arrivals, among whom was an elegantly dressed lady of mature years. I bowed and bid her welcome. 'Queen Ingrid of Denmark,' somebody hissed in my ear, 'the Danish Queen Mother.'

'Good morning, Your Majesty.' I caught on, just in time.

'Good morning,' responded Queen Ingrid with a smile. 'I do hope you are going to take such good care of us as Mr Hansen did. My daughter and son-in-law are often here.' Daughter and son-in-law? Of course – ex-King Constantine and Queen Anne Marie of Greece!

Two days later I was dealt a royal flush; not one but three queens – and three kings – making themselves at home in The Causerie. There were the Kings of Norway, Greece and Spain, and Queens Ingrid, Anne Marie of Greece and Sofia of Spain. As they served themselves from the smorgasbord buffet, I rang Eve upstairs and demanded: 'What on earth do you call an ex-king?'

She wasn't sure either, but said she imagined 'Once a king, always a king. Assume "your Majesty"'. She was right, Kings and queens are easy: you don't have to run the gauntlet of remembering whether a prince or princess is 'Your Royal Highness', 'Your Highness', 'Your Serene Highness' or even 'Your Imperial Highness', depending on the throne they represent.

People are often curious about what it's like to meet celebrities, Royals, heads of state. Once you have the protocol right, you soon realise that however important they are, most people want the same things when they visit a hotel: a warm welcome, recognition, attention to their needs. (But the higher the rank, the deeper the bow . . .) I have seldom met anybody who did not respond to this, and when they did not, there was usually a reason: illness, depression, sadness and only very occasionally, ignorance.

An elderly American couple came to stay for a week at Claridge's. The wife was charming, her husband utterly objectionable. Nothing we could do was right. The receptionist showed him five different suites and in the end he settled for the first one he had been shown. He was cantankerous with the waiters, obnoxious in the foyer, rude to the valet. I was appealed to on more than one occasion and approached the man with as much tact as I could muster, determined he was not going to rattle me. He tried, and I refused to give way to the angry retort that was on the tip of my tongue.

On the day they left, while sir was settling their account, his wife asked if she could have a word with me. She wanted to thank me and the staff, she explained, for being so unfailingly kind to her husband. He had been seriously ill for six months and although now well enough to travel, the prognosis was not good. This would probably be his last trip.

This illustrates why I always train young people to look for the reason behind unreason. Be 'other minded' and you usually find an explanation for even the worst behaviour.

Royalty and heads of state are seldom difficult or demanding, although the recently elevated can be trying, as was Major Ronald Ferguson after his daughter became Duchess of York. From being a client of charm and consideration, he became demanding and aggressive. The Duchess and her father had been regular lunchtime visitors to the Causerie since she was a small girl, always looked after by Gert Nielsen, the Danish head waiter who is also a top international breeder and judge of boxer dogs. Gert paid the Duchess the ultimate compliment of naming one of his bitches Fergie during her wedding year. . .

The Queen and the Queen Mother were unfailingly charming and thoughtful. I recall the Queen Mother aged 89 stepping out of her limousine. As I waited to escort her into the hotel, she inclined her head in the direction of her – somewhat younger – lady-in-waiting and said, 'Let's just wait for dear Mary. She's not too good on her feet.'

When she lunched at Claridge's, the Queen Mother would eschew the private entrance and walk in by the front door, smiling as she slowly made her way through the main lounge. Without any prompting, everybody in the room would stand while she passed, as a small mark of respect for a great lady. The Hungarian Quartet would strike up *Teddy Bears' Picnic*, one of her favourite tunes, and she would beam at the musicians as she passed.

190

Only Dame Barbara Cartland failed to respond to the Queen Mum's charm – and that was due to her failing eyesight. Dame Barbara, a great supporter of Claridge's, lunched there every Wednesday on smoked salmon and pojarski of chicken. Dressed in flowing pastel chiffon and teetering in sling-back high-heeled shoes, her heavily powdered face looking, as somebody once put it 'as though two black crows had crash-landed into the white cliffs of Dover', she is hard to miss.

Every week I would meet her in or greet her at her table near the door, and she would flirtatiously bat those awesome eyelashes at me. I was flattered – until I overheard her say to the restaurant manager: 'Who *is* that nice young man who always comes and chats to me?'

One Wednesday when the Queen Mother walked through the restaurant she spotted her fellow-nonagenarian and paused by her table to nod and smile. Dame Barbara took no notice but was heard to mutter, 'Who was that, dear?' to her discomfited lunch companion.

Like Her Majesty the Queen, the Queen Mother's down-to-earth side includes the enjoyment of food and wine. The Queen Mum enjoys an apéritif before luncheon. Usually Dubonnet and gin – but 'easy on the Dubonnet', we're advised. She appreciates a glass of white wine and perhaps a glass of red with her meal, but refuses sweet wine with the pudding, sometimes saying: 'Oh no thank you, no more wine . . . perhaps a small glass of champagne if there is any?'

The Queen and Prince Philip enjoy a very dry martini before dinner and wine with their meal, but one lunchtime visit Prince Philip took us by surprise by asking for a brown ale! Not much call for that at Claridge's, and the barman had to search his store cupboards for a dusty bottle – and pray that HRH didn't ask for seconds. Princess Margaret favours Famous Grouse whisky with mineral water and two cubes of ice. Except, that is, when on the wagon, when she insists on mixing for herself a cocktail of lemon barley, fresh lemon juice and soda. One way, I suppose, to ensure your drink is never spiked.

While she is not my favourite Royal, I have a creeping sympathy for the Princess: it's difficult to imagine how tedious many Royal engagements must be without the uplifting effects of a judicious amount of alcohol.

At the same time, strong drink is often responsible for the appalling behaviour of the self-styled aristocracy. Like most hoteliers, I have often tolerated and sometimes been enthralled by eccentricity.

But there are limits. At Claridge's the limit was reached by an ostentatiously wealthy European and his wife . He was of Mediterranean descent, she was of central European origin (probably Transylvania, my wife unkindly remarked) and considerably younger than her husband. They made a profession out of enjoying themselves. Her wardrobe, which took up a small corridor, was catalogued in order of designer from Amies to Yves St Laurent. They rose late, partied late and returned late in the chauffeured limousine they retained throughout their visit. I thought I had heard everything when it was reported by the night manager that sir, arriving 'home' in the small hours, had relieved himself in one of the floor-standing ashtrays by the door of the lift (and only a few steps away from the gents cloakroom) but it wasn't the first time. Previously it had been a plant pot. Madame was spoken to and assured us it would not happen again.

However, one weekend a quiet American couple who had been enjoying dinner rushed out of the restaurant mid-meal, clamouring for fresh air. The husband explained to the head waiter who followed them that they had just seen a man in the party at a table close by unzip his trousers and relieve himself on the dining room carpet.

The offenders were disagreeable, complained constantly, and I felt Claridge's could do without them. They had been threatening for long enough to stay elsewhere. After the incident in the restaurant I approached the Managing Director for permission to show them the door, but the decision was to take no action, since we were well into a period of recession and could not afford to turn away guests who paid top prices for the best suite.

Another eccentric I had little time for was Lady 'Bubbles' Rothermere, who would clamber out of her limousine in ballgown and sneakers, clutching her shoes in one hand, a bottle of Cristal Brut part-consumed in the other, to tide her over until she could commandeer fresh supplies. Heaven help any new waiter who did not understand her slurred appeals for more as the evening went on.

The elderly owner of one of the largest private estates in Switzerland was a contender for the title of most irascible guest. She complained about everything, from the cost of a phone call to her friend Margaret Thatcher's dress sense, always haggled over her room rate (as the mega-wealthy often do) and even after we allowed her a reduced rate, was never satisfied. After countless threats she took herself off to the Connaught, stayed for four nights and said that was even worse and she would require her old room back forthwith!

She used to sit in the foyer and subject anyone who approached her to a very obvious once-over. Nobody had any style these days, she complained. Yet she always seemed to wear exactly the same outfit, a Chanel suit, and the same jewels, whenever she went out, day or evening. She enjoyed dropping into conversation that she had lent her sable hat to the Prime Minister for her official visit to Moscow. I often wondered if Lady Thatcher enjoyed her company so much because she made almost as much fuss of Mark Thatcher as his mother did. He would have been a hot contender in the 'most ill-tempered' stakes. His Texan wife Diane seemed a sweet girl, but his arrogance and lack of even the most basic courtesy made him the antithesis of his parents. Denis was always a wonderful guest, cheerful and considerate and apt to refer to 'my darling wife', and Lady Thatcher in her Prime Ministerial days was unfailingly courteous, as she had been when I first met her at the Athenaeum Hotel when she was Education Minister.

It was a source of great satisfaction to me to be able to welcome to Claridge's a number of visitors I had helped look after at other hotels in years past. I remembered Mrs Vernon Sangster, and her late husband, the football pools magnate and racehorse owner, from the Adelphi Hotel in Liverpool after the war, when they used to host a lavish annual party. At one of these I was taken aside by Sam Wood, who told me he had been listening to a young girl with a wonderful voice practising for a performance at the party. 'You've got to listen to her,' Sam said, knowing my fondness for music. 'She is going to be a star.' Just before cabaret time I stationed myself behind a screen in the Derby Room and listened to this beautiful soprano voice. The singer was Julie Andrews. She, too, became a regular guest at Claridge's, as charming and considerate as she was lovely, looking at least 20 years younger than any woman of similar age.

We were fortunate in having a high proportion of repeat guests at Claridge's, but when I first took over the reins there were also several permanent residents. These can be the bane of a hotelier's life, but it's easy to see both sides. When people, usually elderly, live in a hotel suite it becomes their home, full of treasured possessions if not always their own furniture. They expect more say in the way things are run than occasional visitors; they dislike change; tend to regard staff as personal retainers. They may resent it when favourite chairs or vantage points are taken by other people, and they expect to be first in line for the attention of management and staff. Sometimes hardest of all to cope with, they suffer from menu fatigue. No matter how fine the cuisine or how brilliant the chef, if you eat it three times a day for years, it can pall.

We were fortunate in our permanent guests. Although they were elderly and often infirm, they were in the main aristocratic rather than autocratic. Sir Malin and Lady Sorsbie towards the end of their lives would invite Eve and me to take a glass of sherry before dinner, for which they dressed formally every night, although they dined alone in their suite. They had both led fascinating and adventurous lives in Africa, Sir Malin had been a pilot with the Royal Flying Corps and a founder of BOAC, and Lady Sorsbie, American by birth, had had numerous adventures, some of them bringing her close to violent death, during her years in Africa. After a stroke confined him to a wheelchair and restricted his speech, Sir Malin refused to leave his suite, and spent his last years living above us at Claridge's.

Sir Anthony and Lady Hornby also lived there until their deaths, which, like the Sorsbies', came fairly rapidly one after the other. Sir Anthony was a charmer and a scholar and must once have been a most handsome man, Lady Hornby a former ballet dancer of some renown.

The last of our permanent residents was Mr Richard Shannon, a racing man of advanced years but robust health for most of my tenure. Even he, sadly, became very ill and frail and required a round-the-clock nurse for the last few months of his life. After the deaths of those five, we refused requests from people who wanted to take up permanent residence at Claridge's.

The twin to Sir Hugh Wontner's penthouse was retained year-round by Greek shipping millionaire Stavros Niarchos. The suite's walls were hung with his own works of art, the bathroom and bedroom stocked with supplies of his copious medications. Occasionally he would lend the suite to friends, like the late Yul Bryner's widow, when they came to London on short visits, but Niarchos himself would use it only once or twice a year.

We always received word in advance of his visits, and at Christmas his secretary would distribute lavish gratuities to the staff, but it used to strike us as such a waste of a luxurious and spacious suite. It still had to be serviced every day, the bed- and bathroom linen changed, air-conditioning kept in order. It irked us even more on sunny summer days, when I was obliged to stay in London at weekends, that here was a beautiful roof terrace complete with recliners, flowers and plants for shade, and absolute privacy, not being used, while we had only Hyde Park in which to take the sun.

Only once did we yield to the temptation to 'borrow' the Niarchos roof terrace. It was midsummer, 80 degrees, and I had to work over most of the weekend. On the Sunday afternoon I said to hell with it, the hotel is quiet, there's nobody in either penthouse – let's just go up and sunbathe for an hour or two.

We entered the penthouse, double-locking the door behind us, and walked through the sitting room and out of the French windows, then set up two recliners in the sun and stripped off. I dozed happily and Eve looked at the Sunday papers, but she didn't feel comfortable. After less than an hour she urged me to get dressed and leave. We gathered up our things, folded the sunbeds and stepped over the threshold just in time to hear somebody banging on the sitting-room door. Thinking fast, Eve grabbed a pencil and notebook off the desk and pantomimed taking notes while I hastily flung open the door – to admit a florist, watering can in hand, who had come up to tend the flowers and planters on the terrace (at least, that's what she said).

* * *

One of the things I love most about running hotels is that no day is the same as any other. There are very few aspects of the job that I disliked, with the possible exception of paperwork. I am convinced paperwork not only proliferates – it breeds! Haven't you noticed that if you leave two pieces of paper in your in-tray and turn your back, there are 17 when you look again? I have always believed in 'management by walking about' on the basis that every minute spent on paperwork is a minute spent away from the guests, the staff – all those elements that make up the heartbeat of the hotel.

I am suspicious of hotel managers, who are after all innkeepers, who hide in their offices behind mounds of paper or a VDU, or spend hours of every day in 'meetings'. Of course in today's world there are letters and memoranda to be read and written, reports to be formulated, numbers to be crunched and forecasts to be made, *ad nauseum*. The days are long gone when the innkeeper could stand in front of his inn, apron around his ample paunch, arms folded across his chest, beaming a warm welcome or waving a cheery farewell. Still, office work remains a chore, one to be got through when time away from the real business of hotel-keeping allows.

There is no such thing, then, as a typical day. You *may* start the day by popping into the office to cast an eye over the log books which record incidents from each department from the night before, and which form the basis of the morning meeting a little later. Then, the lift up to the top floor to inspect all the room service points on each floor.

Are the breakfast rolls warm? Have the orders fallen behind, need we transfer staff from another floor to help out? How do the room-service breakfast trolleys look – silverware and glasses clean and sparkling? The correct glasses used for orange juice? And the coffee: is it fresh and strong enough, the toast warm and crisp?

Down to the kitchen next, to shake hands with the breakfast cooks, test the scrambled eggs. Something positive, to show you're interested. Enquiring at the same time how your early morning staff are today, taking a genuine interest in their welfare, their families.

For me, a visit to the goods receiving bay now and again is a must, to make a random check of the quality of goods coming in, even if it's only one item. Then, remembering that the outside of the building is the first thing the guest sees, I might take a quick walk around the front and back of the hotel. Are the correct flags being flown? Are they clean, unfurled properly – and the right way up? Revolving doors should be gleaming, brasses polished, and the doormen immaculate with shined shoes, top hat at the right angle and, most important, a welcoming smile.

Breakfast service is in full swing in the restaurant by now, and I may discreetly check a couple of tables, notice if the lighting is correct, carpets free of crumbs, and staff uniforms standing up to close scrutiny in the early morning sunlight. Being sure to notice, too, if any business guests look impatient or cross or seem to be trying to catch a waiter's eye. An unsatisfactory breakfast experience can start the day on the wrong foot – and lose you customers.

Into the front hall then to see if the cashiers are looking wide awake and that somebody with tact and knowledge is around to answer questions and say farewell to departing guests. If *you're* there, then *you* do it. Quarter to nine and you've got 15 minutes to have your own breakfast. Just after nine, a briefing meeting with key heads of department, using the log books which I have introduced into every hotel I managed, to review the previous 24 hours and to plan the next. To keep the meeting truly brief – nobody sits down. This backfired once when a new female department head sagged to the floor after a few minutes. We ascertained that she was not pregnant but a week or two later, she did it again! I'm sure her father branded me an ogre, but if young people can't keep on their feet for ten minutes then a hotel is hardly the right place for them. The morning meeting is one of the best forums for encouraging ideas for improvement from key staff. When you speak, you learn nothing. When you listen, you learn everything.

This might be a day for room inspections – but only after the mail is dealt with. Correspondence used to be a leisurely affair; reservations were made, often far in advance, by letter, dealt with manually and responded to within the week. With the advent of the telephone, then telex and now fax and E-mail, everything demands instantaneous response. Letters of complaint, though you hope there won't be many, also deserve a same-day reply, even if it is just to say: 'Thank you for letting me know. We are very sorry, investigating, and will send a fuller reply within the week.'

The technical services manager or maintenance engineer, housekeeper and assistant manager might now be waiting to view today's block of rooms for inspection, and together we record our findings on the state of the furnishings, the decor, the plumbing, the cleanliness, and anything else that needs attention, so that a prioritised plan can be made and action taken by the appropriate departments. When I started work in hotels, a good housekeeper would don white cotton gloves and run her fingers along flat surfaces, ledges, tops of cupboards and window sills. I still believe in the 'white glove test', though sharp eyes will suffice. Rest assured, if you don't have the sharp eyes, somebody else will. One of the banes of a hotelier's life is the annual visit of the guidebook inspector. Murphy's law dictates that the Michelin inspector, who checks in anonymously, always ends up with the worst room in the house. The AA inspector doesn't get his morning newspaper. The RAC man leaves his shoes outside the bedroom door and they don't get cleaned (though with some of the shoes they wear it's difficult to tell. . .) It takes all the diplomatic skills you possess to talk them round next morning when they declare themselves after paying the bill. It's so easy to tell people what is *wrong* with their hotel. Most of the time we *know* what is wrong. The difficult thing – and the reason inspectors are inspectors and not hoteliers (though some are failed hoteliers) – is to put all of them right immediately.

It may be nearly mid-day now, and the chef expects a visit to discuss the menus and to look at the printed menus for any special parties – has the content, the French, been checked? Together we take a look at the banqueting suites which have been set up for luncheon, and speak to the senior staff.

At least twice a week I lunch in the staff restaurant, but when time is short I just take a look at the hot dishes and the cold buffet before calling in on the restaurant managers to see who is expected for luncheon and which guests need to be met in by me. Wednesday at Claridge's was Barbara Cartland's day for lunching in the main restaurant, other celebrity guests had their regular days for visiting the Causerie, but if Princess Diana or the Duchess of York were to lunch informally with friends, we always had a tip-off from the Palace.

A quick inspection of the restaurants, then, a look at the splendid sweet trolley and a mental note to congratulate the chef patissier who has done such a good job. Good patissiers are the hardest of all chefs to find and to hang on to. Encouragement, as always, helps.

The luncheon hour is a time for the manager to be around in full public view, to give a personal welcome to guests as they arrive, to encourage future bookings for meals, meetings, social gatherings. A good hotelier is a good salesman, too, and it's no good having the finest facilities in the world if the guests don't know about them.

By 2.00 you feel you've earned your own lunch. On a particularly busy day this might be a sandwich at your desk or if you're lucky, one course in your apartment followed by an hour with your feet up and the newspaper. Late afternoon you hope to spend 15 or 20 minutes each with the sales manager, the personnel manager, the financial controller and the IT manager. It's no good having style without profits, and a top-flight accountant is essential. Equally, in today's computerised world, the information technologist is indispensable. The biggest difference between them is that whereas new ledgers and adding machines were mere drops in the ocean and seldom needed replacing, the IT manager is always asking for unbelievably expensive new computer hardware and software. According to him, the normal lifespan of a computer is measured in months rather than years, and his budgets read like science fiction.

In the afternoon there is often a meeting scheduled with, say, the other general managers in the group, or with local organisations, charities, or head office. These could be convened to discuss a range of topics from plans for a new London rail service to a charity ball, through major refurbishment of the hotel, to sales and marketing budgets for the company. When that is over I find it a calming exercise to look in on afternoon tea service in the main lounge. Is business brisk, or does it seem quieter than usual? Why might this be? Points to discuss with the lounge head waiter, the sales people and the receptionists and porters. Do they all 'sell' the hotel's afternoon tea?

In city hotels tea is a useful as well as an elegant occasion. We should never underestimate the importance of the ladies who shop. They can be great ambassadors for the hotel, bringing business to the restaurant and the banqueting suites. Also, it's a constant source of puzzlement to me that more business people don't take advantage of grand hotels for entertaining. People tend to think in terms of expensive luncheons or dinner, but who would thank you for three courses in a local bistro or wine bar, when they could be entertained for the same outlay – or less – to a sumptuous British breakfast; lavish afternoon tea with sandwiches, home-made scones, cakes and pastries; or an elegant glass of champagne with canapes to the sound of music in the early evening?

Before the end of the afternoon, you might snatch an hour or two to deal with the mail and sort out the paperwork. Don't imagine for a moment that you'll be left alone to get on with it! With an open door policy people know they can come to your office at any time – and they do. There might be dozens of interruptions in the course of the afternoon, and most deserve to be dealt with on the spot. Meanwhile, guests will be arriving and departing and some will demand your personal attention. The office staff leave for the day in the early evening, and you nip upstairs or home for a quick shower and change of clothes.

Back in the hotel before the main business of the evening begins, I like to spend time with the restaurant and banqueting managers, the wine butlers and the chef; try to visit every department in the kitchen before dinner, to have the finished dishes described to me and use a teaspoon to test the sauces. This not only encourages the cooks, but gives me the confidence and the ability to describe dishes to a guest. The restaurant managers will have briefed the waiters, who should also have tasted some of the dishes. How do the banqueting rooms look? Who is on the guest list? Are the musicians ready to strike up for the evening? Soon you will be able to enjoy one of the most satisfying aspects of a hotelier's life: watching your guests have a wonderful time knowing that you have been instrumental in stage-managing the show.

Before going off duty for the night I like to have a final walk around, just feeling the pulse once more. This is *my* style of hands-on, face-to-face 'management by walking about'. Other hotel managers might argue that it's out of date, and that 'empowerment' of more junior staff, while they sit in their office as a kind of adjudicator and advisor, to impartially chair meetings, is a management style more in keeping with the 1990s. In my opinion – and I have experienced the technique at first hand in many hotels in the US as well as a few in this country, 'empowerment', rather than shared responsibility, fosters mediocrity. The hotels stand out like a beacon where somebody is clearly in charge to offer firm leadership and authority. Think of an army without leadership, where soldiers are 'empowered' to act for themselves, and think of chaos.

13

'The Privilege and Pleasure That We Treasure Beyond Measure'*

In our 'annexe to Buckingham Palace' banqueting once again played a major role, just as it had in the Adelphi Hotel and the Midland in Manchester.

State banquets were, if not exactly ten a penny, frequent and always exciting occasions. The hotel, and the staff, positively preened before a special event. The air of suspense was palpable for the whole day in anticipation of the satisfaction that comes from the most elegant occasions being stage-managed with streamlined efficiency.

Protocol demands that when foreign heads of state come to London on an official visit they stay at Buckingham Palace as guests of Her Majesty for only three nights, usually Tuesday, Wednesday and Thursday. After that, the VIP visitors would normally stay at either their embassy or at Claridge's. On the first or second night of their visit they are entertained by the Queen at a royal banquet, and the visitors reciprocate with a banquet to return Her Majesty's hospitality. Claridge's is often chosen for this because of the expertise the hotel staff have gained over the years in entertaining royalty and heads of state.

My ten years at Claridge's saw banquets hosted by the Heads of State of Poland, Mexico, Zimbabwe, Malawi, United Arab Emirates, Gambia, Turkey, Saudi Arabia, Nigeria and Morocco, and a host of official visits where the monarch or president might call on Her Majesty or the Prime Minister, but stayed at the hotel with their entourage. These included President Mubarak of Egypt, the Crown Prince and Princess (later the Emperor and Empress) of Japan, and a delegation of Chinese members of parliament. Virtually all the world's reigning monarchs and ex-monarchs

---

*Gilbert & Sullivan, *The Gondoliers*

stayed on purely private visits, as did Presidents Bush, Reagan, Carter and Nixon. All four were perfectly charming guests, but while President Nixon made one of the finest after-dinner speeches I ever heard, addressing a high-powered audience for 40 minutes without notes, President Carter's speech wins the medal for the most tedious and uninspired.

State or official banquets often bring in their wake diplomatic 'incidents' which tax patience to the limit.

A former President of Nigeria flew in his lady cook to teach our chef how to make the President's favourite soup – a potent concoction of cabbages, potatoes and sausage, which he wanted to serve to Her Majesty at his official banquet. Our chef, Marjan Lesnik, a young Slovenian whose own diplomatic skills left little to be desired and who was well aware of Her Majesty's predilection for simple food, especially at dinner, managed discreetly to turn this into a veritable 'dainty dish to set before the Queen' even if it was not quite appreciated by the President.

Worse – much worse – was to follow on the occasion of the most memorable banquet which King Hassan of Morocco gave in the Queen's honour in 1987. In this job you learn to expect the unexpected. Arrangements for the banquet were made with the usual skill and seemingly effortless aplomb of Claridge's impeccably trained staff. We had been visited by the Lord Chamberlain and representatives from the embassy to settle preliminary details: the provisional numbers to attend, the protocol, outline table arrangements, menu and wines (or in this case, fruit juices), the flowers and, of course, security. The Moroccans' initial request to fly in live lambs, goats and pigeons for the traditional couscous to be served at the banquet was politely and firmly refused. Our Southdown lamb and wood pigeons from our best suppliers would, we assured them, meet with their approval.

From then on, arrangements began to assume, if not nightmarish, certainly bizarre, proportions. We made every effort to ascertain exactly how many guests would be attending, precisely which dishes would be served and, since Morocco is a Muslim country and therefore no alcoholic beverages would be required, which drinks. The response was always the same. His Majesty's major domo with a disarming smile would tell us: 'The King will decide.' Assuming the King's decision would be faxed through from Morocco well in advance of the event, Andrew Phillips, the usually unflappable banqueting manager, and the whole team waited. And waited. King Hassan arrived in England and stayed with his entourage in Brighton for a few days before his official visit. Still we heard nothing. 'Please do not worry,' the major domo assured us at each fresh enquiry. 'The King will decide.'

By the time the King had moved to Buckingham Palace and *still* had not decided, we were becoming seriously anxious. These affairs are planned down to the last detail. When the Queen comes to dinner, nothing is left to chance. With only 48 hours to spare, we were given most but by no means all of the information we needed. Last-minute details of table service, guest lists and other items would be confirmed 'very soon, very soon, Mr Jones'.

The King's entourage had by then moved into Claridge's – ministers, doctors, advisers, secretaries – with their own team of male and female cooks straight from the King's palace kitchens to prepare their meals in our chef's domain. The cooks, squatting cross-legged on the tiled floor, constantly clamoured for more space, more utensils, more help. They had been billeted in an assortment of London hotels, but as more and more people connected with the King arrived from Morocco, not eligible to stay at Claridge's but with seniority over the cooks, so these poor devils had to give up their accommodation. On my last walk around the hotel at midnight, I stumbled across heaps of sleeping people wrapped in djellabas and sprawled over the stone-flagged passage leading to the fire exit in Brooks Mews, or squatting outside the bedroom doors of the Moroccan visitors.

On the day of the banquet, the uniformed and plain-clothes police arrived in unmarked vans, dog handlers and sniffer dogs checked all the public areas of the hotel and the bedrooms and suites above the banqueting area. The labradors and spaniels would go wild every time they discovered chocolate wrappers in a wastepaper basket, but to our relief they never managed to sniff out anything more alarming.

The banqueting suites were made ready: hundreds of yards of white linen tablecloths starched 'stiff as a nun's knickers on the day of judgement' arrived from the Savoy laundry on rollers so they could be spread directly on to the tables without creases. Silver place settings and candelabra were polished, glassware sparkled, as did the chandeliers overhead, each place setting was laid precisely in alignment, glasses in a straight line, floral arrangements in the Moroccan national colours not so high as to obscure guests' views of each other or of the top table. Chairs were placed carefully not to disturb the folds of the tablecloths which draped to the floor, and each one tested to make sure no springs were broken, no creaks could be heard, and no splinters on the legs or tacks in the upholstery could snag the gowns of the ladies. Waiters, security-cleared and ready to change into black trousers, starched white jackets and white gloves were painstakingly briefed, haircuts and shoes inspected.

Mid-afternoon. The atmosphere electric with anticipation as it always was before a royal event, when the banqueting manager dashed into my office almost purple in the face.

'Sir! Sir!' he yelled, ignoring the fact that I was on the phone. Sensing an emergency I made my excuses and hung up. 'A coach has just pulled up outside the banqueting entrance. It's full of waiters. Moroccan waiters. In white robes and fezzes and curly-toed slippers. They say they've come to serve the banquet!' Into my mind came the words of the Chairman's lady when first she spied a coach at the side entrance to the hotel. 'A *charabanc*?' she intoned in the manner of Dame Edith Evans' 'a *handbag* . . .?' 'At *Claridge's*?'

At the last minute, explained the major domo, the King had decided . . . and ordered his personal staff to be flown over in his private jet to serve the banquet Moroccan-style. I did not look forward to explaining to our own brigade – who were by now, like racehorses in the slips, ready and rarin' to go – that their plum jobs had been snatched from under their noses. Our banqueting team took great pride in performing well on royal occasions. They would not like this.

British compromise won the day. The Moroccans, I decided, would serve the couscous and our staff would clear it away and serve the sweet.

Then we heard the King had made another last-minute decision. No cutlery would be required. It was traditional on formal occasions in Morocco to eat with the fingers. I drew the line. Her Majesty – *our* monarch – would have knife and fork and spoon as she always did. I instructed the staff to leave the silverware on the table but – just in case – to add silver finger-bowls strewn with rose petals to each place setting.

The banquet commenced, the couscous was served in giant earthenware pots, and we all held our breath. Fingers crossed behind my back, I waited to see what Her Majesty would do. There was an audible sigh of relief when, after only a momentary pause, she graciously picked up a spoon and fork, turned to King Hassan with a smile and said: 'May I help you?'

Because the affair was a 'dry' one, only mint tea, fruit juice and mineral water were offered. The mint tea was prepared in the room by

204

the Moroccan waiters using ornate silver samovars. After the main course they also placed floor-standing silver filigree incense burners in front of the top table. The perfume soon hung like a pall over the entire room, and we could see guests attempting discreetly to waft it away. We turned the air-conditioning up to full strength, but the whole ground floor area was soon permeated with the smell of burning incense, as was my suit next morning.

I felt certain the Queen and Prince Philip would have fortified themselves with an apéritif before leaving the Palace, but for the members of the Royal Household who, like us, were on duty throughout the evening and not dining with the royal party, I made sure there was a vacuum flask of very dry Martinis in my office, constantly replenished (and just as constantly emptied) to fortify them for the rigours of diplomacy.

As always, the Queen was an easy and unfussy guest. She puts people at their ease by never leaving them in any doubt about what needs to be done. At table, when the meal is coming to an end, we are trained to watch for her fingering her handbag. When she does that, it's a sign to us to throw open the doors connecting the banqueting suite with the withdrawing rooms where coffee – in this case more mint tea – and petits fours are served. The Queen will then circulate and speak to the people she hasn't talked to before, spending a relaxed moment or two with each before once again sending one of her 'signals', this time looking with slightly raised eyebrows towards the exit doors until someone, either I or a member of the Royal Household, who watch HM discreetly throughout the evening, gets the message – pretty swiftly if we've any sense. I stand by the open door until the Queen and her host make their way out. I then accompany them to the royal limousine and wait until Her Majesty is driven away.

The week before King Hassan and his entourage of 75 moved into Claridge's, his Paris decorator had arrived to 'transform' our Royal Suite. He intended to completely redecorate, but since the suite had only recently been redecorated by top designer David Laws, I once again had to draw the line and summon up another British compromise. We would allow the paintings on the walls of the suite to be replaced by works of art from the King's personal collection. Priceless objets d'art of silver, gold and glass were placed around the room, his own monogrammed ashtrays replaced ours, and Moroccan rugs were laid over our fitted carpet. The King's stereo system was installed, the air perfumed lavishly with l'Espace. And a giant adjustable throne, mounted on a pedestal and mirrored on three sides, set in the middle of the royal dressing room. At least that's what we thought it was, until the designer explained it was the King's personal barbering chair.

The King's own mattress was to be brought in, too, but the designer was apoplectic when he discovered it was lumpy and His Majesty had not slept well. We replaced it with one of Claridge's own de luxe, hand-made, ultra-firm mattresses and, with the tale of the princess and the pea in mind, we waited. His Majesty slept that first night at Claridge's 'as though on a cloud'. So well, in fact, that he ordered 24 mattresses to be made for him in the Savoy's factory in Mitcham, 12 to be delivered within the week.

Contrary to what we might have expected, King Hassan II was an agreeable and considerate guest. On the morning he left, a Saturday, he ordered all the staff who had looked after him to be lined up in the front hall so he could thank them personally. That was a problem, since most of the staff who had worked such long hours during His Majesty's visit were taking much-needed weekend leave. We rounded up everybody on duty – chambermaids, waiters, restaurant brigade, receptionists, porters and cashiers – and hoped he wouldn't notice. His Majesty shook everybody by the hand and departed in the royal limousine. At the back door, the group's luggage was loaded into an eight-wheel truck whose driver was heard to remark: 'All this just for bed and breakfast . . .'

A royal emissary the following week delivered lavish letters of praise and generous gratuities to be distributed with the King's thanks. He asked me if I would accept 'a small gift, a rug' and where I would like it delivered. Taking the description at face value, I thanked him and said the hall porter would be pleased to take it in for us. What arrived a few days later, carried between two hefty delivery-men was a fine carpet big enough for me to expect Cleopatra to emerge when it was unrolled. It graces our dining room today, and is never referred to as anything but 'the King's carpet'.

I think the happiest banquet hosted by a visiting head of state was that of the Polish President Lech Waleska in 1991. As is customary, the guest list included every available member of the Royal Family, most of the Cabinet, and leading members of the church and the establishment. It was a special privilege to observe the former shipyard electrician looking splendid in white tie and tails entertaining Her Majesty the Queen, and clearly relishing every minute of it. He seemed never to stop talking even during the banquet, yet Her Majesty looked more relaxed than I had ever seen her on these occasions, so he must have been good company. The beaming smile hardly left his face from the moment he greeted the Queen to the moment he waved goodbye at the ballroom door to the last guest. He walked back into the hotel, arm around his wife, with huge cigar and equally huge grin both firmly in place.

The question of who greets whom only once presented any difficulty for me. My job is to greet the royal or presidential personage as they step out of their limousine, and to escort them into the hotel, where their official host performs the formal greetings and introductions. I was briefed when I first arrived at Claridge's: 'You may shake hands with anyone you like, but not with Her Majesty.'

A photograph taken at the time shows me bowing to the Queen, hands plastered rigidly to my sides, as she steps smiling on to the pavement. The reason I look like a tailor's dummy is that I was trying so hard to behave contrary to my nature, which is to shake hands with everyone. To my discomfiture, the Queen immediately held out a dainty hand to be shaken, and by the time mine had windmilled into position, the moment had passed.

Perhaps I was lucky that on the night I failed to shake hands, Her Majesty was in a particularly happy frame of mind. Her middle son had been married earlier that day to Sarah Ferguson, and the Claridge's party was a private one hosted by the Queen's cousin, Lady Elizabeth Anson, for 'a few close family and friends' – 650, to be precise, including all the crowned heads of Europe, Nancy Reagan representing the President of the United States, and our entire Royal Family minus the bridal couple and the Queen Mother. Octogenarian bandleader Lester Lanin flew in from New York to play the Royal Family's favourite dance music. The ballroom and the banqueting suites were decorated in cheerful sunflower theme, and the combination of the toe-tapping music and the silk-canopied dance floor proved too much of a temptation; I sneaked my wife into the 'Royal Enclosure' and danced a foxtrot unnoticed, close-packed as commuters on a London underground train amongst the Queen and her family. Only those without soul could resist the rhythms of Lester Lanin, who never left the bandstand during five hours of continuous music. You had to be eagle-eyed to see the musicians discreetly glide off one at a time for a very short 'natural break'.

We left to return to our own guests and festivities in the hotel restaurant just as breakfast was being served at midnight, with all the Royals' favourite dishes – bacon, eggs and sausages, black pudding, fried bread and tomatoes; devilled kidneys, scrambled eggs with smoked salmon, kedgeree, fish cakes and baked beans. Washed down, of course, with copious quantities of champagne.

In the restaurant, hotel guests from all over the world enjoyed their own post-wedding celebrations at a spectacular dinner which included lobster and consommé, quails' eggs with truffles, baby lamb from Kent, and *Boite de Bijoux* Windsor, a favourite dessert of the Queen's which our chef had created in her honour – a jewel case fashioned from crisp biscuit pastry, filled with fresh berries, elderflower and champagne sorbet, and served with a purée of fresh raspberries.

The Queen spent much of the earlier part of the evening sitting on a green velvet love seat in the foyer of the banqueting suite with Nancy Reagan, watching television replays of the wedding. Royal-watching is a popular sport with the Royals, who like nothing better than to watch 'home movies'. When the Queen and Prince Philip celebrated their Ruby Wedding at Claridge's, black and white newsreel footage of their own wedding was relayed on monitor screens around the room.

Mrs Reagan nearly provided the only jarring experience on Prince Andrew's wedding day, when the US Embassy informed us that she would be arriving with 12 armed secret service agents. Only after we convinced them that our monarch had just two security men with her at all times did the embassy agree to reduce Nancy Reagan's minders – to four.

On these occasions hotels must make available a 'Royal retiring room', usually a suite of rooms on the first floor, and one for each male and each female member of the Royal Family. The rooms are almost never used, nevertheless we always had the head housekeeper, in black evening dress, standing by, to curtsey and lead the way in. For the Queen Mother, special hairpins and grips, face powder, silver-backed hair brushes as well as the usual lotions and potions were always provided.

Not all banquets at Claridge's were state or Royal occasions. And not all of them went as smoothly as we would have liked.

A lavish dinner and dance had been planned for 200 guests. At 6.30 p.m. final preparations in the ballroom were complete. The hostess arrived with the place cards. And the ceiling fell in. Not quite that suddenly, you understand. It began with a trickle of water down one wall at the back of the room. Within a few moments the trickle had become a flood. A workman repairing some ancient plumbing on the floor above had hacked through a mains water pipe. Soon the flood had become a Niagara. Every other banqueting suite was in use.

I started barking out orders, one to each person in the room: 'Turn off the water.' 'Divert the hostess.' 'Close the ballroom doors.' 'Send for scaffolding.' 'Call in the off-duty staff from their rooms to help mop up the floor and re-lay the tables.' 'Ring round the local hotels and borrow water pumps.'

That afternoon I had admired a huge display of flowers backed by trellising in our florist shop's window. I sent an assistant manager with keys to fetch the entire display. The housekeeper was told to bring every inch of net curtaining from store.

With the help of a motley band of willing on- and off-duty staff I got the scaffolding erected, draped it with dozens of yards of net curtaining, moved the band platform in front, and arranged the trellis, flowers and plants to make a dramatic display.

I then went to face the hostess, by now naturally anxious to check the room before her guests arrived, which could be any minute, and not understanding why she had been denied access. I let her do the talking and she did not give me a chance to explain. Perhaps just as well. I led her into the ballroom and her first comment was how beautiful the bandstand looked. 'What a *wonderful* bower of flowers! But Mr Jones, I did not order them. I hope I won't find them on the bill?'

I assured her they would be with the compliments of the management.

At one o'clock the band packed up and the guests left. Less than five minutes later, the combined movement of all our fingers uncrossing and the breeze from our sighs of relief must have been the last straw: the entire ceiling caved in under the weight of water.

The contractors who appeared early next morning sucked their teeth, shook their heads and declared the repairs would take a month. Once again I crossed my fingers behind my back and explained there was to be a Royal party in a week's time. We could move our other bookings, but not that. Again the slow shake of the head. 'Sorry, guv. No can do. No way. Impossible.'

I breathed the words that back then could still perform magic: 'Princess Diana.' She was to be guest of honour at a charity gala in seven days' time.

The contractors went into a huddle. Their chief came back and said. 'All right, sir. It means the lads will have to work round the clock, but for her – we'll do it.' She had that effect on people from all walks of life, but to observe her special gifts with those who needed cheering or reassurance was an even greater privilege.

Princess Diana's gift of communication with the sick and dying took on a very personal significance when a good friend and fellow-hotelier Jonathan Dale-Roberts was terminally ill with Aids in London's Middlesex Hospital. Jonathan had been general manager of the Hyde Park Hotel in London and, latterly, of the Continental Hotel in Sharjah. He returned home to face the final stages of his long illness. We had been told his death was a matter of a few weeks away, then a few days, then imminent. With his twin brother and sister-in-law we kept up a bedside vigil, sometimes spending the night on a nearby bed in the ward, at Sister's invitation, so somebody would be with him at all times. Jonathan lost consciousness and remained in a coma for several weeks – nobody could explain why he lingered.

On a sunny July day in 1991 Princess Diana visited the Middlesex with Barbara Bush, one of the most popular US First Ladies. Their official tour was almost over when one of the nurses from 'our' ward slipped out as the two VIPs were walking downstairs. 'Please – could you just step in and say hello to my patients? It would mean so much to us.' Without hesitation – and much to the consternation of the security men, Diana and Barbara strode into the ward, and while Mrs. Bush chatted to the young men in the main ward, Princess Diana was led into the side room which Jonathan occupied. She asked for a chair, sat down beside him, took hold of his hand and spoke quietly to him for a few minutes, calling him by his name and talking in a way that showed she firmly believed, as we did, that even in his coma he might still hear. Now and then she addressed a remark to his brother and his wife standing at the side of the bed.

Half an hour after the royal visit, we had a call from the hospital: Jonathan had died within ten minutes of Diana leaving his bedside. How appropriate that seemed for a man and a hotelier who in life would never have missed a royal visit!

In the early years of her marriage to the Prince of Wales, Princess Diana remained almost painfully shy, despite getting the biggest cheers from any crowd which assembled on her frequent visits to Claridge's. Her head hung and she always seemed to be looking down. However, it wasn't long before she visibly gained in confidence and self-assurance, and no woman ever sparkled more. Huge sapphire-blue eyes would gaze at you directly, her complexion was perfect English rose, lips which usually quirked upwards in a smile, palely coated and glossed. Even the nose sometimes criticised as too big looked simply noble to me! After our first meeting I became as besotted as the rest of the world.

During the time that Charles and Diana still looked at each other fondly, the pair attended a luncheon at Claridge's and arrived, uncharacteristically, a few minutes late. I met them as usual as they got out of the royal limo and escorted them inside. 'I hope we're not too late,' whispered Diana in an aside, inclining her head towards her husband who was talking to the host of the party. 'He needs to go to the loo!' I told her there was the customary Royal Retiring Room prepared on the first floor, but as we walked past the gents' cloakroom of the Ballroom, she asked: 'Can't he just go in there?' I agreed, Diana tapped her husband on the elbow, whispered to him, and we all waited outside while the Prince did what a Prince had to do.

The only time I can recall a Royal Retiring Room being used was during the King of Greece's 'multi-purpose party' in July 1986, when all Claridge's public rooms were used for this lavish royal family gathering. After dinner an aide came to tell me the Queen, Princess Di and the Duchess of York wanted to visit the Retiring Rooms.

The first-floor suites which had been set aside, one for each of them, necessitated a long walk from the banqueting room to the main elevator, which had an attendant. Instead, I decided to escort the royal ladies myself to the rather small, automatic elevator known as 'the ladies lift' which was much closer. I would operate the lift for them and keep my fingers crossed that it didn't break down, which it did from time to time. It was a tight squeeze, with Her Majesty and their Royal Highnesses in ballgowns and me in white tie and tails. They were all in high spirits, the Queen and Princess Di teasing Fergie about her rather over-elaborate flounced and bare-shouldered 'frock'.

When we reached the first floor I shepherded my royal flock through the long corridor where the head housekeeper, in long black evening dress, should have been standing by the door of the Royal Retiring Room. Instead, I saw her relaxing on a settee chatting to a chambermaid. I began waving my hand in a signal to her to get to her feet, hoping the royals behind me couldn't see. The housekeeper just stared, as if she couldn't imagine what I was doing there and why the G.M. was flapping his hands about. I was rather taken aback, since this lady was our resident authority on curtseying! She had herself been presented at Court, and was always called on when any visiting Americans were invited to the Palace, to instruct the ladies on how to curtsey. We were almost upon her when she caught on, leapt to her feet and appeared almost frozen with fright before she managed just in time to drop to a graceful curtsey before opening the door to the Retiring Room. Judging from the peals of laughter coming from inside and the fact that they didn't reappear for some minutes, the royals were clearly enjoying their relatives' special party.

One afternoon when Diana was due to attend a charity luncheon I walked outside to take a look at the crowd which always assembled when the Princess was expected. They were good-humoured, anxious to catch a glimpse from as close a vantage point as they could find behind the barriers, security men and photographers. I chatted with a few of the onlookers and discovered two elderly ladies so eager for a close-up view of Diana they were positively quivering with excitement. They had been standing there for nearly three hours and had travelled all the way from Brisbane, Australia, primarily to see the Princess at whatever official engagements she had scheduled that week. Each clutched a small bouquet of flowers to present to her. I thought such patience and perseverance deserved reward, and talked the Royal detective into making sure they kept their spot immediately behind the barriers. The detective also had a word with the Princess, and when she emerged an hour later she walked straight up to the two Australian ladies and chatted to them as though they were old friends, beaming down at them and saying how much she appreciated their having come 5,000 miles.

The ladies clearly enjoyed their conversation and were quite animated – until, that is, the Princess got back into her car, when one of them without warning, overcome by excitement and hours of standing, collapsed. She came round quite quickly, and I invited them both into the hotel for tea. They would, they said, remember that day for the rest of their lives: meeting Princess Di and enjoying afternoon tea at Claridge's as guests of the management!

Often the hosts of the events the Princess attended were men old enough to be her grand-father, but you could watch the twinkle appear in their eyes, the spring come into their steps, the moment they were confronted by this dazzling young woman who had the gift of making the person she was talking to feel they were the most important person in the world. She always addressed me by name and greeted me with a handshake and a huge smile, and said how much she enjoyed returning to Claridge's. Every member of staff she met during the event got a special word from her and she never failed to thank them, especially the junior members of the team whom few people noticed.

One of the Princess's charities held an auction at Claridge's, and many of the patrons and wealthy wellwishers donated jewellery and personal effects to be sold to the highest bidder. Towards the end of the evening, it was clear that although the auction had gone well, everybody had enjoyed themselves, and all the items would be sold, the organisers had not quite reached their target. Diana despatched her personal detective to Kensington Palace to fetch a porcelain trinket box which, if memory serves me right, belonged to Queen Mary. He was back within half an hour, the Princess's 'treasure' was auctioned for far more than it was worth, and the charity exceeded its target.

Diana's generosity of spirit never failed to impress me. From the beginning she was beloved by the crowds who assembled to catch a glimpse of her, and always got the loudest cheer, the biggest smiles, the most bouquets. Always, if there were small children or handicapped people or men or women in wheelchairs, Diana would make a bee-line for them and with a big smile immediately get down on one knee to be on their level while she chatted with them.

Even at Buckingham Palace Garden Parties, where the competition is stiff, Diana was the centre of attention. These are formal and formalised affairs – the kind for which the invitation and the 'having been' is vastly more enjoyable than the event itself. Several thousand people wait for up to an hour to be ushered through the Palace gates, under the archway, through a reception area and on to the lawns behind. There they mill about expectantly with fixed social smiles, tight with excitement, for another half-hour, ladies in new frocks and large hats purchased or borrowed for the occasion and seldom worn again, gents in grey or black morning suits. Except, of course, for the self-consciously left-wing making their token protest by sporting serviceable navy serge or grey flannel suits. The brilliant plumage of the ladies is matched here and there by splendid red, navy and gold-braided military uniforms and the traditional dress of diplomats from the African nations. All this is fine, of course, when the weather is. However, the English summer being what it is, sometimes it rains. Then, the squelch of stiletto heels aerating the Palace lawn and the combined aromas of wet wool, damp grass, and soggy feathers is all around you.

The members of the Royal Family on duty emerge from their Palace quarters to a fanfare from the military band, and the massed guests are shepherded into receiving lines four or five deep, with VIP and diplomatic guests put into cordoned-off pens at the end. A Palace official will tactfully 'pull out' somebody here and there and ask if they would like to be presented. He will then ask for a few personal details. As the Queen or Prince Philip or the Princesses make their stately way along their assigned rows, they may pause for an instant to say hello in a general way or briefly greet a few individuals. Then they'll chat for a moment or two with the guests pulled out by the Equerry.

'How far have you travelled today?' Or 'How long have you been in the Fire Service (or the Red Cross or the Army)?' they might ask. Perhaps, to the Mayor of a small town, 'We were there some years ago. You have a splendid Art Gallery. And the people were so kind . . . '

At the second Royal Garden Party we attended the line formed up to meet Princess Diana was twice as deep as that for all the other Royals. The rain was unexpected and torrential, all around us a sea of wet chiffon, uncurling hair-dos and damp trouser cuffs. Most people had umbrellas but they weren't terribly effective against the downpour. Diana, eyes sparkling, laughing and animated and utterly natural as always, ignored the fringe of blonde hair plastered to her forehead and held *her* umbrella to shelter the people she spoke to, while Palace officials did their best to keep her covered with theirs! She stopped before any disabled person for a special word.

One of the few embarrassing moments in which Princess Diana featured was when she was guest of honour at a luncheon for six in Claridge's restaurant hosted by H.M. King Constantine of Greece. We were asked to reserve the table immediately in front of the centre pillar, near the main entrance of the restaurant. At about 10.30 that morning it was reported to me that some evil-smelling liquid was oozing from the cracks in the marble cladding of the pillar. When the engineer removed the slab or marble, we discovered a crack in the ancient soil pipe behind. By 11am the aroma emanating from it could hardly be described as Chanel No. 5. Work began immediately to repair the damage, and the maintenance manager worked non-stop to erect a temporary covering over the pillar and hand-paint it to look like marble. Getting rid of the smell was more difficult. Windows were flung open, fans switched on, air conditioning turned up to maximum, and air fresheners, sprays and pot-pourri used lavishly. Mopping-up operations were completed just minutes before the special luncheon guests arrived, but if Princess Diana noticed how fragrant the restaurant seemed that day, she was sensitive enough not to remark on it.

214

In the late 1980s the hotel hairdressing salon was run by Princess Diana's personal hairdresser. He would go to Kensington Palace each morning the Princess was in London, and travelled with her on official and State visits overseas. Although protective and discreet where the Princess was concerned, he admitted to my wife one summer that the Princess of Wales was 'dreading' her upcoming four weeks holiday with 'the Firm', half of it to be spent on board the royal yacht Britannia. 'The last time she went,' he said, 'she cried every day. There are just too many egos on board. They fight all the time – just like any other family on holiday with the in-laws. There'll be black tie dinners in the officers mess, boring picnics on remote Scottish islands.

'All the Princess wants to do is spend a week or two at Highgrove with the boys, but she says the press would crucify her for not being with the Royal Family on the yacht or at Balmoral.

'She wanted to take her mother and sister and all the children to the Caribbean again, but she was told she would be criticised for that, too. She said: "Why does nobody ever think of me and what I want?"'

* * *

The Sultan of Brunei, owner of The Dorchester, held his children's birthday parties at Claridge's. For each one, our ballroom would be transformed – into the Land of Oz approached by a proper Yellow Brick Road one year; Alice's Wonderland the next, with white Shetland ponies and little carriages, and our banqueting waiters dressed as playing cards. My wife must have looked surprised when she saw our dignified banqueting head waiter, the late Bruno Ivaldi, the best I had known since Sam Wood, in such a get-up. He looked at her solemnly but with a glint in his eye. 'Mrs Jones,' he said. 'We'd dress up in bikinis for our guvnor if he asked us to . . .' Once they had a lavish circus theme with big top in the middle of the ballroom and Janet Jackson providing the cabaret. On another occasion when I was thankful to be on holiday, they transformed our grand ballroom into a Ninja Turtle Sewer complete with turtles.

A City stockbroking firm made another amazing transformation when they held a 1920s Prohibition Party for their staff and clients. The elegant entrance to the banqueting suite became a Chicago alleyway with trash cans, mangy (but not real) cats, ragged washing strung out on lines, and sleazy doorways with spyholes, on which guests dressed Al Capone-style with flapper-skirted molls on their arms, knocked then breathed the password before being admitted. Inside the 'speakeasy', smoke-filled and noisy, cocktails were served in thick china cups, and an adjoining room housed an illegal gambling den. Around midnight, they staged a most convincing kidnapping of the company president – and our banqueting manager – by thugs wielding machine guns. They roared away in three 1920s American cars, and an hour later returned their hostages, badly beaten up and bleeding, clothing ripped and realistic head and body wounds which must have alarmed any passing hotel guest.

King Constantine's multi-purpose party was a more elegant affair, a dinner to celebrate the King's forty-seventh birthday, the Queen's fortieth, their daughter's twenty-first, and the recent birth of their fourth child. Who says the royals don't make a little money go a long way!

The party proved more of a challenge than any of us had anticipated. The guest list included virtually every crowned head in Europe, clutches of ex-monarchs, and a couple of hundred mere titles. As the arrangements progressed, the numbers increased. We would be stretched to accommodate 350 guests for a champagne reception, formal dinner and dancing afterwards. The numbers reached 450 and the King admitted to me that every time he met somebody, he would invite them to his party.

Reluctantly, and for only the second time in Claridge's history, we assigned not only all the banqueting suites and the Foyer but also the restaurant to the King's guests, leaving only the Causerie, the smaller of the two restaurants, to cater for residents.

Sir Hugh made no secret of his displeasure that I had taken the decision to use the restaurant and Foyer and to cater for such large numbers, but I told him our hands were tied because each time King Constantine informed us numbers were up, the invitations had already been sent out.

Giles Shepard, the Managing Director, supported me but Sir Hugh was very annoyed. He felt we could not provide service up to the usual Claridge's standard for such large numbers. I, on the other hand, was confident our very experienced staff would rise to the challenge.

Sir Hugh said he knew the King sufficiently well – 'His Majesty used to greatly admire my daughter, you know, before either of them were married' – to send a hand-written letter saying he did not agree with the expansion of the numbers and if His Majesty insisted then the hotel would not be responsible for the standards of service.

Sod's Law dictated that this missive was delivered to His Majesty just five minutes before his guests arrived, as he emerged from the hotel suite he was using as a dressing room. The King was not amused. But then neither was I; the final guest headcount was just under 500. The story had a happy ending, for Claridge's marvellous staff *did* rise to the occasion, and the King's letter to me afterwards confirmed that his party had been a great success.

* * *

Life at Claridge's was not all balls and banquets! While we had our share of celebrity visitors, many film stars, pop singers and publicity-seekers found Claridge's too staid and too discreet for their liking, while our sister hotel, the Savoy, was linked up more closely to the media machine. The Savoy is altogether more glitzy. Show business people love it, while the stars who come to Claridge's tend to choose it because there they can be shielded from unwanted attention.

There are exceptions. Elizabeth Taylor stayed while she launched her new perfume, Passion, and her new boyfriend Larry Fortensky who later became (and subsequently un-became) the latest Mr Elizabeth Taylor. Miss Taylor's secretary was an infuriating woman. Nothing our patient and professional staff did was right for her or, she said, for Miss Taylor. They didn't like the suite, the food, the service. Their visit was punctuated by a stream of complaints. And yet, after they returned to the US, I had a letter from Elizabeth Taylor telling us how much she had enjoyed her stay and how well the staff had looked after her.

Clint Eastwood unwittingly caused a panic among the first-floor housekeepers. Romolo, our Peruvian room service waiter, who had a most mischievous sense of humour, told the maids to be careful: that Mr Eastwood had Clyde, the orang-utan from the film *Every Which Way but Loose*, with him in the Royal Suite. The maids went in a body to the head housekeeper and refused to clean or even enter the suite while 'that animal' was there.

Romolo was an incurable tease, and new chambermaids were initiated when he pressed into their hands a thick wad of paper money, winked and said: 'Mr X in room 123 left this for you with his thanks.' The maid would pocket the money and only later discover she was clutching 20 crumpled and obsolete Peruvian notes.

Waiters, maids and valets at Claridge's were a breed apart, trained in traditional style to perform services that only the super-rich and the aristocracy now expect. Evening maids, in smart black and white uniforms, were called dress maids because they were trained to help

217

ladies to dress for the evening, and to pack, using copious quantities of tissue paper, or unpack for them. Valets would perform the same service for gentlemen guests, and room service waiters, maids and valets could be summoned at the touch of a button.

Guests as a rule were equally considerate of the hotel staff. A chambermaid appeared red-faced and flustered in the sitting-room of a titled lady. 'Oh madame, I'm so sorry,' she stammered. 'I've looked everywhere – under the bed, in the wardrobes and the bathroom and I simply cannot find his Lordship's other slipper.'

The guest put down the morning paper and gently explained. 'My dear, it's perfectly all right. The reason you cannot find his other slipper, you see, is that his Lordship only has one leg . . .'

Concern over showing utmost courtesy to our guests occasionally got our staff into trouble. Reg Voller, a somewhat large and very bald-headed enquiry clerk, decided the only response to the head bow of a Japanese businessman for whom he had done a small service, was a similar bow of his own. The Japanese bowed further. Reg bowed lower still. And so it continued until there was a resounding *crack* as poor Reg's forehead hit the high desk behind which he stood.

The chief enquiry clerk at the time was a gentlemanly fellow called Stan Bassett, one of those true hotel professionals with a photographic memory and an aptitude for producing the right thing at the right time, no matter how obscure. The chairman had complained at a meeting that his fountain pen was obsolete because it was so old nobody sold refills. Word got back to Stan Bassett. Within minutes, he rummaged in his deep desk drawer and came up with a couple of pen refills he had bought for Sir Hugh when he first acquired the pen – 24 years earlier!

Only rarely did guests take advantage of Claridge's reputation for such personal service. One who should have known better is a distinguished Scot who always stayed in the same relatively spartan single room, which surprised me until I learned that it reminded him of his boarding school. He was shown up to this room by a new and very good-looking 6-foot-something male receptionist who said innocently, 'If there is anything else you require, sir . . .'. The illustrious Scot replied: 'What I'd really like is to give you a good spanking!'

Far worse was the American who stayed in a suite with his wife and asked first the young male cloakroom attendant then the room service waiter if they would massage cream into his sore backside. Both refused, naturally, and the man was asked to leave. But my job was made more difficult because the cloakroom attendant had stupidly kept the £20 tip the man had handed over before making his lewd request.

For every difficult guest there are a hundred who make our business a pleasure. The unfortunate thing is, those who make the most fuss take up so much of a hotelier's time.

Asked to name a few memorable guests, I would include a cross-section of personalities from the regal to the raucous. While Claridge's might be the grande dame of London hotels, she was always able to lift her skirts and live a little. The old lady loved a good party – and was an incurable romantic. She loved it when Harry Connick junior filled the suite of his girlfriend with hundreds of red roses. And when Lenny Henry and Dawn French came straight from their respective theatres late at night to celebrate St Valentine's Day in one of the art deco suites. The hotel seemed to smile, as we all did, when it welcomed the likes of Leslie Caron and Audrey Hepburn, Ginger Rogers, Dame Margot Fonteyn and Walter Matthau, Jack Lemmon and Julie Andrews. And *we* smiled when Sammy Cahn, writer of the *Love and Marriage* lyrics, wrote in his note of congratulations on my move to Claridge's, 'Jones and Claridge . . . go together like a horse and carriage.' I smiled, too, when the charismatic and ageless Sidney Poitier, visiting with Hollywood mogul Marvin Davis a year after I retired, greeted me in the Foyer with 'Mr. Jones are *you* a sight for sore eyes!'

Spencer Tracey said: 'When I die I don't want to go to Heaven, I want to go to Claridge's.' And I feel sure Katharine Hepburn will have forgiven the fact that she was required to use the staff entrance and to dine in her suite in the days when ladies were not allowed to be seen in the hotel wearing trousers.

There was a less warm welcome for one of Hollywood's not-so-grande dames. When I returned from a weekend away one of our receptionists told me a famous opera singer had checked in. Her name was Brigitte Nilsson. And yes, she *did* sing, but not in the way he anticipated. This Brigitte Nilsson was the 6-foot, blonde ex-wife of Sylvester Stallone, and the song she sang was reported to me next day by the wife of an elderly diplomat. She said: 'Mr Jones, I don't know what they were doing in that room last night, but after a lot of crashing about she – well – *screamed*, and it lasted for sixteen seconds.'

It wasn't only the rich and famous who misbehaved. A Nigerian woman summoned the night manager at 3 a.m. and complained that £3,000 was missing from her room. In the few days she had been staying with us, she had been ordering up to 12 bottles of champagne a day and admitting different men to her suite until late at night. She was encouraged to leave early next morning, admitting she must be mistaken about the missing money when advised that the police would be called.

On more than one occasion in the early hours of the morning after a ball our night porter or security staff would almost trip over a couple copulating on the Aubusson carpet in the French Salon. Asked to desist, one young man merely looked up over his shoulder and said: 'Hang on just a minute, will you?'

Celebrity guests now and then caused disruption where none was intended. The actress Jane Seymour was mortified when she let the huge bathtub overflow – easily done as they filled swiftly and silently – flooding two rooms on the floor below and resulting in three rooms being taken out of service. The Japanese were the worst offenders, and floods were common when businessmen would run their bath then leave the bathroom to watch the news on CNN or make a telephone call. Just two minutes was all it took for the great tubs to overflow, and five was sufficient to flood the room below. This became such a problem that a famous Jak cartoon in the *Evening Standard* showed a Claridge's waiter in lifebelt, goggles and flippers delivering room service to a Japanese guest.

Long before I arrived at Claridge's Eleanor Roosevelt was in residence when five hundred US servicemen staged a demonstration at the US Embassy nearby in Grosvenor Square, in protest at the delay in sending them home after the war. Fifteen of them took it upon themselves to march on to Claridge's, where they asked to see Mrs. Roosevelt. Somewhat perturbed, the concierge asked if they had an appointment. 'No sir. Just say it's a bunch of GIs,' was the response from the Texan sergeant.

Mrs. Roosevelt agreed straight away to see them. 'Tell them I'll be right down.' If the hotel staff were surprised, the GIs were not. 'We just told her,' said the Sergeant, 'that we wanted to go home. And she said she would help.'

During my own tenure Joan Rivers, always a favourite when she stayed with us in London, announced in the middle of her television show, 'There's good news and there's bad news. The bad news is: my husband was nearly electrocuted this morning when he plugged in his electric shaver to the wrong voltage. The good news? It happened in the Royal Suite at Claridge's . . . '

A minor but agreeable vote of confidence in Claridge's was given by writer William Safire in one of his New York Times columns. Bemoaning the lack of anything other than Gideon Bibles to read in hotel rooms, he wished they would provide something useful 'like a dictionary. Some hoteliers care,' he wrote. 'Bill Marriott, a good egg, dropped me a note to say he'll lend me a dictionary next time I stay at one of his hotels. In London, if I needed all 13 volumes of the Oxford English Dictionary, I would call downstairs to Ronald Jones, general manager of Claridge's, and get action.'

The traffic in compliments wasn't all one way, though. Mr. & Mrs. Trent from New York had been Claridge's guests for 30 years before I took over, and I soon learned it was Mr. Trent's custom to smoke the last cigar of the day comfortably ensconced in the leather armchair in front of the fireplace in the front hall. Our night porter, the late Melvin Silcox, used to tell him: 'Sir, if the hotel caught fire I wouldn't let the London Fire Brigade over the threshold until Mr. Trent finished his cigar!'

Some guests behave entirely properly yet still end up embarrassing you. Such was Zelda Fischer, an inoffensive-looking matron from Boston. She asked to interview me for a small magazine she published called 'Good Credentials' and I made the arch mistake, in a frantic moment, of not insisting on seeing a copy before agreeing. Some months later I was sent a little cream-coloured brochure with my portrait on the front cover and the 'interview' and my biography taking up the first four pages. Two pages further on, the Personal section contained gems like these:

'This beautiful Irish redhead (mid-30s) adores Jewish men!' And 'Exquisite blonde, mid-30s, a delightful mix of intellect and playfulness . . . ' Another entry was headed: 'Did your mother tell you to wait for a Jewish doctor? You'll be glad you waited when you meet this tall, funny, handsome MD – 35. Please be Jewish, 25–34, and taking care of yourself. You may wind up with a doctor in the house!'

And my favourite. 'How does he stay so fit? He looks better than most men of 50. Why do 30-year-old women beg to meet him? What is the secret of this 60-year-old hunk?' When Eve saw that one she paid me the compliment of threatening divorce! Nothing to do with me, though. I had just inadvertently given an interview to the head of America's latest and very expensive lonely hearts club, staying at Claridge's while she tried to secure a foothold for her business in the UK.

14

'My Object All Sublime'*

The glamour side of hotels is just one of their many facets. Others are more mundane. Taking over even the grandest hotel is like moving into a new home. You have looked it over, fallen in love with it, but as soon as you start living in it, you are overwhelmed by all the improvements it needs.

Just like home, you start with the kitchen. You have a budget, exceed it, double the figure you first thought of, wait twice as long as you anticipated for the builders to arrive, only to end up tearing your hair out, spending more, waiting longer. And, hopefully, ending up with the kitchen or the home of your dreams.

In Claridge's case, the kitchen budget expanded from £3.5 million to £4.8 million and the work took several years to complete.

When I first arrived, my priority was the refurbishment of the guest bedrooms and suites. There were nearly 200 rooms, including 54 suites, every one a different shape, size and configuration, every one decorated and furnished differently. A nightmare for a hotelier – look at the Four Seasons or the Hilton or Marriott hotels, and however comfortable and nicely furnished the bedrooms are, they are pretty well standardised, one room much like another. At Claridge's many of the bedrooms were in a sorry state, and most were well below the standard I expected in one of the world's grandest hotels.

Whoever had been responsible for interior décor had a lot to answer for: sludge-coloured walls, mud-coloured carpets, 1950s 'contemporary' furniture that I wouldn't have wished on a lodger in a Blackpool boarding house. Somebody described it as 'faded elegance' but there was nothing elegant about this degree of fading.

Bleak as some of the bedrooms looked, they were nothing compared

*Gilbert & Sullivan, *The Mikado*

with the back-of-house and basement areas. The staff facilities at this grand luxe hotel were worse than those I remembered from the Adelphi Hotel in Liverpool during wartime. They were outdated, worn-out, dirty and a disgrace.

There were five 'tiers' of staff dining: the managers' private dining room was a converted garret bedroom on the sixth floor. Food cooked in the basement kitchen was sent up in a lift at 12 noon and sat stewing on an ancient hotplate until all the managers had had their lunch, usually well after 2 o'clock. The restaurant head waiters, true to tradition, had the best deal, under a domed ceiling in a private dining room behind the restaurant. Chefs and cooks made do with lunch or supper standing by their stoves. Heads of department and clerical staff had the use of the Couriers' Room in the basement, with waitress service. Adjacent to that was the staff hall, where the remainder of the personnel ate at long tables covered with oilcloth, seated at benches. The food came from the main kitchen and was left on a clapped-out iron stove and hotplate for as long as it was needed. The staff hall reminded me of the workhouse in *Oliver Twist*, except nobody ever asked for more. There were not too many complaints, however, because in pride of place was a beer-dispensing machine, which was responsible for the 'tired and emotional' condition of staff I came upon lolling around in corridors during my first few days.

My priorities changed: first, get rid of the beer machine. Then switch my attention from redecorating the guest bedrooms to a total replanning of the back-of-house and basement areas, including the ancient kitchens. The guests might not see the results, but with a better-cared-for and self-respecting team, I knew the service to the guests would automatically improve.

During the next few years we constantly upgraded our personnel department until we ended up with two of the finest personnel managers any hotel has ever known, Jane Chilman and Ann France, now over-seeing personnel at the Lanesborough and Royal Garden Hotels respectively. I persuaded the directors to let me bring Irene Kail, our nursing sister from the Athenaeum Hotel, to Claridge's, where she set up a small occupational health department. Sister conducted pre-employment medicals, trained kitchen staff in environmental health and safety procedures, and operated a counselling and welfare service for the staff, bringing in physiotherapists, osteopaths and chiropodists for weekly clinics. At a time when staff turnover was an acute problem for London hotels, Claridge's had unquestionably the lowest.

Plans were drawn up for a £3.5 million reconstruction of the kitchens, room service stations on each floor, staff changing rooms and rest rooms, and a new single-status cafeteria with its own kitchen.

The renovations became like a diabolical game of chess. As one area was closed for refurbishment, that department had to be moved into another area and kept operating at full tilt. As each phase of the work began, unforeseen hazards were encountered, and as these were dealt with, so we would decide we might as well make other improvements rather than come back in two or three years and start all over again.

We found pillars that had deteriorated and no longer supported the ceilings above; hidden staircases that had to be removed; floors that had crumbled almost to dust. Claridge's is a Grade A listed building, and every step we took had to be approved by the local authority. This wall would have to be preserved, that doorway could not be covered over or demolished, the character of the original 1898 building must be preserved – quite literally at all costs.

The mâitre chef des cuisines Marjan Lesnik had come to Claridge's the year before me, and the new kitchen was the implementation of his dream. He was closely involved with the design and planning at every stage, travelling the UK and Europe to find the equipment that would last, if not a lifetime, certainly well into the next century. This alone would have been a full-time job, but all the while chef Lesnik and his brigade of nearly 80 chefs and cooks continued to oversee the preparation, in often makeshift conditions, of up to 1,000 meals a day for the two restaurants, room service and banqueting salons.

My senior assistant manager at the time was Rudi Jagersbacher, an ambitious and tough young Austrian who is now a Vice-President of Hilton International. The three of us would often work far into the night, and could hardly wait to get on to the job soon after dawn next day. We all three – Slovenian, Austrian and Englishman – relished a unique opportunity to contribute to the revival of a great British institution.

Claridge's new kitchen was so state-of-the-art it became an exhibition in its own right. I had personally inspected kitchen equipment at the top hotels in Paris – the Ritz, the Bristol, the Crillon and the George V among them – and chef and I had together decided upon the Rorgue stoves we inspected there. I recall watching the chef in l'Hotel Bristol pushing a huge copper pan across the top of the stove and seeing it glide smoothly all the way from one end to the other, so precise was the engineering. That stove was already several years old, which clinched the deal in my mind.

We issued invitations to visit us 'At Home on the Range', showing groups of hoteliers, journalists, chefs and hotel guests around the upstairs restaurant kitchen with the Rorgue range and the main kitchen with its 'Gucci stove', nicknamed because of its smart red and gold livery. One piece of equipment they preserved, however, was an old stove from the last century which could roast a whole sheep or a side of beef. This is still used for banquets, now clad with the same red and gold livery as the new stove.

For the restaurant staff the new kitchen meant that for the first time in nearly a hundred years, waiters would not have to run up and down 22 stairs to collect every dish for the restaurant.

Within a year or so of opening, the staff restaurant had won an international award from an American magazine; the kitchen designer won an award; the kitchen won an award. At long last, Claridge's staff had a workplace worthy of their skills.

As the reconstruction was reaching its final stages, we encountered a problem that had nothing to do with the fabric of the building. We had planned to create a new staff entrance at the back of the hotel in Brooks Mews. Sir Hugh used the fire-escape staircase and ground-floor corridor, whose exit door led into the mews a few yards east of the staff and goods entrance, for his private comings and goings. We would look to see whether his Rolls was parked outside the front entrance or the Mini tucked alongside the back-door fire escape, nicknamed 'the Chairman's entrance', to get some idea of whether the Chairman was in residence officially or not. Sir Hugh was insistent that this entrance should be retained 'in case Royalty or other distinguished personages might need to leave the hotel avoiding the public areas'. Apparently Queen Maud of Norway had used it to escape the press. She died in 1938.

I was asked by Giles Shepard to approach Sir Hugh for approval of the last stages of the refurbishment, including the new entrance, but Sir Hugh urged me to look for an alternative. Faces were saved all round when we discovered a hidden staircase and supporting pillars which would need to be strengthened, and crumbling floors and ceilings. Escalating costs prevented the final part of the plan being implemented. Sir Hugh kept his special entrance.

This came to the notice of the world at large in a 1991 *News of the World* story with a photo spread showing a young friend of Sir Hugh's in a Claridge's bathrobe, and another showing them walking hand in hand near the Savoy. This friend had been introduced to me in the hotel.

'She is an artist, like you, Mr Jones! And the daughter of a Brigadier,' Sir Hugh had said, which seemed to make everything quite respectable in his mind. The *News of the World* revealed that she worked for an escort agency called Aristocats. The newspaper headline was: 'QUEEN'S CRUMPET ADVISER, 83 AND A TART AGED 24', referring to Sir Hugh's honorary appointment as Clerk of the Royal Kitchens – a gift for headline writers. The story described the meetings of 'Sir Hugh and hooker Mandy in the penthouse', and made much of the fact that at Claridge's and the other Savoy hotels, hookers are most definitely banned.

Although many of the older staff and the managers knew about Sir Hugh's peccadilloes, he was usually fairly discreet, taking his 'young friends' out through the Chairman's entrance. This time, however, the scandal became public, and many of us never quite forgave him for making a laughing stock of the hotel and the people who worked there.

The morning after the *News of the World* allegations, Sir Hugh kept his head down and did not make an appearance in the hotel. We didn't really expect he would make his regular Tuesday morning visit, either. However, he turned up chipper as ever, with no mention of the weekend's unpleasantness, and when I told him I was expected at the Savoy for a meeting at 11 a.m., he astonished me by offering for the first time to drive me there. I folded myself into his little mini to undergo one of the most hair-raising journeys I ever experienced in central London.

Sir Hugh's attitude to other road-users might have been 'ignore them and they'll go away'. And, sensibly, they did. The car screeched around Berkeley Square on two wheels, wove and ducked through traffic jams, and cut in front, behind and alongside anything that threatened to get in its way. I understood, as I emerged ashen-faced in the Strand, why he had not used his gold-coloured Rolls-Royce.

Presumably to take my mind off his driving, Sir Hugh regaled me with his views on naughtiness and the media. The young lady had been set up by the press, he declared. She was utterly respectable, came from a good family, father a brigadier, and 'there was nothing – absolutely nothing – *sexual* about our relationship.' I tried to suppress a smile as I recalled the *News of the World* photographs in which the 'young lady' posed in the bathrobe and described how she had taken a bath in his penthouse after staying the night. The media, asserted Sir Hugh, had a great deal to answer for. He much preferred the French system. I thought

226

he meant the French system of naughtiness being taken pretty much for granted, but no, he meant their privacy laws, which prohibited media intrusion into the personal lives of public personages.

Soon after this incident Sir Hugh emerged from a private talk in my office with Carol Price, wife of former US Ambassador Charles Price and a director of Claridge's, saying indignantly: 'That lady seems to think I lead a dissolute lifestyle!'

Sir Hugh seldom regarded rules as applying to him. In 1987 a letter in the *Evening Standard* complained that the writer, a fit man of mature years, had been refused admission to Forest Mere health hydro, which belonged to the Savoy group, because they did not accept guests over the age of 70. Sir Hugh was at that time a few months short of his eightieth birthday – and a regular visitor to Forest Mere.

It was difficult not to see the humorous side of his private life, just as it was impossible not to admire his professional achievements well into old age.

Special orders were in place for servicing the Wontner penthouse. At 7.30 China tea and a Cox's orange pippin were taken to Sir Hugh, on a trolley on which his six newspapers were laid out either in a brown envelope to the left of the tea service or folded underneath. The written instructions included the message 'Do not speak unless spoken to'. Regular breakfast service must include 'Sir Hugh's pasteurised milk poured into jugs the night before so the cream rises to the top'. The valet who looked after Sir Hugh's clothes was allowed into the penthouse at 9.30 each morning and between 7 and 8 in the evening, but the maid could not enter before 10.30 a.m. The radiators had to be drained each day at 4 p.m. because of the peculiarity of the heating system.

Lady Wontner usually stayed for two nights during the week, spending the rest of the time at their country house in Buckinghamshire or at their summer home in the Scottish borders. Her habit was to arrive on Tuesday and leave on Thursday, unless there was a banquet or dinner to attend with Sir Hugh in his capacity as City Liveryman or former Lord Mayor of London, weighed down and listing to starboard with medals, although we never found out what for. This left Sir Hugh free to pursue his own interests at the beginning and end of each week, his custom being to leave London before lunch on Saturday and return after dinner on Sunday.

Occasionally the regime went awry. As when instructions were left for Mrs X, a guest of Sir Hugh, to be looked after when she arrived at

7 p.m. Mrs X actually arrived mid-morning and was shown up to the penthouse as instructed. She explained that she was an air stewardess, her flight had been rescheduled and she would like to rest. She chose the more feminine of the two bedrooms and fell asleep.

Soon after, Lady Wontner arrived unexpectedly and Goldilocks could not have been more of a surprise. An urgent telephone call was made to Sir Hugh, which resulted in Mrs X being shown to a single bedroom on the fifth floor.

Next day Sir Hugh told me that in future he would like the penthouse to be used more for 'official entertaining', a veiled reference, I assumed, to accusations being levelled by Lord Forte about his accommodation privileges. It had always been his intention, he went on, that the penthouse should be used as a private dining room when our banqueting suites were full.

That was not the only time poor Lady Wontner was surprised in her London home. On at least one occasion she was startled by the unscheduled appearance outside her penthouse window of Brewster, the notorious West End hotel cat burglar, who escaped from prison as quickly as he was put into it.

Towards the end of his life, when under renewed pressure from the Savoy board to quit the penthouse, Sir Hugh prevailed upon me to write, in his presence, a letter to Sir Anthony Tuke, Chairman of the board, explaining why the penthouse would be difficult to let. He dictated the letter, I signed it, but Sir Anthony and the board guessed without having to ask me, that I had done so under pressure.

In truth I was grateful for Sir Hugh's views on the subject of living in, since it meant that Eve and I were able to live on the premises, as I had done since I first became a manager, when most managers of five-star hotels did. Giles Shepard would have preferred all the managers to live out, but after inspecting the house that might have been allocated to us in Bourdon Street, with windows and doors on all three floors heavily barred to prevent intruders entering after climbing up drainpipes or over the roof, we opted to stay put.

We were grateful for the many privileges that living in conferred, but privileges come with a price tag: my salary was a fraction of that paid to living-out managers and indeed to my successor at Claridge's, who lived out with his family. We were happy to give up our privacy in exchange for the benefits of hotel service; 15 different people had keys to our suite, and since all of them were doing a job for our benefit, there was no question of asking them to wait for us to answer a knock on the door. Staff knew they could 'knock and enter' in order to service our apartment quickly and therefore not delay service to the guests. We didn't need our innumerable towels or our bedlinen to be changed every day, but to have issued separate instructions for our apartment would have made matters more complicated for staff – easier to fall in with whatever arrangements were in place for the regular servicing of guest accommodation. We were also happy to entertain hotel guests in our suite to make them feel they were at home and among friends, especially if they were travelling alone or were regular visitors.

And if it meant no jeans and tee-shirts but being reasonably presentable and in Eve's case, made-up, from 7.15 in the morning, when the first 'caller' appeared, until midway through the evening, when dinner was cleared away, then so be it. Our permanent suite at Claridge's was on the first floor, over the bins and the loading bay outside the staff entrance in Brooks Mews, and since work began underneath our windows at 6.30 a.m. Monday to Friday, it would not have been the most popular guest accommodation. But we considered ourselves fortunate to have it. Living in only becomes a problem when you have small children. It gives them a distorted sense of values and puts constraints on their freedom.

I have always been on call 24 hours a day, and although the young managers are loath to admit there are situations with which they could not deal, it was useful for them to know I was there should they need me. They would ring me only occasionally: a guest at death's door; a chambermaid who had drunk too much or been crossed in love, threatening to jump from a seventh-floor window. Living on the premises also meant I could be around when a special arrival needed my attention, and in the office dealing with paperwork early in the morning before other people were up and about; I could make my rounds of the hotel, front and back of house, from top floor to basement, shaking hands with the night staff going off duty and the early morning staff arriving. I could check on special parties or banquets late into the night, keep my finger firmly on the pulse of the hotel. Eve and I slept in a different room of the hotel at every opportunity, so we could evaluate everything from a guest's viewpoint. In the morning, we'd make a list of items that needed dealing with and I'd hand it to the appropriate department – housekeeping, maintenance and so on. On no occasion do I recall there being fewer than a dozen points, and usually there would be many more. All my assistant managers, many of them now general managers of other grand hotels throughout the world, have been trained to do this.

The transition from the Athenaeum Hotel to Claridge's had been tougher on my wife than it was on me. I had experienced many hotels of this style. Claridge's had nothing that the great railway hotels in their heyday did not have. The formality, the grandeur, were exactly what I expected. Eve, although she had married into the industry, lived in the Athenaeum Hotel for seven years, and had been writing about hotels for far longer, found much had changed. The directors of Rank Hotels had always treated her with friendliness, courtesy and respect and recognised the role she played in my life, both personal and professional. At Claridge's she was barely acknowledged – often not even that – or spoken to by either my Managing Director or Chairman. Even the flowers sent by Giles Shepard on the day we arrived, to the apartment that was to be our home, were addressed solely to me.

At the Athenaeum, a smaller and more modern hotel, my approach had been strictly hands-on. Eve was an invaluable asset in attending functions in-house and outside, entertaining guests at lunch, tea or dinner, and hosting cocktail receptions for 'fam trips' – familiarisation tours for groups of overseas travel professionals. We regularly entertained hotel guests on Friday evening for cocktails, to give them the personal welcome that was lacking in many other hotels. The Americans in particular loved it, and felt the Athenaeum was truly their home away from home. As Harold Rosenbluth, one of the doyens of the travel business in North America put it: 'You two are giving visitors what they can't get in any other property – you!'

Claridge's was a different matter. Traditionally the management did not fraternise with the guests, whose average age at that time seemed to be firmly in the senior citizen category and virtually all of whom were either titled, had aristocratic pretensions or, at the very least, were endowed with old money and had stayed at the hotel for years. These were not people who needed 'stroking'; their social lives were complete without us, who were, when all was said and done, paid servants. I have witnessed more times than I can count the demise of hoteliers who looked upon guests as friends. There inevitably came a time when the hotelier forgot his 'friends' were paying the bill. The friends never did.

The move for Eve engendered a feeling of being cut off from the guests and from the staff, too. We had a strict rule in both hotels that Eve never gave orders directly to any member of staff except those who looked after our apartment. There could be only one boss, and staff should never be put in the position of taking conflicting instructions from or of having to give priority to the manager's wife. Most of them had been in situ for years, there were nearly 550 of them, and the personal contact was not – at first – welcomed.

I worked 14 or 15 hours a day, six days a week. Weekends were reduced to one day off – if we were lucky. Sunday became a day for catching up with paperwork, thinking and planning in peace and quiet with no interruptions.

Eve had given up running Friends in London, which looks after overseas visitors, meeting them at the airport in chauffeur-driven limousines, planning sightseeing, supervising shopping, arranging baby-sitters or specialist guides. She also arranged their hotel accommodation, and considered it unsuitable that she might be bringing clients to Claridge's in limos other than Claridge's own, and charging them for the privilege. Friends in London was taken over by her close friend and partner Mary Bailey, and thrives under her direction.

Eve was also an award-winning freelance journalist specialising in hotels and restaurants, and while she carried on with this, she herself took the decision not to write anything controversial about hotels while I was at the helm of Claridge's.

She did not feel at home there. When we arrived by taxi on the afternoon of Saturday 3 November 1984, we both not only dressed up to the nines, complete with hat and gloves, but actually hired a Louis Vuitton cabin trunk to move our things in. We felt we couldn't arrive somewhere so grand with our tattered luggage. It did not take long to discover the guests' luggage was a far more battered and motley collection than ours!

We were welcomed by Michael Bentley, the long-serving deputy manager. A good meeter and greeter of VIP guests, he was nevertheless considered by both Sir Hugh Wontner and Giles Shepard unsuited to the role of general manager. As a compensation he was allowed the title of 'manager', while I would become Director and General Manager, but his role would remain that of a senior assistant until he left Claridge's, once again with a new general manager, soon after I retired.

The rest of that day had been like another wedding day. Michael Bentley escorted us through the front hall, flames from the open fire

231

reflected in the polished black and white marble floor. A curving staircase wide enough for two ladies in ball gowns to walk side by side led up to the floors above. Through a glass and gilt arched door, the Foyer (never called the lounge at Claridge's) where liveried footmen (never waiters at Claridge's) in velvet knee-breeches served afternoon tea. A uniformed attendant operated the old-fashioned lift, complete with upholstered seats, which took us to the second-floor suite that had been temporarily assigned to us. Decorated in pale yellows and pastel blue, with chintz draperies, it was all much prettier and more relaxing than we had imagined. It was also banked with the most unbelievable array of flowers we – and the hotel florist – had ever seen in one room. Baskets and bouquets and potted plants and posies – there must have been two or three dozen separate arrangements from well-wishers all over the world. It might have felt a little like an undertaker's parlour had it not been for the happy messages of congratulations and welcome. We were served afternoon tea on silver and fine china with tiny sandwiches, home-made scones with jam and clotted cream, and miniature pastries.

We took an hour or two to unpack and open one of several bottles of champagne which had been left for us, each in a silver ice bucket, by friends in England and the USA. And another hour to look at all the greetings cards and telegrams. In the marbled bathroom we christened the tub which would have accommodated a *ménage à trois*, and the waterfall shower, cocooned ourselves in enormous thick white towels and bathrobes, and dressed for dinner. We remember that dinner: a *bavarois de légumes* whose taste, texture, colour and sauce were perfection; a *petite marmite*, one of my favourite broths; then venison Baden Baden, good meat well-cooked with redcurrant and pear garnish. Beautifully presented, each ingredient tasting of itself. No sauce or garnish over-fussy or too rich.

The sweet trolley was more mixed, I recall, with good-looking Dutch apple pie but chocolate and coffee mousse with an unattractive skin on top. A vast selection of cheeses on a trolley of their own, but I'd have preferred to see just half a dozen perfect cheeses and have the waiter know how to describe each one. I would eventually stop the practice of serving complimentary *friandises* or petits fours *before* the sweet so that guests could fill up on those and not buy a third course. And I was disappointed that no liqueur trolley was brought to the tables around us. I would make sure the waiters knew my motto: 'Not seen, not sold'.

So good overall, and with so much additional potential. I couldn't wait to tackle this new job.

I changed few of my initial responses to Claridge's as the pressures of the job intensified and I uncovered the vast amount of work that had to be done to bring the hotel up to scratch. I would wake at 5 a.m., be in the office or around the hotel at 6.30, and apart from half an hour for lunch, would not return to our suite until 8.30 p.m., by which time I was fit for nothing but a light meal in front of the television. Our regular visits to the theatre, to concerts and weekends away, became pleasures of the past. Until, that is, we bought our first tiny cottage in the Cotswolds, near Moreton-in-Marsh, early in 1985.

Eve drove down to meet the removal van, which parked in reverse on the downward slope of our driveway. Midway through the move, it became clear that all was not well with our furniture, which had been stored for several months. First one container then another was unloaded. Sofas and armchairs were saturated and stained, polished wood furniture ruined beyond repair. Personal belongings were unrecognisable.

Between bouts of hysteria, Eve spoke to the head man at the removals depot. An investigation would be carried out – first thing on Monday morning. This was late afternoon Friday. My wife explained that we had been looking forward to spending our first weekend in our new home, but that was now impossible. The bed was ruined, and the blankets. We would book ourselves into the village inn for the weekend at their expense.

We needed that cottage bolt-hole more than we had expected. But the strain of the first year at Claridge's, which had manifested itself in rows we were quite unaccustomed to, began to ease off as we both came to feel more at home in our new surroundings. Eve continued to work as a freelance journalist and a lay magistrate, eventually going back to 'school' to work for her certificates and diploma in wine studies. The guest profile relaxed, as more younger people appeared, and Claridge's began to exhibit the warm and friendly welcome I insisted upon for everybody who crossed the threshold – provided they could pay the bill, dressed properly and behaved themselves. I like to think that by the time I retired, neither Alan Bennett the playwright nor Anton Mosimann the world's favourite chef would have been ordered round to the staff entrance. Mr Bennett because he 'didn't look like a Claridge's guest' and Mr Mosimann because 'he was a chef visiting another chef'. Hotel staff, no doubt about it, can be the worst snobs of all, but I was determined the warmth of Claridge's welcome and the friendliness of the staff would soon equal the excellence of the service and the elegance of the surroundings.

We gradually got to know more of our guests and were aware of those who would welcome an invitation to drinks or dinner, and those who would be outraged at the idea.

In her book *The Historic Hotels of London* in 1986 author and critic Wendy Arnold made me feel we were on the right road. She wrote:

> Happily, England's most prestigious hotel has recently undergone a miraculous transformation under its new General Manager, Ronald Jones.
>
> Nothing, heaven forbid, has been radically altered. But the liveried retainers, though stately and dignified as ever, have become once again attentive and concerned . . .
>
> Ronald Jones has great pride in this historic building and his trust and confidence in his staff have inspired them. This is a newly impressive Claridge's.

The staff were responsive and eager for the changes that in their hearts they knew were vital. Some had loyally followed me from the Athenaeum Hotel; my Secretary Pat More, the head linkman Mario Utelini, the nursing sister and others. Many of them however had worked at Claridge's for 30 or 40 years. More than a few were second- or even third-generation, like Bill Capelan, one of the linkmen, as uni-formed doormen are called in grand hotels, who came to Claridge's as a young lad to work alongside his mother and his grandmother.

Claridge's upholsters its own furniture, makes its own curtains and, as part of the Savoy group, manufactures its own superb beds, grinds its own coffee and washes its own laundry. The company no longer chooses (on the hoof) and ages its own beef, buys its own wine, or prints its own literature, but it did all those things, too, until recent years.

I was concerned that with such traditions behind them, the staff would be reluctant to change, but they were on my side, eager for the improvement in business they knew would follow. Tourism was flourishing in London in the mid-1980s, the pound was strong against the dollar, and the Savoy group's profits were in good shape. The staff, like the directors, were anxious that the fabric and the traditions of the hotel should be preserved. I convinced them that together we could retain the best of the old while implementing a little of the new.

There were a few bad apples in the barrel. A banqueting manager whose large gins I used to find in the fuse boxes, in cupboards, four or five glasses at a time. He claimed it was water; my nose and his breath proved otherwise. A doorman caught even after two warnings selling tablecloths and shirts from the boot of his car parked outside the hotel. Even a housekeeper with a conviction for pushing and using hard drugs.

I learned that potential guests had been put off coming to Claridge's by the attitudes they encountered. How a US admiral who walked in one day without luggage (he was taking a walk from his hotel, having decided on the spur of the moment to extend his stay in London) was shown the door despite there being rooms aplenty. A lady judge we knew from Louisiana had called to make a reservation and her enquiry was met with the reply: 'Have you stayed at Claridge's before, madam?' She said she had not, and was told immediately: 'I'm sorry. We have no accommodation.'

I had encountered this attitude myself when, as general manager of the Royal Garden Hotel, I had promised my secretary and an assistant manager tea at Claridge's as a birthday treat. We walked unchallenged into an empty Foyer, sat at a table and were ignored by the solitary waiter. Eventually I went over to him and politely asked for tea.

'I'm afraid we don't serve tea to non-residents, sir.' was the response. I asked to see the manager. The waiter returned and said the manager was 'not available'. The assistant or duty manager, then? 'He is in a meeting, sir.' Again politely, I urged him to get the assistant manager out of the meeting. He did, and once again we went through the 'residents-only' ritual.

In vain I appealed to his better nature by explaining it was the lady's birthday and she was very disappointed. To no avail I cited the Act that decreed a bona fide traveller should be given sustenance by a hotel. I wasted my breath when I pointed out there were no residents in sight of the deserted ground floor of the hotel.

Only when I asked to be put through on the telephone to Sir Hugh Wontner was there instant capitulation! We were grudgingly escorted to the furthest recesses of the empty Reading Room and served the worst afternoon tea I can remember.

To be fair, this does not tally with Eve's experience when she escorted a respectable American couple to the hotel for Friends in London. She met them with a chauffeur-driven limo at the airport, and noticed they were being trailed by an unkempt youth with bedroll, tee-shirt and torn

235

jeans. Just as she was about to bar his way into the back of the Rolls, the American lady turned to face him and said: 'Zachary, you sit here opposite me.' Eve was horrified at the prospect of taking this sulky apparition through the hallowed portals of Claridge's, and she knew that only one double room had been booked.

The reception brigade in tailcoats and pinstriped trousers didn't turn a hair. We do not have a room for the young gentleman just at this moment, she was told, but if he would like to take a seat . . . Within minutes, Zach was shown up to a room adjoining his parents'. A jacket and tie – a selection is kept for such occasions – were offered and reluctantly accepted.

When we introduced weekend terms and added-value breaks to the hotel, staff – especially younger staff, surprisingly enough – were concerned about attracting 'the wrong type of people'. What if, they asked, those guests, unused to hotels like ours, turned up in jeans and trainers?

'Send for me,' I suggested. 'Or show them up to their room yourself and in the lift, say: "I'm sure you're aware of our dress code in the public rooms, sir, but if by any chance you haven't packed a jacket and tie, we have a selection of jackets and designer ties which we will be happy to lend you."'

Diplomacy in all its guises has long been one of Claridge's strong points. I quickly learned not to make hasty judgements. We were all worried about the growing crowd of shouting, banner-waving demonstrators which gathered in Brook Street for the arrival of the President of Mozambique. It was only after somebody alerted Scotland Yard that one of the waiters explained that the placards actually said 'Welcome' in Portuguese!

Claridge's first computer came on-line in January 1985, and it was fun to compare it with the communications and billing systems that were in operation in the first hotels I worked in. There, waiters in the restaurant or room service would pull up a speaking tube on the end of a hose, blow down it to make a whistling noise to attract the attention of the kitchen, and verbally order the food. The kitchen would transfer the speaking tube from ear to mouth, confirm the order then yell it to the appropriate chef's corner. Later, the waiters would put the written check into a cylinder with an opening on one side, and shoot that down another tube to the kitchen. If the kitchen was not below the restaurant and the pull of gravity couldn't be used, then a pneumatic system, based on the same principle but using compressed air, was installed.

The computer was followed by new air-conditioning in the restaurant, then the cleaning of the marble and brickwork around the hotel entrance. A new personnel office complex was added in Brooks Mews, behind the Savoy Training Centre, and staff accommodation redecorated. A Remanco computerized billing system was introduced for food and beverage operations, and the ballroom and reception salons redecorated and carpeted. At last, by 1990 two-thirds of the hotel bedrooms were refurbished.

Throughout my career I had suffered from directors' wives and mistresses being allowed to get their hands on interior décor. Only the top designers would be good enough for Claridge's.

Tessa Kennedy, with a background in theatre design, created some wonderfully dramatic suites in Scottish Baronial, Hollywood and Provençal style. She transformed the ladies' cloakroom to a 1920s boudoir using the original fixtures and furnishings. And the smallest double room in the house – almost impossible to let except at short notice – was given her Biedermeyer treatment and became the favourite of many of our regular visitors.

David Laws, whose designs were popular at 10 Downing Street and Buckingham Palace, gave the art deco treatment to several suites of rooms, reviving the original 1930s design of the 'new wing'. John Stefanides, a favourite of Princess Margaret, transformed some of our most difficult rooms and suites – always on time and within budget. Trisha Wilson of Dallas brought a surprisingly restrained, open feel to a large suite on the first floor. She had stayed frequently at Claridge's and we knew her well before she started work on the project, but nevertheless there were fears of a 'Dallas' look. We need not have worried. Trisha, like her fellow Americans, stayed at Claridge's precisely because it was so British, and had no inclination to change that.

One thing included in every designer's brief was that the bathrooms should be restored to their original opulence. Black and white marble, beautiful ceramics, rare art deco vitrolite wall coverings: nothing was ever thrown out at Claridge's. I recalled how infuriating it had been for the new owners of the Ritz in London to discover all the wonderful 1920s bathroom fittings had been dumped. Ours were intact – huge chromium 'waterfall' showers the size of soup plates, art deco taps, original washbasins and bidets. We tried to forget that the plumbing itself was nearly a hundred years old and the several million pounds it would cost to renew it.

I sometimes felt like the curator of a living museum, as one treasure after another revealed itself. Nothing had been thrown out – but much had been hidden, under layers of paint, bricked up in old glass stores, hidden in cellars. Beaten copper panels on the main staircase, obscured by decades of black paint, were restored by specialists at the Victoria and Albert Museum. We uncovered a 1911 mural hidden behind wall mirrors in the French Salon. And I was encouraged to commission Christopher Ironside shortly before he died, to produce exquisitely engraved mirrors depicting the Judgement of Paris and complementing those which Basil Ionides had created for the restaurant in 1930.

Shortly before I retired I achieved a ten-year ambition. I had discovered in the archives an illustration of the unique decorated plaster panels which had brought light and life to the great dome atop Claridge's Foyer. We commissioned an artist to have these copied as a *trompe l'oeil frieze* painted around the dome, enhanced by state-of-the-art computerised lighting, to make the elegant Foyer one of the loveliest rooms in Europe.

And yet, some of the least expensive alterations or additions proved most effective: a small forest of plants in the restaurant and posies of fresh flowers on every table, with silver-shaded lamps and candles in silver candlesticks in the evening. The waiters were given new uniforms, and menus for pre- and post-theatre suppers introduced into the Causerie. I was again able to indulge my love of music. A Hungarian quartet had been introduced into Claridge's as an experiment in 1902 and still played (not with the same musicians, elderly though some of them are) during luncheon and dinner, making Claridge's the only hotel I know to have orchestral music during the early part of the day. The atmosphere when the quartet played in that glorious room was vibrant, and I was sad to learn that soon after I left, the lunchtime music was stopped as an economy measure.

I introduced a pianist, Ian Gomez, for the nights when the 'Hungarians' took their break. I also tried to reintroduce dinner-dances on Friday and Saturday evenings with a small dance band, but appeals to Sir Hugh fell on deaf – or at least unmusical – ears. Restaurants were for dining, he insisted, not dancing. The argument that business would greatly improve since the restaurant was desperately quiet on those two evenings failed to move him, even after I discovered that dinner-dances had been held in the restaurant before World War II.

A few months after Sir Hugh's death in 1992 dinner-dances resumed and our weekend restaurant business increased dramatically.

My swansong just before retiring from Claridge's was to commission a recording of the Hungarian quartet, for which I wrote the sleeve notes. It seemed only just that their special brand of 'Palm Court' music should be available to a wider public, and as a memento to hotel guests. At least three of the team of eight who make up the quartets were septuagenarians. Louis Mordish, one of England's best-known cinema organists, composer and accompanist to Dickie Henderson for many years, only joined the Hungarians in his seventy-fifth year in 1984, and played regularly at Claridge's until his death in 1996 at the age of 87. Arthur Gerard, one of the finest violinists I have known and a graduate of the Royal College of Music, was a veteran of the musical-comedy theatre, where he worked with the outrageous Douglas Byng and met most of the great composers and performers of the post-war years. He performed frequently on radio and television, too, and despite being profoundly deaf he rarely played a false note in the ten years that we listened to his virtuoso performances. Thank heavens we still have Arthur with us on CD. Art, the base player, was well into his seventies, and could recall a long career with famous dance bands such as Sidney Lipton's. Several of these veterans had played with the BBC Light and Concert orchestras.

I admired the younger musicians, too, music teachers by day, who helped sustain the tradition of musical comedy and operetta, the songs of Ivor Novello and Noël Coward, of Gershwin and Cole Porter, alongside colleagues who remembered the originals.

The task of reshaping the hotel was endless but the rewards were great: some took the form of the small gifts which visiting heads of state bestowed at the end of their stay – silver sake cups from the Crown Prince and Princess, now the Emperor and Empress, of Japan; a bronzed tray from President Mubarak of Egypt; a Polish crystal rose bowl from Lech Waleska after his presidential visit; embroidered tablecloth and napkins from the Chinese; and from the President of Malawi, Malawi gin and some boxes of excellent tea, coffee and macadamia nuts. Other rewards were less tangible but more important to all of us who loved the hotel: seeing an increase in younger visitors; hearing old and new guests remark on the improvements and the restoration; and being recognised internationally through a series of awards.

In 1987 *Travel & Leisure* magazine named Claridge's one of the Ten Best Hotels in the World in the Grand Tradition – surely the most cumbersome title of any award known to man. But greatly appreciated, since it gave a tremendous boost to all the people who had worked so hard at upgrading both the welcome and the fabric of the hotel. For Eve and me, it meant a trip to New York to receive the award, as guests of American Express. When Bobby Short played and sang after dinner on the night of the awards ceremony, we thought we had died and gone to heaven. The next evening we were hosted by our good friend Donald Smith, the cabaret impresario. I sat next to Celeste Holm and Al Hirschfeld, the theatrical cartoonist, and we listened to impromptu performances by Steve Ross, Jeff Harnar and David Staller, Anne Francine, Gwen Verdon, Julie Wilson and Margaret Whiting. Then we *knew* we had gone to heaven, but felt very much alive.

In 1989 I was voted Hotelier of the Year, at which I reminded my peers who had shown their confidence by voting for me that it had taken me just 44 years to become an overnight success! In 1990 there followed one of the most important events of my life: being awarded the OBE by Her Majesty the Queen, for services to the hotel industry. In 1990, too, the hotel won the award of the Art Deco Society of Florida for our restoration work. Another brace of awards followed in 1991, first the National Clean Kitchen Award, which recognised our back-of-house team, the kitchen porters and the washing-up staff who do such an essential job without ever being seen by a guest. That was followed by Claridge's being named Britain's Best Hotel in the *Courvoisier Book of the Best*.

In 1992 we received the Best Hotel in Britain nomination from the American Express magazine; in 1993 we were Five Star Hotel of the Year to the RAC. And the year I retired brought the RAC's Blue Ribbon.

The most potent award, however, was knowing that we, the staff and I, had brought the hotel through the worst recession in living memory without going into the red. And the unforgettable tributes paid to me and to Eve when we left: a concert at which staff members sang or performed to music provided by the orchestra of Bullerswood, the school we had 'adopted'. A 'This is Your Life' presentation at which they played *Nobody Does it Better*, which had all of us in tears. And the gift of a computer to facilitate the writing of this book.

Together this amazing team and I had galloped through the boom years of the 1980s, increasing business and ploughing profits back into the restoration of one of the world's most exciting hotels. Our directors had fought off bid after bid from predators who threatened the very existence of Claridge's and the Savoy Hotels. We rode high on a wave of success. At the same time, everybody was aware that lean years were approaching. There would not be the capital sums available for investment into the fabric of the building. Tourism in London would be decimated and business travel from the US and elsewhere drastically curtailed. Margins would have to be shaved and the pattern of business would change: businessmen who before might stay a week, would now leave after two or three nights; those who brought their wives now travelled alone; others who always reserved a suite were booking single rooms – hoping they would be upgraded to reward their loyalty to our hotel when others were offering grossly reduced rates.

We always looked on reducing rates as a very last resort, and instead would use every contrivance the marketing people could come up with: added value at weekends and one- or two-day programmes where breakfast or dinner, sometimes both, would be included along with flowers, chocolates, champagne and canapés. Reservations for regular guests would be upgraded whenever possible, from a small double room to a larger, from a larger double to a suite of rooms. Giles Shepard's suggestion of complimentary limousine transfers to and from airports worked well, especially for North American visitors, as did the offer to press clothes on arrival without charge.

On the down side, Claridge's could no longer enjoy the luxury of retaining staff years past retiring age. Streamlining without loss of service to the guests was essential, and Claridge's must have been one of the only hotels in London which was able to do this through increased efficiency and purely natural wastage; there were no redundancies, no sackings, no job losses, and the older employees – some into their eighties and one over 90 – understood they would have to make way in order to preserve jobs for the younger people who needed them more.

We embarked on a programme of job enlargement, training staff to do more than one job or to work in more than one area in order to increase flexibility. For them it also meant additional skills and qualifications to add to their CV.

The recession proved a challenge for all of us, but the person who suffered most was Giles Shepard, Managing Director of the Savoy Group. He was treated shabbily by his fellow directors and by certain elements of the press – most notably those who had benefited from his hospitality. His task in steering not just one hotel but the entire company through the recession was an unenviable one, and one which he

241

accomplished, with Forte snapping at his heels, perhaps at the sacrifice of short-term profits but without compromising the standards, style or quality of the hotels.

To see another managing director take over as the recession ended must be galling in the extreme. I at least had the satisfaction of knowing that my successor would take over a hotel that was in better shape than any centenarian should be, with a string of awards that should stand it in good stead through the remainder of its century, and a staff that is as dedicated and loyal as the institution that is Claridge's deserves.

In the words of Christopher Moritz from Los Angeles, who was nine years old and had just stayed at Claridge's for the first time: 'This is the hardest place I've ever had to leave!'

AFTERWORD

'Everything That's Excellent'

The Claridge's years were great years, but not necessarily the greatest. There were other years and other hotels to compete for that title. They were certainly the best possible climax to an eventful and exciting career, and to an important chapter of my life.

No hotel or hotel group is going to remain the best. Buildings decay, environments change, companies fold or get taken over as fortunes decline. The needs and desires of the public alter with the times they live in. I am more fortunate than most hoteliers alive today in that I have seen and been part of the very best years of two of the greatest hotel companies in history: the railway hotels that became British Transport Hotels, and Savoy Hotels. They blazed a trail of excellence that few have been able to follow.

I have also witnessed the decline of the first company, although several of its grand buildings still stand: two of them – Gleneagles and Turnberry – remain the best of their kind. I hope not to be around to witness the decline of the second great hotel company, for although it is inevitable it should not be imminent. Perhaps 50 years from now a hotel director will write in his memoirs, to the disbelief of young readers: 'Ah yes, I remember the days when the Savoy and Claridge's were truly grand hotels.'

And what of life after the grand hotels? My wife, afraid I would suffer withdrawal symptoms from half a century of making things happen, created such a workload for our small company I haven't drawn breath and long for a day off!

I have been invited to lecture to hotel management students and business organisations in the UK and Europe, to advise hotels in England and the USA, and to write for various publications. Oxford

---

*Gilbert & Sullivan, *Iolanthe*

Brookes University has paid me the compliment of appointing me a Visiting Fellow at the School of Hotel and Restaurant Management. Eve and I have sailed the world's oceans as guest speakers on wonderful cruise ships and the QEII. The Royal Shakespeare Company at the Barbican Theatre has taken me on as a supernumerary and I've relished appearing as senator, citizen, soldier and judge in *Measure for Measure, Julius Caesar, Richard III* and *Hamlet,* experiencing life backstage and on-stage with one of the world's great theatre companies. There hasn't been much time for piano lessons, painting and sculpture – but I've fitted them in, too.

Best of all, I was appointed non-executive director of a country hotel I have greatly admired for years, the Dormy House in Broadway. The proprietor and the young general manager there flatter me that they reap the benefit of my experience. I marvel at how they keep their hotel busy and profitable during the leanest times and I luxuriate in learning something new every time I visit.

Now, I am told, there are other books to be written and I cry *more time, more time . . .*